The Wind Blows Where It Wishes

THE WIND BLOWS WHERE IT WISHES

Selected Works on Spirit Baptism, Spirit Preaching,
Tongues and Initial Evidence, Subsequence, Cessationism,
Xenoglossy, Glossolalia, and Other Spirit-related Topics

ROBERT W. GRAVES

DIOMEDEIDAE PUBLISHING
CANTON, GEORGIA

The Wind Blows Where It Wishes: Selected Works on Spirit Baptism, Spirit Preaching, Tongues and Initial Evidence, Subsequence, Cessationism, Xenoglossy, Glossolalia, and Other Spirit-related Topics

Diomedeidae Publishing – Canton, Georgia USA

Cover design by J. D. King.

Library of Congress Control Number: 2023952482

PAPERBACK ISBN: 978-0-9960445-4-7
HARDCOVER ISBN: 978-0-9960445-5-4

Contents

"The wind blows where it wishes, and you hear its sound, but you do not know where it comes from or where it goes. So it is with everyone who is born of the Spirit."

JESUS
Recorded by John
the Apostle
(3:8 ESV)

Preface

Two roads diverged . . .

I felt like an interloper. Straying so far afield. Why was I sticking my nose where it did not belong? It belonged in English literature, my field of study, not theology. Give me Milton and Shakespeare, Wordsworth and Coleridge, Melville and Twain, not Augustine and Aquinas, Luther and Calvin, Bultmann and Barth.

Why did I venture so far afield, especially given the beauty of literature and the exhausting boredom of theology? Well, I offer two replies to that question: (1) Theology is only boring if there is no God, especially no Spirit who connects humans to the triune Godhead; (2) The study of literature can also be quite boring under the wrong circumstances, for example, if one loses sight of the object being studied and, say, immerses himself in the study of literary theory.

As mentioned, my choice of study was English literature, the closest I came to studying theology or Bible in college were my courses in Greek (Classical and Koine), taken to fulfill my foreign language requirement in graduate school. Thankfully, however, whether one studies theology or literature there can be much overlap; after all, the Bible is literature. Furthermore, many early works of English literature are filled with biblical allusions and even theology, for example, John Milton's *Paradise Lost* and John Bunyan's *The Pilgrim's Progress* (more recently, C. S. Lewis's *The Screwtape Letters*). Many of the principles applied in literary interpretation would also apply to interpreting the Scriptures.

I am not trying to justify dipping my toes into the waters of biblical studies; I still consider myself an interloper. But, at the time, the 1970s, I felt justified because the existing Pentecostal literature did not sate my need to understand and, thus, be able to explain and defend the experience I just had, that is, being baptized in the Holy Spirit and speaking in other tongues. *This* put me on a trajectory that landed me in the waters of biblical studies. (I was saved in 1969, and defending my faith became integral to my new life. Apologetics was of great interest to me, as chapter 14 regarding the reliability of the Bible's message will attest. But when I was baptized in the Spirit in 1972, complete with a glossolalic experience, the defense of this new spirituality became my focus.)

In the '70s, the works of Stronstad, Menzies, Ruthven, and Keener were nonexistent, and the anti-Pentecostal works of Dunn, Bruner, Stott, Gaffin, Hoekema, Gromacki, Unger, and the popular work of MacArthur were on the bookshelves. I grew tired of waiting; the earliest of the new-generation Pentecostal works would not arrive until 1983 (Hunter's *Spirit-Baptism: A Pentecostal Alternative*) and 1984 (Stronstad's *The Charismatic Theology of St. Luke*).

Since 1947, the standard defense of Pentecostalism had been Carl Brumback's *What Meaneth This?* But it was quite elderly now and answered few questions that were being posed by current anti-Pentecostal scholars. I discovered Bill MacDonald's "Glossolalia in the New Testament" in 1979, possibly the first defense of Pentecostalism's doctrine of Spirit baptism to be published in a scholarly, evangelical journal (1964), but it was only ten pages long in the *Bulletin of the Evangelical Theological Society* (twenty in its pamphlet reprinting by Gospel Publishing House).

In 1979, I discovered the very helpful pastoral book *The Glossolalia Phenomenon* (1966), edited by Wade Horton. I would not find the first book-length, substantive defense of Spirit baptism and the continuity of all the spiritual gifts until 1980 (although it was published in 1968). It was written by Princeton Theological Seminary graduate, Neo-Pentecostal (Baptist) scholar Howard M. Ervin. After reading Ervin's book, I half-jokingly mentioned to someone that if I had discovered it earlier, I might not have chosen to dedicate a lifetime to exploring this subject. If, on the other hand, Stronstad's *The Charismatic Theology of St. Luke*, Menzies's *Empowered for Witness* (1994), and Ruthven's *On the Cessation of the Charismata* (1993) had been available to me in 1976, I believe the trajectory of my studies would, indeed, have shifted.

But that's not the way things happened, and after studying the topic of Spirit baptism and cessationism for several years, including interviewing Pentecostal scholars such as Anthony Palma, Horace Ward, Charles W. Conn, Stanley Horton, Howard Ervin, M. G. McLuhan, and Paul Elbert and exchanging correspondence with Elbert, Ervin, Gordon Fee, Horton, Palma, McLuhan, MacDonald, and William Menzies, I started writing things down. My first essay was "Tongues Shall Cease: A Critical Survey of the Supposed Cessation of the Charismata," published in 1983 in *Paraclete: A Journal Concerning the Person and Work of the Holy Spirit*"; five other essays would follow in *Paraclete*. They are all reprinted in this volume; some would be repurposed as chapters in my 1987 book, *Praying in the Spirit* (updated and enlarged in 2016). Other articles would be published in various Pentecostal and non-Pentecostal periodicals. (Still, nearly half of the pages herein are either unpublished or their circulation has been very limited.)

Eventually, the works of scholarship of the pentecostal movement evolved to elite status—what I mean by that is (1) today they are on par with the biblical scholarship being produced by the best scholars in Christendom; and, by implication, (2) as a layman, my contribution had to take a different form, more in the fashion of support personnel, which is why, in 2005, I initiated the formation of The Foundation for Pentecostal Scholarship, Inc.

This is also the reason that my last two works were compilations of Pentecostal and Charismatic scholars. I am referring to *Strangers to Fire* and *The Kingdom Case against Cessationism.*

As a free-lance, Christian writer, I also published popular articles and short stories only tangentially related, for the most part, to Pentecostalism; some of these you will find at the end of this volume as bonus chapters.

As a Pentecostal, I couldn't end this book without the inclusion of my testimony. It was the first piece I published—very fitting for a Pentecostal. It was written for a youth publication (and reprinted in another). It was also re-written for an adult publication and published as a handout to prisoners. As you'll discover, I started low in life, but finished high, seated with Christ in the heavenlies, from whence he poured out the promise of the Holy Spirit. *. . . And that has made all the difference.*

Introduction

The original purpose of the chapters of this book was either to provide information and reasoning, or, in the case of the bonus chapters, to provide entertainment or to stimulate reflection. In other words, I wanted the reader to think, laugh, or cry. You'll have to judge whether I've succeeded.

The chapters that were originally published in print (the first footnote of each chapter should tell you) remain original with possibly only insignificant changes, for example, the addition of the Bible version quoted, or the deletion of "NIV" since it is the select version used throughout when not referenced. If a substantial updating occurs, it will be reflected by a footnote that is bracketed. Articles that appeared only online (again, the footnote will tell you) may have been thoroughly revised and updated.

In the more academic chapters, the reader may notice that I sometimes retained an earlier citation of a paper but, also, inserted a later publication of the same work in an anthology, so there will be two sources for the work cited. I hope that this will not cause confusion but simply give the reader more sources to choose from if they wish to find the referenced source.

Please enjoy the read, I pray.

1

The Forgotten Baptism[1]

Waters that divide, they have been called, referring to the various modes of water baptism. Some churches sprinkle; others pour; most nonsacramental Protestants immerse. But despite the method, the act is universally identified as water baptism.

Could there possibly be a hamlet nestled somewhere in America where a water baptism has not taken place? Or a clear stream whose waters have not ritually bathed a believer?

Water baptism in the name of the Father, the Son, and the Holy Spirit is a distinctive practice of Christianity. The Lord himself commanded his disciples to go into all the world and baptize believers (Matt 28:19). Wherever there are Christians, there are baptized persons.

Wrapped in camel's hair and desert dust, John the Baptist came calling his listeners to repent of sin and be baptized. But when Jesus came to John, John's ministry of water baptism diminished. And John had the distinct privilege of proclaiming what would seem to be a greater baptism.

Greater than water baptism? Greater than the rite every Christian is commanded to undergo? Greater than this distinctive feature of Christianity known from Bangor, Maine, to San Diego, California, and on every continent?

---

[1] Originally published in the *Pentecostal Evangel* (May 24, 1987): 6–7.

Will you believe the words of John the Baptist himself? All four Gospel writers recorded John's words. The earliest, Mark, inscribed in the first paragraph of his book the words of the Baptist to his disciples: "I indeed have baptized you with water: but he shall baptize you with the Holy Ghost" (1:8 KJV).

Luke made it clear that John believed his ministry would be superseded by Jesus's, and his water baptism surpassed by the baptism of the Messiah: "I indeed baptize you with water; but one mightier than I cometh . . . he shall baptize you with the Holy Ghost" (3:16 KJV).

Call it the missing or forgotten baptism, for who has heard of it? Catholics perhaps envelop it in confirmation; Reformed churches and Baptists telescope it into conversion. Usually, one must dig deeply into their theological writings to uncover mention of it. And if found, mention is in response to a 20th-century movement which has emphasized, as did John the Baptist, this baptism performed by Christ—the Pentecostal baptism in the Holy Spirit.

The Assemblies of God takes seriously John's proclamation that, even as he baptized in water, Christ would baptize believers in the Holy Spirit.

John did not think water baptism was enough, nor did Jesus, for he commanded his water-baptized disciples to remain in Jerusalem until they were baptized in the Holy Spirit, thus empowered for ministry (Luke 24:49; Acts 1:5–8).

Peter's words which recommend water baptism (Acts 2:38) are made with one thought in mind: Believers need to receive this gift of the Holy Spirit. Repentance and water baptism place them in such a position.

Have you been baptized in water? Fine, Jesus commanded it. But how do you know you have been baptized in water? First, you knew what water baptism was; then, you were conscious of the physical experience that matched your mental conception—you felt the waters of baptism.

Have you been baptized in the Spirit? There is no reason you would be less conscious of it than of water baptism. After all, it is a greater baptism performed by a mightier Baptizer.

Paul implied believers could know they have been baptized in the Spirit when he asked the Ephesians if they had received the Spirit after they believed (Acts 19:2). That would be a meaningless question if they could not sense such a baptism.[2]

---

[2] [On the matter of subsequence and the aorist participle, see Paul Elbert's *The Lukan Gift of the Holy Spirit* (Canton, GA: The Foundation for Pentecostal Scholarship, 2021), 96–102, and Howard M. Ervin's *Conversion-Initiation and the Baptism in the Holy Spirit* (Peabody, MA: Hendrickson Publishers, 1984), 61–66.]

This Baptism is perceptible to you, and its evidence is observable by others. "But ye shall receive power, after that the Holy Ghost is come upon you . . ." (Acts 1:8 KJV). This power, though personal, will spill over into your public ministry and life-style.

Because this evidence was perceptible to others, the twelve disciples could direct the church to choose men for service who were "full of the Holy Ghost" (Acts 6:3 KJV). And Paul could see that certain Ephesian Christians were not filled with the Holy Spirit. Thus, he commanded them not to be "drunk with wine . . . but be filled with the Spirit" (Ephesians 5:18 KJV).

Although faith, love, and joy may be results of the baptism in the Holy Spirit, these are characteristics that may go unnoticed initially, especially by others. And though certain gifts of the Spirit may be bestowed or actuated when the believer is baptized in the Holy Spirit, they may not be recognized and utilized until months later.

Is there immediate, observable evidence to confirm that Spirit baptism has taken place? The long-range evidence has been mentioned, and it is important. But where is the immediate confirmation in the believer's mind? Where is the evidence (the wet clothes of water baptism) to convince the believing community?

Certainly, Simon's reaction to his Samaritan neighbors who received the Holy Spirit demonstrated the presence of an immediate, observable phenomenon that accompanies and verifies the Spirit-baptism event (Acts 8:18). What was the evidence? Pentecostals believe the evidence is the same today as it was for New Testament believers and that it is deducible from New Testament documents.

We assume that Luke, inspired by the Holy Spirit, would not draw a distorted picture of the early church for the later church to follow. If you are looking for facts about water baptism or Spirit baptism, look to Acts. Both are vital parts of Luke's portrayal of the foundational and dynamic church.

Examine all passages where the immediate, observable evidence of Spirit baptism is described. They yield one common denominator—glossolalia, that is, speaking with other tongues as the Spirit gives the utterance (Acts 2:4; 10:46; 19:6).[3]

Have you been baptized in the Spirit? Or has this become the forgotten baptism in your life? Remember:

1. John the Baptist prophesied it (Matt 3:11)
2. Jesus proclaimed it (Acts 1:5–8)

---

[3] [See Timothy Laurito's *Speaking in Tongues: A Multidisciplinary Defense* (Eugene, OR: Wipf and Stock, 2021).]

3. The early church practiced it (Acts)
4. The Spirit demonstrated it (Acts 2:6; 8:18; 10:44–46; 19:6) and
5. We must continue it (Acts 2:39).

With your mind on obedience and your passion on a needy church and lost world, open your heart now and ask your Savior to baptize you in his Holy Spirit. May the baptism in the Holy Spirit be forgotten in your life no more.

2

Why Not Acts?[1]

Has a new Christian ever asked you which book of the Bible he should read first? If so, you probably advised him to start with one of the gospels. After all, the focal point of each gospel is Jesus. And what could be more important in the Christian's life than Jesus?

The logic appears strong, until you ask the question of where in the timeline of Christ's life the new believer should begin. Matthew begins his gospel with Jesus's royal ancestry and goes all the way back to Abraham. Mark begins with a fiery John the Baptist, whose appearance was prophesied by the Old Testament prophet Isaiah.

Luke begins a bit earlier than these with the barren parents of John the Baptist, Zechariah, a priest, and his wife, Elizabeth, Mary's "cousin." John's gospel begins before them all, when the Son of God was the Word, before time began. Each gospel ends not long after the Resurrection, with Luke ending with the Ascension.

All truth about Jesus is important and should be painstakingly studied by every believer, and every book of the Bible should be studied. Still, we must start somewhere or we will never start anywhere.

For the new believer, what better starting place is there than Jesus's last promise to his disciples? "You shall receive power when the Holy Spirit

[1] Originally published in the *Pentecostal Evangel* (April 7, 2011): 14–16.

has come upon you; and you shall be My witnesses both in Jerusalem, and in all Judea and Samaria, and even to the remotest part of the earth" (Acts 1:8).

It is the book of Acts, the second part of Luke's two-volume work, that tells believers how they are to live . . . and die. No other book in the Bible describes the Christian life in such vivid detail and depth. The new believer learns that Jesus's promise of power is not just for first-century believers but "is for you and your children, and for all who are far off, as many as the Lord our God shall call to Himself" (2:39).

This personal power for testimony and mission is the most prominent and prolific theme in Acts. The new believer learns that this power propels him with great joy and boldness of testimony, accompanied with signs and wonders when needed. Luke's descriptions will make the absence of this power in the believer's life glaring and its remedy imperative. If the new believer doesn't have this power, he will want it and expect it after reading Acts, because in Luke's world it is part and parcel of the Christian life.

Luke calls this experience of the Spirit by many names: baptizing, filling, receiving, giving, pouring out, and falling upon. But no matter what he calls it, he describes it as something every believer is entitled to and every believer needs. By portraying Peter and Paul as experiencing it numerous times (2:4; 4:8, 31; 9:17; 13:9), Luke makes it clear that it is something that the believer continually needs and should continually remain open to and expectant of.

In Acts, the new believer learns that miracles, signs, and wonders are not limited to the Jesus of the gospels or the twelve apostles but continue in the life of each believer through the Spirit of Jesus. An unheard-of disciple named Ananias prays for Paul and baptizes him; Paul is healed and filled with the Holy Spirit. An unknown group of believers in Lystra encircle a dead or left-for-dead Paul—he arises and walks away (14:19–20).

In Acts, the new believer learns that *more* signs and wonders are recorded in the lives of believers who are *not* part of the Twelve apostles than are. By telling the story of those believers who came after the Twelve, Luke sends a clear message to later believers—the same Spirit lives and works in you!

Believers such as Philip, Stephen, Apollos, Barsabbas, Mark, Timothy, and Silas witness boldly of the gospel of Jesus Christ, and some establish cells of believers in cities across the region. Paul and Barnabas, although called "apostles" (14:14), were not members of the Twelve apostles, who are not heard of again after chapter 16, as Luke focuses on Paul's ministry and his journey to the center of the Empire.

As Luke describes Stephen, Peter, and Paul witnessing to, defending, or explaining the resurrection of Jesus, his messiahship, or the coming of the Holy Spirit, they refer to Old Testament prophets, kings, and patriarchs.

These references whet the new believer's appetite for more of the word, especially the Old Testament, which points with great elegance, drama, and intricacy to Jesus the Messiah.

In his descriptions of Stephen's martyrdom, Peter and John's arrests, and Paul's stoning, Luke prepares the new believer for the mocking and persecution that he will surely encounter as he fulfills the mandate to testify. Persecution is another prominent theme in Acts. Not to worry, divine guidance is paramount in Acts, as well.

The new believer learns that God may direct believers through visions, angels, prophets, prayer, fasting, church leaders, and events of intervention by the Holy Spirit (16:6–7). Sometimes the Holy Spirit "speaks" to the believer (10:19). By whatever method, Luke makes it clear that, through the Holy Spirit, the Lord is present with the believer.

Luke mentions many other topics that will be of interest to the new believer—salvation, the kingdom of God, praise, tongues, prophecy, exorcism, baptism—nothing to bore the new believer here. The Spirit, who reveals Jesus to the believer, will inspire him to move on to the gospels and the epistles to learn more about the precious Savior and the role of the Spirit in the lives of believers in the early churches throughout Asia.

The book of Acts has twenty-eight chapters. Someone has observed that we are writing chapter twenty-nine today. Since the same Spirit indwells and uses believers today just as in the first century, the church today should have the same look, the same motivation, the same power. New believers, having read Acts, will steer the church in this direction. So why not tell the new believer to start his Bible-reading with Acts, where the high adventure he has started first began?

3

Preaching—The Spirit
and the Human
Dimensions[1]

Two hundred years ago a bishop approached the famous British actor David Garrick and inquired why clergymen "though believing what they preached met with little response, while Garrick, knowing his subject to be only a fable, could rouse his audience."

Garrick replied that actors deliver their fictions with the warmth and energy of truth while ministers "pronounce the most solemn truths with as much coldness and languor as if they were the most trivial fictions."

Garrick was not suggesting that preachers be trained in theatrics but that they deliver a *living* message with *life*.

A sermon is not a monolith of one ingredient. It is a variety of elements, the substance of which receives thrust as the Spirit penetrates the human dimension.

The existence of speech and homiletics courses in Pentecostal colleges implies that pulpit presentation is indeed important—a sermon is more than content. Likewise, the Pentecostal's interest in spiritual phenomena

---

[1] Originally published in *Advance* (August 1986): 6.

reminds us that without the Spirit's anointing, a well-delivered sermon does not measure up to God's ideal.

Delivery and Emotions

For decades, charges of emotionalism have been hurled at the Pentecostal movement. As a result, many preachers have over-compensated by allowing little or no expression of emotions in their delivery. They neither utilize their own emotions nor address the emotions of their listeners. This is a mistake.

If sin is a fact and eternal damnation an approaching reality, how can my emotions be unaffected? If the Resurrection occurred and God awaits His own in heaven, how can I sedately accept this?

Dwight Moody once wished his associate pastor could spend five minutes in hell. He knew such an experience would excite and motivate the most reserved preacher.

Of the various ingredients of delivery, enthusiasm and excitement are not surpassed in importance. These are the contagious elements of delivery—the dynamics that motivate.

Emotions were designed by God, and they are used by God. Social scientists acknowledge that "a person can be convinced of the validity (logic) of a certain action, but yet not take that action until he gets excited (emotional) about it" (H. Charles Pyron, *Communication and Negotiation*). Without addressing the emotions, it is often easy to prove a point *but next to impossible to motivate a person.*

A well-delivered message by definition addresses both mind and emotions. It is ineffective to cater solely to the emotions, and it is ineffective to cater solely to the mind. There must be a blending, a careful balancing, so that from this matrix of mind and emotions develops an interior stirring which the sinner translates into a decisive act, thoughtfully yet tearfully.

Delivery and Anointing

To avoid Garrick's observation that ministers "pronounce the most solemn truths with as much coldness and languor as if they were the most trivial fictions," those who stand behind the pulpit must acknowledge and yield to the Paraclete who stands beside them. To do this, they must realize (1) the need for an effective delivery (including *pathos*, or emotions), and (2) their own divine limitations or the need for anointing—the true Spirit-event beyond man's influence.

If an acquaintance's resurrection from the dead will not persuade the unbeliever (as in Luke 16:30), it is a mistake to believe the lessons learned in Homiletics 323 will alone suffice to convince and convict a wayward world.

Left untouched by the Spirit, rhetoric and logic will not reap the harvest, and theatrics will not save a soul. But when touched by the Spirit, the Paraclete's testimony to the well-preached Word pierces the soul of man with the response, "It's true! It's true!"

"Man has sinned," the preacher says. "It's true!" the Spirit responds.

"Christ has died."

"It's true!"

"God has raised Him."

"It's true!"

"Forgiveness may be yours, and you may reign with Him forever."

"It's true! It's true! It's true!" speaks the Spirit to the sinner.

And with the preacher's unswerving trust in this Spirit-event come the enthusiasm and excitement necessary to motivate a listening world.

In the end, the minister who recognizes the need of the Spirit's anointing upon his well-delivered sermon may hear his parishioners echo other words of David Garrick. Of the great 18th century preacher George Whitefield, he once said, "I would give a hundred guineas if I could say 'oh' like Mr. Whitefield."

Sorry, Mr. Garrick, but such anointing is for the pulpit, not the stage.

4

Praying in Tongues[1]

The Corinthians were speaking in tongues, but in many cases to the wrong audience. "Men can't understand you," Paul wrote. "When there is no interpreter, speak to yourself and to God" (1 Corinthians 14:2, 28, paraphrased). Noticeably, he did not tell them to stop speaking in tongues or to curtail their speaking. To the contrary, he said, "I thank God I speak in tongues more than all of you" (v. 18), and "I wish all of you spoke in tongues" (v. 5). He told others, "Stop forbidding speaking in tongues" (v. 39).

Paul was careful not to quench the interior moving of the Spirit within each member of the body. The solution to the abuse of tongues at Corinth was not disuse but redirection. Once three glossolalic utterances had been interpreted to the Corinthian congregation (v. 27), or if there was no one with the gift of interpretation among the congregation; all utterances were to be directed inward, "to yourself" (i.e., quietly, v. 28) and heavenward, "to God" (v. 28).

Three Implications of Paul's Solution

1. God always listens. Would Paul, by inspiration of the Spirit, order us to direct our prayers to God if He was not listening? We can be sure that though men may or may not listen to us, God always listens. As Isaiah

---

[1] Originally published in *Paraclete* 20.4 (Fall 1986): 14–15.

earlier taught, His ears are not dull to our voice (59:1); and as Peter later confirmed, His ears are open to our prayers (1 Peter 3:12).

2. God always understands. Not only does God listen, but He understands the mysteries our spirits utter (1 Corinthians 14:2, 14). Paul encourages us to speak in tongues to God, who understands when no one else does. He not only understands our glossolalic utterances but the groans and cries of our hearts (Romans 8:26, 27).[2] To Him the slightest tension of our soul, the warmth and wetness of our tears reach linguistic formulation! He is indeed the Great and Ultimate Interpreter.

3. God always answers. Upon request, Jesus taught His disciples to pray, "Thy will be done" (Matthew 6:10 KJV). Later in Gethsemane our Master would practice His teaching: "Not as I will, but as You will" (Matthew 26:39, NKJV). James tells us it is possible to "ask amiss" (4:3 KJV); that is, we may be asking that our will be done.

According to Paul, when we speak in tongues we do not understand what we are saying (otherwise we could always interpret the utterance), but the Spirit helps us to pray, and it is always according to the will of God (Romans 8:26, 27). In other words, our glossolalic prayers cannot but be in the will of God. Thus, it would seem we are assured of an answer from God.

Reasons for Edification

He listens; He understands; He answers! Need we wonder why Paul could say that "He that speaketh in an unknown tongue edifies himself" (1 Corinthians 14:4 KJV)?[3] First, we have a sensitive, attentive audience. Second,

---

[2] [Some do not see a reference to glossolalia in these verses. However, I do not find sufficient force in their arguments and must agree with scholars who argue for the probability of a reference to glossolalia here. (See Gordon D. Fee, *God's Empowering Presence* [Peabody, MA: Hendrickson, 1994], 575–86, and Robert P. Menzies, *Speaking in Tongues: Jesus and the Apostolic Church as Models for the Church Today* [Cleveland, TN: CPT Press, 2016], 139–41.)]

[3] The older anti-Pentecostal cessation or closure model which relegates glossolalia to the Early Church age finds relatively few scholarly adherents today. As an option, some anti-Pentecostals have reinterpreted Paul's words here to mean that tongues-speaking is selfish and undesirable since the congregation is not edified and the purpose of the *charismata*, after all, is the edification of the congregation (John R. W. Stott, *Baptism and Fullness* [Downers Grove, IL: Intervarsity Press 1977], 113–15; Robert L. Thomas, *Understanding Spiritual Gifts* [Chicago: Moody Press, 1978], 33–34, 122, 207–8, 212–20). Incidentally, congregational tongues are dispensed with either by the "prophecy-is-greater" or the "finished revelation" argument.

The answer to Stott et al. is: (1) The use of personal tongues may indeed be selfish at times; for example, at such times when ministry to others is preeminent; (2) A rigorous exegesis of the passage doesn't support the contention that Paul is using irony in verse 4; especially damaging is Paul's reluctance to speak in tongues to the church

we have an empathetic, omniscient audience. And third, we have a benevolent, omnipotent audience. Also, when we don't know how to pray, He supplies the language; when we don't know what to pray for, He supplies direction; and when we do not have the means to provide, He supplies the need.

In the face of the gross abuses of tongues at Corinth, Paul could still recommend this gift for all because of its edifying value (1 Corinthians 14:5). And though the bonds of fellowship among the Corinthians were weak and the misuse of tongues was blatant, Paul valued tongues enough to order those who were forbidding them to stop (v. 39). And if we would follow in Paul's footsteps (1 Corinthians 4:16), we would experience the edifying effects of glossolalia more than all the Corinthians (v. 18). Thus edified, we might minister as Paul ministered.

---

coupled with his confession to speaking in tongues more than all the Corinthians; (3) Stott's interpretation creates a contradiction in Scripture, for Jude commands us to use prayer to edify ourselves (v. 20); (4) There is nothing wrong with seeking inner or spiritual strength. Private Bible study, prayer and meditation, deeds of love all edify the individual; they are self-edifying without being selfish. Even as self-edifying prayer in the native tongue may prepare one to minister to others, self-edifying glossolalia may prepare one for such ministry.

5

A Good Word from the Critics[1]

There are Pentecostals alive today who remember vicious verbal (as well as physical) attacks upon the infant Pentecostal movement. According to Frank Ewart, Dr. G. Campbell Morgan called the movement "the last vomit of Satan."[2]

Henry A. Ironside said he

> . . . could count scores of persons who had gone into utter infidelity because of it. . . . Many more . . . lapsed into insanity. . . . In the last few years hundreds of holiness meetings all over the world have been literally turned into pandemoniums where exhibitions worthy of a madhouse or of a collection of howling dervishes are held night after night. No wonder a heavy toll of lunacy and infidelity is the frequent result.[3]

[1] Originally published in *Paraclete* 21.3 (Summer 1987): 22–25.

[2] Quoted in Robert Mapes Anderson, *Vision of the Disinherited: The Making of American Pentecostalism* (New York: Oxford University Press, 1979), 142.

[3] Quoted in Horace S. Ward, Jr., "The Anti-Pentecostal Argument," *Aspects of Pentecostal-Charismatic Origins*, ed. Vinson Synan (Plainfield, NJ: Logos International, 1975), 106; alternatively, this source may be found in *Strangers to Fire: When Tradition Trumps Scripture* (Tulsa: Empowered Life Academic-Harrison House, 2014), 80.

The movement "was wicked and adulterous," according to Dr. Dixon; R. A. Torrey claimed it was founded by a Sodomite.[4] Its adherents reminded Sir Robert Anderson of Isaiah's "wizards that chirp and that mutter" (Isaiah 8:19).[5]

Something Happens!

Something indeed happens. This has never been denied. Even those who find little or no good in the movement attest to the actuality of the resulting phenomena. Otherwise, they would not have spent elaborate efforts to explain the experience. Kildahl devotes a book to explaining the phenomenon of glossolalia psychologically.[6] In a larger volume Samarin concludes it is a learned response.[7] That something happens has never been denied, but the anti-Pentecostal evaluation and interpretation of that something has radically changed.

John R. W. Stott, respected church leader and critic of the Pentecostal movement, writes, "There can be no doubt that God has used this movement to bring blessing to large numbers of people."[8] Merrill Unger wrote three books refuting Pentecostal practice and doctrine. In one of those books, he stated that "the charismatic revival represents a sincere quest for God's spiritual best in the believer's life."[9]

Joseph Dillow testifies, "I know many men whom I admire highly who speak in tongues. Furthermore, I'm not aware of anything but good that has come from it in some of their lives."[10]

Evangelical leader Russell Hitt describes the reason for his posture on the new Pentecostalism:

> I have come to the position that it is a spiritual phenomenon being used of God very dramatically in some quarters. It is plainly bringing new life and virility to denominations long since pronounced dead or apostate by many evangelicals. Thousands have been ushered into the

---

[4] Quoted in Anderson, *Vision*, 142.

[5] Sir Robert Anderson, *Spirit Manifestations and "The Gift of Tongues"* (Wilmington, DE: Cross Publishing, n.d.), 24.

[6] John P. Kildahl, *The Psychology of Speaking in Tongues* (New York: Harper and Row, 1972).

[7] William J. Samarin, *Tongues of Men and Angels: The Religious Language of Pentecostalism* (New York: Macmillan, 1972), 9.

[8] Stott, *Baptism and Fullness*, 7.

[9] Merrill F. Unger, *New Testament Teaching on Tongues* (Grand Rapids: Kregel, 1971), 2.

[10] Joseph Dillow, *Speaking in Tongues* (Grand Rapids: Zondervan, 1975), 163, 164.

kingdom of God and others have received a new enduement of power, despite the theological question this raises.[11]

Popular author and pastor John F. MacArthur, Jr., wrote the bestselling criticism of Pentecostalism, *The Charismatics*. In the book, MacArthur confesses, "Charismatics truly love Jesus and the Scriptures. . . . I thank God for much that is happening in the Charismatic movement. The gospel is being proclaimed and people are being saved. I also believe that through this movement some Christians are recognizing a certain new reality in Christ and making commitments that they have never made before."[12]

For J. I. Packer, the experience that Pentecostals call the baptism in the Holy Spirit is spiritually valid: it empowers, it sanctifies, it deepens awareness of the Father's love and the Spirit's presence.[13]

The Biblical Validity of the Experience

Pentecostalism's most trenchant exegetical critic, James D. G. Dunn, is not without praise for the Pentecostal theology of Spirit baptism and spiritual manifestations. In fact, he supports the biblical integrity of the Pentecostal experience:

> Like earlier "enthusiasts" Pentecostals have reacted against both these extremes. Against the mechanical sacramentalism of extreme Catholicism and the dead biblicist orthodoxy of extreme Protestantism they have shifted the focus of attention to the experience of the Spirit.
>
> Our examination of the New Testament evidence has shown they are wholly justified in this. That the Spirit, and particularly the gift of the Spirit, was a fact of experience in the lives of the earliest Christians has been too obvious to require elaboration (e.g., Acts 2:4; 4:31; 9:31; 10:44–46; 13:52; 19:6; Romans 5:5; 8:1–16; 1 Corinthians 12:7, 13; 2 Corinthians 3:6; 5:5; Galatians 4:6; 5:16–18, 25; 1 Thessalonians 1:5f.; Titus 3:5, 6; John 3:8; 4:14; 7:38f.; 16:7—the presence of the Spirit was to be better than the presence of Jesus).
>
> It is a sad commentary on the poverty of our own immediate experience of the Spirit that when we come across language in which the New Testament writers refer directly to the gift of the Spirit and to their experience of it, either we automatically refer it to the sacraments and can only give it meaning when we do so . . . , or else we

---

[11] Russell T. Hitt, "The New Wave of Pentecostalism: A Second Look" (n.p., n.d.), 9.

[12] John F. MacArthur, Jr., *The Charismatics: A Doctrinal Perspective* (Grand Rapids: Zondervan, 1978), 13.

[13] J. I. Packer, *Keep in Step with the Spirit* (Old Tappan: Revell, 1984), 225–27.

discount the experience described as too subjective and mystical in favor of a faith which is essentially an affirmation of biblical propositions, or else we in effect psychologize the Spirit out of existence.

The Pentecostal attempt to restore the New Testament emphasis at this point is much to be praised.[14]

On the issue of glossolalia as initial external evidence of the baptism of the Holy Spirit, Dunn writes the following:

> In favour of the Pentecostalist thesis it must be said at once that their answer is more soundly rooted within the NT than is often recognized. It is certainly true that Luke regarded the glossolalia of Pentecost as an external sign of the Spirit's outpouring. In Acts 10:45f. "speaking in tongues and extolling God" is depicted as proof positive and sufficient to convince Peter's Jewish companions that "the gift of the Holy Spirit had been poured out even on Gentiles." The Ephesian "believers" speak in tongues and prophesy when the Holy Spirit comes upon them (Acts 19:6). The only other passage in which an initial giving of the Spirit is actually described is 8.17ff., and it is obvious that Luke has in mind here an eye-catching display of ecstasy—something more than sufficient to arouse the envy of an accomplished magician. It is a fair assumption that for Luke the Samaritan "Pentecost," like the first Christian Pentecost, was marked by ecstatic glossolalia. If so, then the fact is that in every case where Luke describes the giving of the Spirit it is accompanied and "evidenced" by glossolalia. The corollary is then not without force that Luke intended to portray "speaking in tongues" as "the initial physical evidence" of the outpouring of the Spirit.[15]

Only by postulating that Paul, not Luke, is the spokesman for today's church does Dunn save his own non-Pentecostal theology.

Dunn's examination and ultimate rejection of the Pentecostal theology of Spirit baptism leads him to the brink of a doctrine of Spirit baptism that is less palatable to him than Pentecostalism's. Since his examination verified that glossolalic utterances did indeed accompany Spirit baptism, and since Spirit baptism is equivalent to conversion, then spiritual manifestations should accompany conversion. (Only by

---

[14] James D. G. Dunn, *Baptism in the Holy Spirit: A Re-examination of the New Testament Teaching on the Gift of the Holy Spirit in Relation to Pentecostalism Today* (Philadelphia: Westminster, 1970), 225, 226.

[15] James D. G. Dunn, *Jesus and the Spirit: A Study of the Religious Experience of Jesus and the First Christians as Reflected in the New Testament* (Philadelphia: Westminster Press, 1975), 189, 190.

dispensationalizing glossolalia to primitive Lukan Christianity does Dunn escape the force of his own argument.) In this context, Dunn pays a final compliment to Pentecostals.

> Accepting that the gift of the Spirit is what makes a man a Christian, how do he and others know if and when he has received the Spirit? In what ways does the Spirit manifest his coming and his presence? What indications are there that the Spirit is active in a congregation or in a situation? Clearly these are questions of first importance at all points of Christian life and activity. And in case it should be thought that I have been less than just to the Pentecostals let me simply add in reference to these questions that Pentecostal teaching on spiritual gifts, including glossolalia, while still unbalanced, is much more soundly based on the NT than is generally recognized. [16]

Conclusion

The observable evidence of the Pentecostal baptism in the Holy Spirit—a love and devotion of the Scriptures, a fervency to proclaim the gospel, a deeper Christian life, a greater sense of the reality of God, an enduement of power, spiritual invigoration, revitalized churches, and even healed marriages—has overwhelmed would-be critics of the Pentecostal-charismatic movement (listed evidence are taken from anti-Pentecostal writers). Although they press for a more careful and articulate formulation of Pentecostal theology, today's critics are now quick to concede that it is a movement of God's Holy Spirit—a movement whose experiences are right out of the New Testament.

---

[16] Dunn, *Baptism*, 229.

6

The Johannine Anointing:
Focusing on Truth[1]

In 1977, after a consideration of all New Testament literature, J. K. Moon gave this classic Charismatic/Pentecostal, albeit eclectic, definition of the anointing:

> The anointing is the special presence of the Holy Spirit in the life and ministry of God's servant which produces an inspiring awareness of the divine presence. His entire faculties are enhanced (heightened illumination, courage, wisdom, discernment, faith, guidance, memory, vocabulary, emotions, intellect, and physical performance) beyond natural abilities. The Word of God is quickened to accomplish its regenerating, healing, edifying, and sanctifying objective. And those ministered to are invested with a God-consciousness. . . .[2]

For most Protestant Christians the word *anointing* has this univocal meaning, the rich meaning with which Luke impregnated it in his usage of its verb form in association with the empowerment of Jesus when the Holy Spirit descended upon him (3:22; 4:18). According to Luke, when the Spirit

---

[1] Originally published in *Pneuma Review* 8.1 (Winter 2005): 6–9.
[2] "The Holy Spirit in Preaching," *Paraclete* (Fall 1977): 26.

came upon Jesus, he experienced the power (4:14) and fullness (4:1) of the Spirit, which enabled him to victoriously endure satanic attacks, to preach the gospel, to effect inner-healing (4:18), to do good, and to heal those oppressed of the devil (Acts 10:38). However, John also spoke of an anointing, and his description, defying Moon's definition, is much different than Luke's.

The Lukan and Johannine Anointings

In 1981, David Bundrick specifically addressed the Johannine anointing and isolated it, rightly so, as one particular kind of anointing, i.e., distinct from the Lukan anointing. Bundrick hinted at the distinction when he wrote that, "While emphasis today is placed upon 'the anointing of the teacher,' this text [1 John 2:18–27] demonstrates that 'the anointing upon the student' is vital."[3] But neither Moon nor Bundrick clearly defined and delineated both the Lukan and the Johannine anointings.

The distinctive marks of the Lukan anointing are the accompanying, might acts of God (such as, healings, exorcisms, evangelism). The Johannine anointing, on the other hand, is the *chrisma* (only John uses this word in its noun form). Its effect is more internal and thus hidden from the view of others. (It is not to be confused with Paul's unrelated term *charisma*.) It cannot be said that the Lukan anointing abides, and it cannot be said that all Christians have it, whereas the Johannine anointing (*chrisma*) is had by all Christians (1 John 2:20) and abides (1 John 2:27). The Johannine anointing *teaches* and lends assurance to the believer that he has the truth and should remain *in Christ* (1 John 2:27; cf. 2 Cor. 1:21–22); the Lukan anointing enables one *to be a teacher* and lead others *to Christ* or further *in Christ*. Whereas the Lukan anointing is evidenced by external, mighty deeds of God for the performance of God's will, the Johannine anointing is the quiet, inner witness of the Spirit, which certifies the truth of a teaching.

Unfortunately, Moon's definition above blurs the distinction between the Lukan and the Johannine anointings, as Moon co-mingles the functions of the two anointings. In the opening quotation, note that Moon's first three sentences refer to the classic Pentecostal anointing, whereas the last sentence refers to the "chrismatic," i.e., Johannine anointing: "And those ministered to are invested with a God-consciousness. . . ." (Although, even here, Moon writes as though this God-consciousness comes from the instrumentality of the anointed minister rather than from the *chrisma* of the Holy One, i.e., Jesus, see 1 John 2:20.)

---

[3] "Ye Need Not That Any Man Teach You," *Paraclete* (Fall 1981): 17.

The Johannine Anointing for Today's Christian

In the first century, John was writing to Spirit-endowed believers (3:24; 4:13) who were being seduced by super-spiritualists, whom some have identified as Gnostics; however, John identifies them as *antichrists* (such a one denies the Anointed One, the *Christos*, 2:22). Inasmuch as the *chrisma* serves to certify the truth of "all things" (2:27), false statements to the contrary would be *anti-chrisma*, making John's "antichrist" identification both logical, rhetorically pleasing, and apropos. The common thread in the various branches of Gnosticism was and still is the Gnostic's claim to greater and higher knowledge, usually of an esoteric and thus unverifiable origin and nature. The Gnostics of John's day were denying the humanity and incarnation of Jesus. This eventually led to the denial of the efficacy of the atonement and the trinitarian concept of the godhead.[4] The teachings of today's super-spiritualists eventually deny the sovereignty of God, the Lordship of Christ, and the servanthood of the believer. These historic, biblical doctrines are denied by many teachers today who place man at the center with God in orbit around him.

Unfortunately, Pentecostals, more than other Christians, have gravitated toward these unscriptural teachings. Therefore, a reminder of the Johannine anointing from Pentecostal leaders would be in order. John reminded his readers of the teachings they received in the beginning; these were the truths in which they should continue (1 John 2:24). In the beginning, they had received an anointing, but some were discarding it and opening themselves up to seducing teachers. They left their beginning and no longer relied upon the Teacher or Paraclete (John 14:26) who, in fact, gave them their beginning through the teachings of the apostles (1 John 1:1–5a; 4:5–6).

Conclusions

Though Luke and John both speak of a *chrisma* (Luke using its verb form), the contexts do not suggest a univocal usage of the term. Whereas the Lukan anointing results in usually visible manifestations of the Spirit, the Johannine *chrisma* is an inner witness to the truth of a teaching. The function of the Johannine anointing is to confirm these truths within the hearer, especially as they relate to Jesus (1 John 2:22–23; 4:1–3; 5:5–10; cf. John 14:26; 16:14–15). The text (1 John) seems to indicate that this function of the Spirit is operable in all believers, who have been given the Spirit (3:24; 4:13).

---

[4] Bundrick, "Ye Need Not," 15.

These spiritual concepts are not in competition, neither are they mutually exclusive. Our prayer should be for both: may the fire fall, expanding the kingdom, and may our minds be illumined, securing truth within us.[5]

---

[5] I would like to express my gratitude to Professor Paul Elbert (Church of God Theological Seminary) for his insightful comments on an early draft of this article.

7

The Jerusalem Council and the Gentile Pentecost[1]

The immediate capitulation of the Jerusalem council to Peter upon hearing the Gentiles had had a "Pentecostal" experience suggests at least two important points: (1) a limited practice of glossolalia by non-Christians, and (2) a normative experience of glossolalia by Christians. The sudden capitulation to Peter's defense is a matter of biblical record (Acts 11:18). When the council heard the Gentiles had received the Spirit, "they held their peace" (KJV), "they stopped their criticism"(TEV), "their doubts were silenced" (NEB). A. T. Robertson writes that "Peter's statement of the facts made an unanswerable defence. . . . The wrangling . . . ceased."[2] "Nothing could be said to counter Peter's argument," writes F. F. Bruce. "Their criticism ceased; their worship began."[3]

---

[1] Originally published in *Paraclete* 18.1 (Winter 1984): 4–8.

[2] *Word Pictures in the New Testament* (1930; repr., Grand Rapids: Baker, n.d.), 3:155.

[3] *The Book of the Acts*, NICNT (repr., Grand Rapids: Eerdmans, 1981), 236; cf. Ernst Haenchen, *The Acts of the Apostles: A Commentary*, trans. Bernard Noble and Gerald Shinn, ed. Hugh Anderson and R. McL. Wilson (Philadelphia: Westminster, 1971), 359, 362, and I. Howard Marshall, *The Acts of the Apostles*, TNTC (1980; repr., Grand Rapids: Eerdmans, 1983), 198.

The Gentile Pentecost and Pagan "Tongues"

With the burgeoning of the Pentecostal/charismatic movements has come an increased scholarly interest in what may be considered the distinctive Pentecostal phenomenon, tongues. Unfortunately, this at times has translated into exaggerated claims of glossolalia discoveries. These claims restrict tongues neither temporally nor geographically: "Pagan tribes all over the world have been speaking in tongues for centuries," says Joseph Dillow.[4]

Non-Christian glossolalia has been uncovered in 20th-century B.C. Mesopotamia; in 12th-century B.C. Egypt; in Babylonia; in Greek mystery religions; in Plato's dialogues; in Virgil's Aeneid; in Tahiti, Haiti, Borneo, Hindu-Kush; in the South Pacific, Italy, Japan, Greenland, Australia, Africa, Asia, North and South America; among Jews, Hindus, Buddhists, Shintoists, Moslems, spiritualists, and so on.[5] However, most of these reported instances of glossolalia turn out to be something other than tongues. In an unfortunately unnoticed master's thesis, A. A. Lovekin convincingly argues that many recent glossolalia "finds" are either (a) significantly different from New Testament (and 20th-century Christian) glossolalia, or (b) lacking in the details which are necessary to determine glossolalic utterances. Lovekin writes,

> There is no well documented instances of phenomena similar to apostolic glossolalia in either the preceding or contemporary pagan, or Jewish religions. The only similarity is a quality of ecstasy noted in prophecy which is present in the experience of the glossolalist. But this is not of equal degree because the ecstatic prophet has to lose consciousness and this is nowhere to be found in apostolic glossolalia.[6]

---

[4] *Speaking in Tongues* (Grand Rapids: Zondervan, 1975), 189.

[5] Louis S. Bauman, *The Tongues Movement*, rev. ed. (Winona Lake, IN: BMH Books, 1963), 5; John T. Bunn, "Glossolalia in Historical Perspective," in *Speaking in Tongues: Let's Talk About It*, ed. Watson E. Mills (Waco, Texas: Word Books, 1973), 36–47; Donald W. Burdick, *Tongues: To Speak or Not to Speak* (Chicago: Moody Press, 1969), 65–67; Robert G. Gromacki, *The Modern Tongues Movement*, rev. ed. (1967; Nutley, NJ: Presbyterian and Reformed Publishing Co., 1972), 5–10; John F. MacArthur, Jr., *The Charismatics*, 108–12; Chris W. Parnell, *Understanding Tongues-Speaking* (Nashville, TN: Broadman Press, nd.), 16, 18, 35; Charles R. Smith, *Tongues in Biblical Perspective*, rev. ed. (1972; Winona Lake, IN: BMH Books, 1973), 15–21.

[6] "Glossolalia: A Critical Study of Alleged Origins, the New Testament and the Early Church" (MA Thesis, University of the South, 1962), 40; cf. G. W. H. Lampe, *God As Spirit: The Bampton Lectures, 1976* (Oxford, UK: Clarendon Press, 1977), 53–54. The point to be made here is not that ancient pagans never exhibited glossolalia, but rather if they did it was on a very limited basis, restricted to priests, priestesses, and

While researching the linguistic aspect of glossolalia, W. J. Samarin also faced the problem of unsubstantiated claims of glossolalia. Concerning those claims and the results of his own research, he writes,

> I would like to make the strong hypothesis that artificial, human like languages—in other words, glossolalia as I use the term—are rarely found in societies that have had no contact with Christianity. This claim would reject other ones to the contrary, on the grounds that what is unintelligible or unlike human language to an observer is not to be automatically designated "glossolalia."[7]

The immediate capitulation of the Judaists to Peter bears out our belief (and the implications of Lovekin and Samarin) that non-Christian glossolalia was scarcely known by New Testament Christians. Otherwise, Peter would not have had an "unanswerable defence" and the Judaists would not have "kept their peace" upon hearing of the Gentiles' Pentecostal experience. They would, in fact, have had a devastating rebuttal: "The Gentiles received evil spirits and spoke in pagan tongues!" Thus, it seems reasonable to infer from the Jerusalem council's abrupt submission to the Spirit that pagan tongues were not as pervasive as some detractors of the Pentecostal movement have suggested. Such would have destroyed the credibility of New Testament tongues as an evidential sign.

Glossolalia Was a Normative Christian Experience

If the first implication denies the wide spread phenomenon of glossolalia among pagans, the second seems to confirm the normality of glossolalia among New Testament Christians. Glossolalia would not have served as a credible sign of Spirit-baptism if it were not a repeated and thus normative Christian experience. If the only occurrence of glossolalia had been at Pentecost, tongues would have hardly been the incontrovertible evidence which silenced the Judaists, many of whom had never themselves experienced tongues (according to the anti-Pentecostal argument). Thus, F. D. Bruner's argument that the "tongues of Pentecost" convinced the circumcision party of God's acceptance of the Gentiles is fundamentally flawed. Bruner contends that tongues were "not the normal initiatory experience of the church

---

those holding similar positions. The fact remains that if anti-Pentecostal arguments from the purported similarities of pagan and Christian glossolalia lose their force when confronted by radical differences, they pale into oblivion when confronted by the decreeing of glossolalia by Almighty God who has freighted tongues with rich, spiritual meaning in the proper Christian context.

[7] *Tongues of Men and Angels*, 222.

and that its only correspondence was Pentecost."[8] His proof from Scripture is that "Peter does not say that the Holy Spirit came upon Cornelius's household 'just as he always does with everyone'" (194). Gardiner clarifies Bruner's argument, writing:

> When Peter defended his visit to Cornelius' house before the council at Jerusalem he had to reach back eight years—clear back to Pentecost—to find his comparison—"as I began to speak, the Holy Spirit fell on them, as on US AT THE BEGINNING " (Acts 11:15). He couldn't say "as on all the churches ever since Pentecost," because that wasn't the case! (54–55).

There is, of course, good reason why Peter did not say this, namely, Cornelius's experience in Caesarea was the *initial* outpouring on the Gentiles just as the apostles' experience in Jerusalem was the *initial* outpouring on the Jews. The epochal experience of the Gentiles finds its counterpart not in the everyday experience of the Jewish initiates since Pentecost but in the epochal experience of the Jews at Pentecost. These are the precedents and the archetypes to which every Jew and Gentile should hearken back and in which they should long to participate.[9] (It is also possible that Peter was speaking directly to leaders of the council who had participated in the Jerusalem Pentecost; in which case he would logically point them back to *their* baptism in the Spirit. Marshall adds that the pointing back to Pentecost rather than to the first converts from Judaism prevented any "second-class citizens" label from being attached to the Gentiles [197].) Thus, Bruner's scriptural proof for his conclusion that "after Pentecost the Pentecostal

---

[8] *A Theology of the Holy Spirit* (Grand Rapids: Eerdmans, 1970), 195; cf. George E. Gardiner, *The Corinthian Catastrophe* (Grand Rapids: Kregel, 1974), 9, 54–55.

[9] One might rightly ask why tongues seemed to coincide with conversion in Cornelius's case. The two distinct experiences of conversion and Spirit-baptism were divinely telescoped, it seems, so the outward sign of tongues would provide the irrefragable evidence necessary to convince the hardest heart at the Jerusalem council. Note that this was a unique occasion, having no parallel in Scripture. To make the Gentile Pentecost the norm as some have tried (MacArthur, Jr., *The Charismatics*, 99) is to make the exception the rule. The entire Christian experience (in this world) is of a stratified character. It commences with conversion and culminates with a heavenly transformation. In between are experiences which may interact with each other in various ways. The Pentecostal baptism in the Spirit finds itself between the *archē* and the *telos* of the believer's earthly existence. In Cornelius's case, for the sake of signification, Spirit-baptism was made to occur simultaneously with conversion, for which there is no immediate outward sign. Since one must *first* receive (the regenerating work of) the Spirit (Romans 8:9) before he qualifies as a candidate for Spirit baptism, the Jerusalem council, upon hearing of the gentiles' Pentecostal experience, could logically conclude God had granted the gentiles "repentance unto life, . . . purifying their hearts by faith" (Acts 11:18; 15:9).

manifestations [of glossolalia] were not only not normative but probably not known" (194) is unconvincing.

Though arguing from what is not said is normally a risky business, we can say it is at least interesting that tongues are not mentioned in Peter's (or Luke's) retelling of the Gentile Pentecost (11:4–17). Yet the occurrence of glossolalia was supposed to have been the compelling sign which immediately silenced the Judaists (even as it astounded and convinced Peter and the other eyewitnesses). That Peter (or Luke) would forget to mention that the Gentiles spoke in tongues is inexplicable, unless perhaps tongues had become established as the normative outward sign of Spirit baptism, rendering any mentioning of it superfluous. Notice also Luke does not state the council inquired how Peter knew the Gentiles had been baptized in the Spirit (11:15, 16). Did they presume glossolalia was present at the Gentile Pentecost? Did Luke assume his readers would make the presumption? If so, why?[10]

Conclusions

The credibility of glossolalia as a sign of Spirit baptism would have been severely weakened if (1) pagan tongues had been as prevalent as many anti-Pentecostals purport, and (2) Christian glossolalia had occurred only once before the Gentile Pentecost, i.e., at Pentecost 8 years earlier. Since the glossolalia attending the Gentile Pentecost was accepted as a valid sign by the Jerusalem council, pagan tongues were probably not a widespread

---

[10] To reply that Peter probably mentioned tongues but Luke omitted them doesn't explain why Luke writing by inspiration of the Holy Spirit did not mention tongues. It is possible that Peter's allusion to Pentecost in Acts 11:15, 17 might suffice to suggest glossolalia to the Judaists. But if true, this may imply that, in the mind of the New Testament Christian, Pentecost was not the epochal salvific event that Dunn, Bruner, and others posit, but rather the genesis of the charismatic ministry of the believer. There seem to be only two explanations that justify Peter's or Luke's omission of the incomparable evidence of tongues: (1) tongues had been established as the sign of Spirit baptism; (2) Luke saw no need to mention tongues in what is now known as chapter 11 after just mentioning them in the previous chapter. The second solution seems weak, given the importance of the council meeting, the swift surrender to Peter's argument, and Luke's statement that "Peter began and explained everything to them precisely as it had happened" (Acts 11:4). Both of these solutions contain presumptions on Luke's part. The first states that Luke presumed his readers would not be misled by the omission of tongues since Spirit baptism, by nature, includes tongues. The second states that Luke presumed his readers would not be misled by the omission of tongues since he so recently mentioned them. Actually, there is no reason to create a disjunction; the solution could contain both presumptions without negating either.

phenomenon, and Christian glossolalia was in all likelihood a normative, Christian experience.[11]

---

[11] Marshal as much as admits that in Acts tongues is the inevitable sign of Spirit baptism. However, since he conflates Spirit baptism and conversion and assumes people do not speak in tongues at conversion today, he is forced to use silence and Paul to (mis)interpret Luke (*Acts*, 194; cf. James D. G. Dunn, *Baptism*, 229). Marshall also errs in not considering that Paul nowhere discusses tongues, but rather the abuse of tongues. Though Paul's treatment of tongues teems with helpful implications, one must go to Luke to formulate a full-blown doctrine of Spirit baptism and glossolalia.

8

Use of *gar* in Acts 10:46[1]

Perhaps the most distinctive (and controversial) doctrine of Pentecostalism is that which asserts glossolalic utterances consistently accompany the initial Spirit-baptism event. Interestingly, a common three-letter Greek particle is used by Luke in a context that lends strong support to this particular Pentecostal doctrine. That Greek word is *gar*.

Here is a noncontroversial word if ever there was one. *Gar* occurs in the New Testament 1,056 times. In the King James Version, it is translated as the coordinating conjunction *for* 1,001 times; in the Revised version it is translated *for* 1,054 times—all but two occurrences of *gar*.[2] In Acts this innocuous little particle occurs about 78 times, and in 74 cases it is translated *for* (KJV).

In the verse that will presently be under examination—Acts 10:46—*gar* is translated *for* in the King James Version, New King James Version, Revised Standard Version, New Revised Standard Version, New American Bible, New English Bible, English Standard Version, New American Standard Version, Today's English Version, New International Version, Douay-Rheims Version, Young's Literal Translation, Phillips, and the Living Bible, which are all the versions I consulted.

---

[1] Originally published in *Paraclete* 22.2 (Spring 1988): 15–18.

[2] H. E. Dana and Julius R. Mantey, *A Manual Grammar of the Greek New Testament* (Toronto: Macmillan, 1927), 243.

General Usage of *gar*

It is apropos at this juncture to allow the grammarians to inform us of the nature of this resolute little word. Dana and Mantey (referencing Kühner) delineate three uses of *gar*: (1) to express a ground or reason (illative usage), (2) to express an explanation, and (3) to express confirmation or assurances. "It is most frequently used in the illative sense introducing a reason. At such times it means *for*."[3]

According to Smyth, "γάρ [*gar*] is especially common in sentences which offer a reason for, or an explanation of, a preceding or following statement. . . . It serves to introduce a cause of, or a reason for, an action before mentioned; to justify a preceding utterance; to confirm the truth of a previous statement."[4] Davis and Robertson write, "Sometimes it [*gar*] is merely transitional or continuative . . . , *but the illative use is plain*."[5] They call it the "chief inferential particle." Elsewhere, Robertson writes, "In a sense it [*gar*] is often causal. . . ."[6]

As a postpositive conjunction, *gar* is always positioned between two clauses. According to the consensus of Greek grammarians, as shown above, interpreters are justified in finding a causal or inferential (illative) relationship between two clauses joined by *gar* and lacking specific contextual ingredients that better support the explanatory or confirmatory sense of *gar*.

Luke's Use of *gar* in Acts

More often than not, Luke uses *gar* as a coordinating conjunction creating a causal or inferential relationship between two clauses. A clear instance of the illative *gar* occurs in Acts 2:15: "These men are not drunk, as you imagine; for [*gar*] it is only nine in the morning" (NEB). The inferential relationship between these two clauses is so evident that some translators have not deemed it necessary even to translate *gar*: "These men are not drunk, as

---

[3] Ibid., 242, 243.

[4] Herbert Weir Smyth, *Greek Grammar*, rev. ed. (Cambridge, MA: Harvard University Press, 1956), 638, 639.

[5] A. T. Robertson and W. Hersey Davis, *A New Short Grammar of the Greek Testament* (Grand Rapids: Baker, 1930) 317, 337, italics added.

[6] A. T. Robertson, *A Short Grammar of the Greek New Testament* (n.p.: privately printed, 1908), 159; see also Robertson's *A Grammar of the Greek New Testament in the Light of Historical Research,* 4th ed. (Nashville: Broadman, 1934), 1191. Blass, Debrunner, and Funk discuss *gar* under the subheading "Causal coordinating conjunctions," *A Greek Grammar of the New Testament and Other Early Christian Literature* (Chicago: University of Chicago, 1961), 235. Arndt, Gingrich, and Bauer write that *gar* is "used to express cause, inference, continuation, or to explain," *A Greek-English Lexicon of the New Testament* (Chicago: University of Chicago, 1957), 235.

you suppose. It's only nine in the morning!" (NIV; see also Phillips and TEV). The Revised Standard Version spells out the inferential relationship with the semi-causal conjunction *since*: "For these men are not drunk, as you suppose, since it is only the third hour of the day."

It is a mistake to see *gar* as a causal conjunction in the strictest sense. Robertson has written, "In sense it is often causal, *but it is not considered a causal conjunction in the formal usage.*"[7] If *gar* were causal in the formal sense, Acts 2:15 would imply the nonsensical idea that the coming of nine o'clock in the morning causes all drunk men to be instantly sober. Instead, the illative *gar* introduces in the second clause the ground or reason that supports the first clause.[8] These men could not be drunk because devout Jews simply do not imbibe excessive quantities of wine by nine in the

---

[7] Robertson, *A Short Grammar*, 159, italics added.

[8] A list of several other instances of *gar* in Acts may clarify the usage of the illative *gar*:

a. "They seized Peter and John, and because [*gar*] it was evening, they put them in jail until the next day" (4:3).

b. "Then said the Lord to him, Put off thy shoes from thy feet: for [*gar*] the place where thou standest is holy ground" (7:33 KJV).

c. "You have no part or share in this ministry, because [*gar*] your heart is not right before God" (8:21). This verse contains an equally important *gar*. Here *gar* appears to support the Pentecostal doctrine of subsequence—that is, Spirit baptism may occur after regeneration. In this verse, if the first clause refers to the Pentecostal experience and the second clause to salvation (regeneration), it would seem that Peter thought that one must be regenerate in order to have a part in the Pentecostal experience. The verse is worthy of investigation.

d. "But Paul cried with a loud voice, saying, Do thyself no harm: for [*gar*] we are all here" (16:28 KJV).

e. "Before he sailed, he had his hair cut off at Cenchrea because [*gar*] of a vow he had taken" (18:18).

f. "And Paul went down, and fell on him, and embracing him said, Trouble not yourselves; for [*gar*] his life is in him" (20:10 KJV).

g. "Paul had decided to sail past Ephesus to avoid spending time in the province of Asia, for [*gar*] he was in a hurry to reach Jerusalem, if possible, by the day of Pentecost" (20:16).

h. "After sighting Cyprus and leaving it on our left we sailed to Syria and put in at Tyre, since [*gar*] that was where the ship was to discharge her cargo" (21:3 Phillips).

i. "Don't give in to them, because [*gar*] more than forty of them are waiting in ambush for him" (23:21).

j. "But now I urge you to keep up your courage, because [*gar*] not one of you will be lost; only the ship will be destroyed" (27:22).

k. "Therefore I encourage you to take some food, for [*gar*] this is for your preservation: for not a hair from the head of any of you shall perish" (27:34 NASB).

l. "But we would like to hear your ideas, because [*gar*] we know that everywhere people speak against this party that you belong to" (28:22 TEV).

morning. This they knew inductively from firsthand experience—a point to remember when we come to Acts 10:46.

Acts 10:46 and *gar*

"While Peter was still speaking these words, the Holy Spirit came on all who heard the message. The circumcised believers who had come with Peter were astonished that the gift of the Holy Spirit had been poured out even on the Gentiles. For [*gar*] they heard them speaking in tongues and praising God" (Acts 10:44–46).

Some eight years after Pentecost, the Holy Spirit was poured out upon the Gentiles. For those Jewish Christians who were not with Peter to witness this event, there were objections—that is, until they were informed the Holy Spirit had fallen on the Gentiles even as He fell on the Jews. "When they heard this, they had no further objections" (Acts 11:18). For those "astonished" Jewish believers who were with Peter when the gift of the Holy Spirit was poured out on the Gentiles, the proof that the Gentiles had received this gift was indisputable: "For [*gar*] they heard them speaking in tongues" (Acts 10:46).

There is no doubt that *gar* in Acts 10:46 is to be taken in the illative sense. That is, it introduces the ground, reason, or proof that the Gentiles had received the Holy Spirit. The question is, how did speaking in other tongues become such a sure sign of Spirit-baptism? It would seem that only a divinely assigned cause-effect pattern would justify Luke's use of *gar* in Acts 10:46 and explain the unopposed acceptance of the Gentiles simply because they had praised God in other tongues. Just as the first-century Jews had inductively learned that men do not imbibe excessive quantities of wine before 9 a.m., so first-century Christians had inductively learned that speaking in tongues was God's appointed evidence that a Christian had been filled with or baptized in the Holy Spirit. Not only is this the implication of *gar* in Acts 10:46, but it is supported by the other passages in Acts where the immediate, observable initial evidence of Spirit-baptism is described. (See Acts 2:4 and 19:6.)

9

Tongues Shall Cease
A Critical Survey of the Supposed
Cessation of the Charismata[1]

"Tongues shall cease." Over 1,900 years have passed since the apostle Paul penned this prediction in a letter to the Corinthians (c. AD 54), and not a few cessationists have argued that the future tense of the verb (*pausontai,* "cease") is no longer warranted—the use of the past tense is now justifiable, or so the argument goes. R. G. Gromacki concludes his book, "'Tongues . . . shall cease' (1 Corinthians 13:8). They have."[2] And according to George Zeller, Paul's injunction not to forbid tongues "no longer applies today."[3]

The Pentecostals and the cessationists both agree that *charismata* as described by Paul and Luke are temporary. The problem arises when one attempts to determine the factor (and thus arrive at an approximate date) responsible for the cessation of these manifestations of the Spirit. For the Pentecostal/charismatic, Scripture, church history, and personal

---

[1] Originally published in *Paraclete* 17.4 (Fall 1983): 20–28. For an updated and expanded version, see *Praying in the Spirit* (Tulsa: Empowered Life Academic-Harrison House, 2016), 73–80, 139–204.

[2] Gromacki, *Modern Tongues Movement*, 143.

[3] George W. Zeller, *God's Gift of Tongues: The Nature, Purpose and Duration of Tongues as Taught in the Bible* (Neptune, NJ: Loizeaux Brothers, 1978), 104.

experience indicate that all the *charismata* are to continue through the Church Age. But for the cessationist, the prophetic, miraculous, "sign" gifts ceased in AD 54, 58, or as some say AD 68/69; still others say AD 70 or 90, 98, or 100, or certainly before AD 200. Some say the cessation was immediate; others claim it occurred over several decades, tapering off gradually.[4]

Since the conjectures about the date of the cessation usually range from AD 54 to 100 (plus a generation or so for the time necessary for the apostles' last charismatic disciple to die or the New Testament to become "available" and "circulated"), if any one of these conjectures is correct, the most any guess could be off the mark is approximately 86 years. This estimate is far from being off 1,900 years, a possibility the Pentecostal must consider. Conversely, it is a possibility the cessationist must consider if the Pentecostal interpretation of 1 Corinthians 13:8–13 has validity.

But the cessationist cannot treat a span of 86 years as inconsequential; ignoring or depreciating this difference is unjustifiable. If the cessationists actually know why (and when) these *charismata* ceased, they must be able to convince Pentecostals and fellow cessationists with compelling exegeses and cogent arguments. Thus far, cessationist rejoinders have lacked these qualities.

The Survey

The first important modern theologian to give detailed consideration to the cessation of *charismata* was B. B. Warfield (1851–1921).[5] Warfield lists four different factors, either proposed or endorsed by him, which he contends were to effect or coincide with the cessation of the *charismata:*

1. When the Apostolic Age passed (6)
2. When the last disciple to whom the apostles conferred a gift died (23, 24)
3. When the whole knowledge of God designed for the saving health of the world had been incorporated into the living body of the world's thought (26)
4. When the revelation of God in Christ had taken place and had become in Scripture and church a constituent part of the cosmos (27)

---

[4] If the *charismata* did cease, it would seem the cessation would have had to have been gradual. Otherwise, we have Christians throughout Christendom discovering that one minute they spoke with tongues and the next minute such was impossible, and all this without a whisper of the day or event preserved for posterity.

[5] *Counterfeit Miracles* (1918; repr., Edinburgh: Banner of Truth Trust, 1972).

Anyone looking for a precisely stated factor and date will receive little help from Warfield.

Douglas Judisch, writing some 60 years after Warfield, gives five factors/dates for the cessation of tongues:[6]

1. In AD 70 (43)
2. With the death of John the Apostle (49)
3. Shortly after John's death (63)
4. When the apostles' last charismatic disciple died (75–76n2), and
5. When the Christian matured in the faith; for Paul it was prior to his writing of 1 Corinthians (83)

For Judisch, tongues passed away first in AD 54, again in AD 70 "with the smoke that arose from the temple afire" (43), and finally, in the second century when the last of the apostles' charismatic disciples died. Thus, *five* different factors are proffered to effect the cessation of tongues! These contradictory factors and dates are only partially explained by proposing two kinds of cessation: (1) cessation of distribution, and (2) cessation of operation.

Warfield and Judisch are not isolated cases. The chart I have prepared (see at the end of the chapter) underscores the cessationists' inability to delineate only one cessation factor (and date). Of the 38 authors in the survey only 16 defend *one* factor/date, and some of these add qualifiers; for example, Zeller writes, ". . . *on or before 70 A.D.*" (90). Criswell says tongues "ceased almost immediately" but fails to anchor the "immediately" to any firm, categorical factor: "The Church grew up and no longer needed the sign."[7]

Thus, even many of these choosing only one factor do not speak with certainty. A few, however, state not only one factor but a definite year with absolute certainty. Gardiner and Schutz are possibly the only two who do this. Both choose AD 70: "When Titus the Roman sacked the city of Jerusalem and dispersed the Jews over the world in 70 A.D.," Gardiner writes, "the reason for tongues disappeared and the gift ceased in and of itself. Since then there have been no Biblical tongues spoken!"[8]

By far the majority of the cessationists choose AD 90–98, when the apostle John penned his last inspired word, as the factor/date of cessation. Others opt for c. AD 100, allowing John to use the *charismata* until his

---

[6] *An Evaluation of Claims to the Charismatic Gifts* (Grand Rapids: Baker, 1978).

[7] *The Baptism, Filling and Gifts of the Holy Spirit* (Grand Rapids: Zondervan, 1973), 122.

[8] *The Corinthian Catastrophe* (Grand Rapids: Kregel, 1974), 36.

death.[9] Still others allow the *charismata* to reach further into the second century, extending them through the life of the apostles' last charismatic disciple or until the New Testament became "available" or "circulated." But even of these three groups (31 individuals) only eight[10] do not hedge their guess—23 choose other factors (and thus dates) as well.

The Problem of Ambiguity

Imprecisely defined terms and concepts make it almost impossible to determine the factor/date some of the date-setters choose. Samples of these enigmatic and problematic expressions are listed below, followed by pointed remarks.

1. *Mature church.* What constitutes a "mature" church? How are we to determine when (if?) the church matured? (Thomas, 108–10; Vander Lugt, 69; cf. Swete, 378–79).[11]
2. *Almost universal acceptance of the New Testament by the church.* Please define "almost universal" and "acceptance" (Walvoord, 174). The canon was not sure until the fourth century!
3. *Faith established.* Define "established." How do we determine when it happened? (Unger, *Baptism*, 140). (This question is appropriate after all the remaining expressions.)
4. *New Testament made available.* Define "available" (Unger, *Tongues*, 96). Does this include translations?[12]
5. *New Testament in circulation.* Define "circulation" (Unger, *Tongues*, 148; R. W. DeHaan, 14). Many languages still do not have the New Testament in circulation.

---

[9] The majority of cessationists believe prophetic, miraculous, "sign" gifts ceased because (1) "the very moment the last verse of Revelation was written" (Ronald E. Baxter, *The Charismatic Gift of Tongues* [Grand Rapids: Kregel, 1981], 63) God's revelation to man (which includes the revelatory gifts) was completed (about AD 96), or (2), the last of the apostles died (about AD 100), ending the Apostolic Age. Many cessationists treat these factors as though they happened simultaneously. Obviously they did not, however close they may have been. But more important, they are two completely different factors, requiring two entirely different sustaining arguments.

[10] A study of other works by those authors would probably prove this figure too high.

[11] See pages 47–48 for full bibliographic data.

[12] Charles R. Swindoll writes this intriguing passage: "Now we must understand that the first-century church was indeed different from ours today. Without God's final word *bound neatly in a clearly printed Bible*, the people of that day had to wait upon God for His truth to be communicated through gifted men" (*Tongues: An Answer to Charismatic Confusion* [Portland, OR: Multnomah, 1981], 11, italics added).

6. *Revelation . . . had become . . . a constituent part of the cosmos.* "Constituent part"? (Warfield, 27).
7. *Revelation incorporated into world's thought.* Define "incorporated" and "world's thought" (Warfield, 27).
8. *Foundational period.* Was the foundation laid before all the apostles and prophets died? Before the New Testament was completed? Did the operation of tongues and other "temporary" gifts cease *within* or *at the end* of the "foundational period"? (Epp, 42; Coppes, 57; Dillow, 115; Schutz, 16, 17; Smith, 84).
9. And finally, the word *cease* must be clarified. It should be made clear whether one is speaking of the cessation of the *distribution* or the cessation of the *operation* of the *charismata*.

If dialogue between Pentecostals and non-Pentecostals is to be meaningful, non-Pentecostal rejoinders must be couched in precise, unambiguous language.

The New Testament Inscribed

For those dating the cessation in AD 90–98 and 100 +, the inscribed revelation of the New Testament plays a momentous role—it is indeed the cessation factor. But even among these there is no agreement upon *why* and *when.* We go from the New Testament being written, to its being "circulated," to its being made "available," to its being "accepted by the church," to its being "incorporated into the world's thought." For some choosing the completed New Testament as the cessation factor, it is only a matter of 1 Corinthians 13:8–10 being fulfilled: "Whether there be tongues, they shall cease . . . when that which is perfect is come. . . ." For these the "perfect" (*teleion*) to come is the New Testament, which culminated when the last letter of Holy Writ was penned.[13] But the great majority of commentaries and many cessationists (e.g., Hoekema, *Tongue-Speaking,* 106–07n8.; MacArthur, 165–66; Vander Lugt, 69) reject this interpretation of 1 Corinthians 13:8–12.

Paul Elbert, arguing for charismatic continuity, has attempted to

---

[13] To some cessationists, the *teleion* is (or includes) the mature church (Criswell, 134; Swete, 378, 379), or mature Christians (Epp, 42; Judisch, 83; H. Carl Shank, *More of Christ: Preliminary Thoughts Concerning a Reformed Antidote to the Current Charismatic Movement* [Cherry Hill, NJ: Mack Publishing, 1973], 23). [I've yet to see a cogent cessationist argument that explains how and why the completion of the Scriptures would effect the cessation of revelatory spiritual gifts since the canon of Scripture was not fixed until the fourth century (much less distributed in completed form) and even today there are people groups without the completed Scriptures in their language and millions more who are illiterate.]

illustrate Paul's understanding of 1 Corinthians 13:8–10. His work thoroughly refutes the position that Unger, Dillow, Thomas, Walvoord, Ryrie, Chantry, and numerous other cessationists take. From the historical, epistolary, linguistic, grammatical, and philological perspectives, Elbert presents evidence that nullifies the classical cessationist argument from 1 Corinthians 13:8–10 and supports the Pentecostal interpretation. A passage from pages 26 and 27 of Elbert's 36-page paper (with 101 footnotes), regarding the Greek voice, reflects the thoroughness which characterizes the entire paper:

> I have examined, roughly speaking, at least two thousand examples of diverse forms of *pauo/pauomai* [*cease*] from the Classics to the Fathers. Aside from a very marked decrease of instances, which were already rare, of detectable reflexive stress upon the onset of Koine, the usage is essentially the same throughout in all forms. My research leads me to clearly corroborate the findings of Veitch-Smyth and to further add the behavioral corollary, which is really implicit in their descriptions, that *when no object is involved* (13:8) *the middle form is universally preferred* (I know of no deviation).[14]

That which is "perfect" can be nothing less than Christ and the eternal state.

For other cessationists opting for the completed New Testament as the cessation factor, the issue is not as simple or clearcut as the mere fulfilling of 1 Corinthians 13:8–10. It is a theological issue of immense proportion. For these, the continued use of revelatory gifts, producing "fresh revelations," infringes upon the sufficiency and finality of Scripture.[15] Pentecostal scholars have yet to answer this charge thoroughly.[16] Perhaps it is

---

[14] See Paul Elbert, "Face to Face: Then or Now? An Exegesis of First Corinthians 13:8–13, "Society for Pentecostal Studies," Springfield, MO, December 1977 (now available in *Strangers to Fire: When Tradition Trumps Scripture*, ed. Robert W. Graves [Tulsa: Empowered Life Academic-Harrison House, 2014], 493–520); see also Elbert's rebuttal of the "dispensational closure model" as it affects the gifts of the Spirit in "The Charismatic Movement in the Church of England: An Overview," *Pneuma* 6:1 (1984): 27–50.

[15] "Pentecostal practice is a *de facto* denial of the sufficiency of Scripture. Pentecostals are unconsciously despising the revelation of God in Christ as insufficient" (Chantry, 27, 33). See also Baxter, 131; Gaffin, 121; Carl Henry, "Evangelicals: Out of the Closet but Going Nowhere?" *Christianity Today* (January 4, 1980): 16–22 and *God, Revelation and Authority*, vol. 4 (Waco, TX: Word Books, 1979), 252, 253, 283, 284, 488, 500; Reymond, 26, 27; Shank, 36.

[16] It is noteworthy, however, that in 1927 Pentecostal scholar Donald Gee was responding (albeit briefly) to this objection: "We hasten to remove any false impression that we expect or claim . . . infallible inspiration to be given today; we believe that in that particular measure it ceased with the completion of the

because the objection seems so outrageously misplaced, given the high view of Scripture the great majority of Pentecostals hold.[17]

Since Scripture says nothing explicitly about the cessation of the charismata (except 1 Corinthians 13:8–10 which decrees them until Kingdom come), an extrabiblical argument must be posited.[18] Thus, for some of the cessationists listed in the AD 90–98 column of the chart, the cessation of the charismata often becomes an assumed a fortiori based upon the following syllogism:

Major Premise:	Extrabiblical revelations undermine the sufficiency of Scripture.
Minor Premise:	Prophecy and tongues produce extrabiblical revelations.
Conclusion:	Prophecy and tongues undermine the sufficiency of Scripture.[19]

As much as the cessationists have tried to make the major premise self-evident, it is not. The key term, unfortunately, is the most nebulous—*sufficiency*. Sufficient for what? The obvious, most general answer is that *it is sufficient for what it was given*. The basic error of the

---

Scriptures. But in the sense in which the spiritual gifts of the Early Church were inspired, we believe inspiration should continue right through this dispensation. We have already pointed out that the spiritual gifts of the Early Church were not regarded as infallible; and it is a fallacy to think that even in apostolic days they were placed upon a level with the Scriptures" (*Concerning Spiritual Gifts*, rev. ed. [1927; Springfield, MO: Gospel Publishing House, 1972], 103).

[17] Unger pays Pentecostals a left-handed compliment when he writes: "It is . . . a strange anomaly that Pentecostals and Neo-Pentecostals champion the gift of tongues for today, yet inconsistently reject extrabiblical prophecies and extrabiblical knowledge by special gifts of the Holy Spirit. Pentecostals, like non-Pentecostals, study the Word and make it the source of their spiritual knowledge and prophetic instruction. They do not rely upon the pronouncements of believers who claim the gift of prophecy or the gift of knowledge today apart from the written Word" (*Baptism*, 142). Note also anti-Pentecostal historian R. M. Anderson's remark that, among early Pentecostals, "revelations were rarely claimed to be entirely new, but, rather, fresh insights into truths residing in the Bible . . ." (*Vision of the Disinherited*, 154). See Larry W. Hurtado, "Why Pentecostals Need the Bible" and Joseph R. Flower, "The Purpose of Prophetic Utterance," *Paraclete,* 6.1 (Winter 1972): 20–21 and 22–25; and Cecil M. Robeck, Jr., "How Do You Judge Prophetic Utterance?" *Paraclete,* 11.2 (Spring 1977): 12–16; [see also Robeck's "The Gift of Prophecy and the All-Sufficiency of Scripture."]

[18] Honest scholarship recognizes that the Scriptures do not teach a cessation of the *charismata* in this Age. Therefore, the better anti-Pentecostal treatises of the future will probably be more theoretical than exegetical (e.g., Carl Henry in theology and R. M. Anderson in history/sociology).

[19] See Dillow, 134.

43

cessationist is lumping the two—inscripturated revelation and revelatory *charismata*—into the same category on the assumption that they were given for the same purpose.[20] There is no scriptural or logical reason for doing this.

To answer the cessationists' objection summarily and tentatively, I would say it is difficult to accept that the very Scriptures decreeing gifts are negated by the gifts. It is also difficult to accept that the Scriptures could replace the gifts—even revelatory gifts—since they perform different functions entirely. Indeed, a major error of the cessationists is that they focus on the source and authority of the *charismata* and ignore their function. Since the Scriptures and the *charismata* have the same source, so the argument goes, they have the same authority; thus, the *charismata* undermine the sufficiency and finality of the Scriptures. But when local prophecies are made subject to Scripture, the Pentecostal asks, "How does this derogate the authority of Scripture? Does it not, in fact, exalt it?"

If a prophecy is from God, it is indeed authoritative; but though all such prophecies have the same origin, it doesn't follow that they have the same function. One function of Scripture is its service as The Standard. But if it alone serves as The Standard, how can prophetic utterances attain its glory or undermine its supremacy? All prophetic utterances are subject to its blazing light. If they survive, they are gold; if not, they are dross and are rejected by the *logos-koinonia*—the community governed by the Word. Pentecostals indeed shout *sola scriptura*—and louder than most.[21]

Scripture is sufficient for what it was given; Scripture is final, not to be contradicted or overridden by local prophetic utterances which are, along with all *charismata*, "For the perfecting of the saints, for the work of the ministry, for the edifying of the body of Christ: till we all come in the unity of the faith, and of the knowledge of the Son of God, unto a perfect man, unto the measure of the stature of the fulness of Christ" (Eph 4:12–14).

Thus, it seems that the cessationists who fall in the AD 90–98 and

---

[20] "It is too restrictive to confine the purpose of revelation solely to the writing of scripture, for it was also given to enhance, complement, amplify, illustrate or personally apply God's truths and to convict or strengthen people. When this was its purpose revelation could parallel recorded truth but it would never contradict it. We know that there were many Spirit-inspired events and revelations during the original apostles' lifetime that are omitted from the Biblical record, for these had a personal, local or passing application (2 Corinthians 12:1–4, 12; Acts 5:12; 6:8–10; 14:3, 4; 21:9; Romans 15:17–19; 1 Peter 4:10)" (Jim McNair, *Experiencing the Holy Spirit* [Minneapolis, MN: Bethany Fellowship, 1977], 48).

[21] [Though in this context this is an accurate statement, I would point the reader to the subsection on page 129 titled "The Formation of the Canon."]

AD 100+ columns on the chart have been unable to prove that the *charismata* did indeed cease when John penned his last inspired word or breathed his last breath; just as those falling under AD 54, 58, 68/ 69, 70 have been unable to prove their hypotheses.

Conclusion

The variety of answers cessationists give to the same questions and their inability to come to terms with each other do not mean all of them are mistaken. One theory could be correct. So, I am not positing that the varieties of theories mean all are wrong. But I would say they demonstrate indecisiveness within cessationist circles and suggest the inability of the cessationists to answer a question which is of immense significance to the church today. The attenuated scholarship of the cessationist begs for precise terminology, convincing exegeses, and persuasive interpretation. Having attained these, the cessationist will either convince the Pentecostal that the *charismata* have ceased—or convince himself that they have not.

PROPOSED DATES OF CHARISMATA CESSATION*

AD 54 1 Cor Written	AD 58 Last Miracle Recorded	AD 68/69 Hebrews Written	AD 70 Jerusalem Sacked	AD 90–98 Last NT Book Written	c. AD 100 Apostle John Dies	AD 100+ NT Circulated
Banks	(gradual)			Banks	Banks	
Baxter	(gradual)		Baxter	Baxter		
		Burdick		Burdick	Burdick	Burdick
				Carter		
				Chantry		
				Cooke	Cooke	
Coppes	(cease in four stages)			Coppes	Coppes	
Criswell	(tongues cease before other gifts)			Criswell		
M.R. DeHaan	(gradual)			M.R. DeHaan		
					R.W. DeHaan	R.W. DeHaan
		Dillow	Dillow	Dillow		
Epp				Epp	Epp	
				Gaffin		
			Gardiner			
		Gromacki		Gromacki		
				Gustafson		
				Hoekema	Hoekema	
Judisch			Judisch	Judisch	Judisch	Judisch
	MacArthur	(gradual)		MacArthur	MacArthur	
				Packer	Packer	
				Pentecost		
				Reymond	Reymond	
		Roddy				
	(tongues cease before other gifts)			Ryrie		
			Schutz			
				Scofield		
				Smeaton		
	Smith					
Swete	(gradual)					
				Swindoll		Swindoll
Thomas	(gradual)			Thomas		
Unger				Unger	Unger	Unger

AD 54	AD 58	AD 68/69	AD 70	AD 90–98	c. AD 100	AD 100+
1 Cor Written	Last Miracle Recorded	Hebrews Written	Jerusalem Sacked	Last NT Book Written	Apostle John Dies	NT Circulated
	Van Gorder (tongues cease before other gifts)			Van Gorder		
		Vander Lugt	(tongues cease before other gifts)			
				Walvoord		Walvoord
				Warfield	Warfield	Warfield
				Williams		
			Zeller			

* BIBLIOGRAPHIC DATA: William L. Banks, *Questions You Have Always Wanted to Ask About Tongues, But . . .* (Chattanooga: AMG, 1978), 34–37; Ronald E. Baxter, *The Charismatic Gift of Tongues* (Grand Rapids: Kregel, 1981), 65–71; Donald W. Burdick, *Tongues: To Speak or Not to Speak* (Chicago: Moody, 1969), 38, 39; Charles Webb Carter, *The Person and Ministry of the Holy Spirit: A Wesleyan Perspective* (Grand Rapids: Baker, 1974), 280; Walter J. Chantry, *Signs of the Apostles: Observations on Pentecostalism Old and New*, rev. ed. (Edinburgh: Banner of Truth, 1976), 50, 51, 53, 60; Ronald Cooke, *Do Miracles Then Continue?* (Hollidaysburg, PA: Manahath, 1981), 81, 84, 86; Leonard J. Coppes, *Whatever Happened to Biblical Tongues?* (Phillipsburg, NJ: Pilgrim, 1977), 60, 61; W. A. Criswell, *The Baptism, Filling and Gifts of the Holy Spirit* (Grand Rapids: Zondervan, 1973), 121, 122, 134; M. R. DeHaan, *Pentecost and After* (Grand Rapids: Zondervan, 1964), 33, 35, 147; Richard W. DeHaan, *The Charismatic Controversy* (Grand Rapids: Radio Bible Class, 1978), 12–14; Joseph Dillow, *Speaking in Tongues* (Grand Rapids: Zondervan, 1975), 106, 107, 115–16, 134; Theodore H. Epp and John I. Paton, *The Use and Abuse of Tongues* (Lincoln, NE: Back to the Bible, 1963), 41–44; Richard B. Gaffin, Jr., *Perspectives on Pentecost: Studies in New Testament Teaching on the Gifts of the Holy Spirit* (Grand Rapids: Baker, 1979), 100; George E. Gardiner, *The Corinthian Catastrophe* (Grand Rapids: Kregel, 1974), 36; Robert Glenn Gromacki, *The Modern Tongues Movement*, rev. ed. (Nutley, NJ: Presbyterian and Reformed, 1972), 128, 129; Robert R. Gustafson, *Authors of Confusion* (Tampa: Grace Publishing Co., 1971), 32; Anthony A. Hoekema, *What About Tongue-Speaking?* (Grand Rapids: Eerdmans, 1966), 110; Douglas Judisch, *An Evaluation of Claims to the Charismatic Gifts* (Grand Rapids: Baker, 1978), 43, 49, 63, 76n., 82–83; John F. MacArthur, Jr., *The Charismatics: A Doctrinal Perspective* (Grand Rapids: Zondervan, 1978), 131, 165–167, 169; A. M. Stibbs and J. I. Packer, *The Spirit within You: The Church's Neglected Possession* (repr., Grand Rapids: Baker, 1979), 33; J. Dwight Pentecost, *The Divine Comforter: The Person and Work of the Holy Spirit* (repr., Chicago: Moody, 1975), 190; Robert L. Reymond, *"What About Continuing Revelations and Miracles in the Presbyterian Church Today?" A Study of the Doctrine of the Sufficiency of Scripture* ([Nutley, NJ]: Presbyterian and Reformed, 1977), 1, 6, 41, 43–44, 53; A. Jackson Roddy, *Though I Spoke With Tongues*, rev. ed. (Atascadero, CA: Scripture Research, 1974), 50; Charles Caldwell Ryrie, *The Holy Spirit* (Chicago: Moody, 1965), 86, 91, 92; Vernon A. Schutz, *Tongues and the Sign Gifts* (Grand Rapids: Grace Publications, n.d.), 16, 17; C. I.

Scofield, *The New Scofield Reference Bible* (New York: Oxford University Press, 1968), 1245n2; George Smeaton, *The Doctrine of the Holy Spirit* (repr., Carlisle, PA: Banner of Truth, 1974), 150; Charles R. Smith, *Tongues in Biblical Perspective: A Summary of Biblical Conclusions Concerning Tongues*, rev. ed. (Winona Lake, IN: BMH Books, 1973), 70, 71; Henry Barclay Swete, *The Holy Spirit in the New Testament* (repr., Grand Rapids: Baker, 1976), 378, 379; Charles R. Swindoll, *Tongues: An Answer to Charismatic Confusion* (Portland: Multnomah, 1981), 9, 11, 12, 20, 21; Robert L. Thomas, *Understanding Spiritual Gifts: The Christian's Special Gifts in Light of 1 Corinthians 12–14* (Chicago: Moody, 1978), 13, 108–13; Merrill F. Unger, *The Baptism and Gifts of the Holy Spirit* (Chicago: Moody, 1974), 135, 136, 139, 140, and *New Testament Teaching on Tongues* (Grand Rapids: Kregel, 1971), 96, 136, 137, 148, 149; Paul R. Van Gorder, *Charismatic Confusion* (Grand Rapids: Radio Bible Class, 1972), 28; Herbert Vander Lugt, *Are Tongues for Today? What the Bible Says About the Sign-gifts* (Grand Rapids: Radio Bible Class, 1979), 69–73· John F. Walvoord, *The Holy Spirit: A Comprehensive Study of the Person ana Work of the Holy Spirit*, 3rd ed. (Grand Rapids: Zondervan, 1977), 69, 174; B. B. Warfield, *Counterfeit Miracles* (1918; repr., Edinburgh: Banner of Truth Trust, 1972), 6, 23, 24, 26, 27, 29, 30; John Williams, *The Holy Spirit: Lord and Life-Giver* (Neptune, NJ: Loizeaux Brothers, 1980), 228; George W. Zeller, *God's Gift of Tongues: The Nature, Purpose and Duration of Tongues As Taught in the Bible* (Neptune, NJ: Loizeaux Brothers, 1978), 62, 63, 89, 90.

10

A Review of *Perspectives on Spirit Baptism: Five Views*[1]
With Excursus on 1 Corinthians 12:13a

Perspectives on Spirit Baptism[2] is a collection of five scholarly essays that define Spirit baptism from five traditions: Reformed (Walter C. Kaiser), Pentecostal (Stanley M. Horton), Charismatic (Larry Hart), Wesleyan (H. Ray Dunning), and Catholic (Ralph Del Colle). Each view is formatted as a chapter, which concludes with responses from the remaining four scholars. The space afforded each view differs widely in some cases. For example, the Reformed view is only 22 pages, whereas the Charismatic view is 64 pages long; the difference (42 pages) is longer than the Catholic view (39 pages). The Pentecostal and Wesleyan views are 48 and 49 pages, respectively. Regarding the responses, there is again a disparity. Horton's responses total only six pages, while Del Colle amasses just over 14 pages (the average was 10 pages).

All the contributors to this volume are terminal-degreed scholars, but *were they the most qualified?* What brings this question to mind are the

---

[1] The review portion of this chapter (with slight changes) was originally published in *Pneuma Review* (August 8, 2014): http://pneumareview.com/perspectives-on-spirit-baptism-five-views/.

[2] Chad Owen Brand, ed. (Nashville, TN: Broadman & Holman, 2004).

credentials of Kaiser and Horton. These are highly distinguished scholars, but their forte is the Old Testament, whereas Spirit baptism is a New Testament phenomenon. Both men are venerable patriarchs of their denominations (Horton, at the time of this writing, will soon be 90) and have high degrees of name-recognition (which publishers desire), but I sensed a lack of edge and freshness in their presentations and responses.

Kaiser starts things off with a historical summary of the responses to Pentecostal theology by John R. W. Stott[3] and James D. G. Dunn.[4] Mysteriously, forty years after Stott's dividing of Scripture into didactic and historical, Kaiser makes the same mistake, favoring Paul's "didactic" passages over Luke's "narrative." Kaiser ignores three and a half decades of scholarship, beginning with I. Howard Marshall (1970) and continuing to this day, that corrects the misguided notion that Luke was merely a historian.[5]

Neither does Kaiser fare well in the department of fairness. In his attempt to connect Spirit baptism with conversion, he quotes Pentecostal scholar R. P. Menzies in order to counter him with a quote from J. B. Shelton (also a Pentecostal), but he unfairly ends the Shelton quote at a point that serves his purpose. Had he continued *with the same sentence*, it would have destroyed his point. Here is Kaiser's quotation from Shelton: "Luke is not averse to associating the Holy Spirit with conversion." Kaiser even omits the ellipses that indicate an opening and closing omission. (23) Here is the complete sentence and following sentence: "Although Luke is not averse to associating the Holy Spirit with conversion, this is not his major pneumatological thrust. Some misunderstanding has arisen when the role of

---

[3] *Baptism and Fullness: The Work of the Holy Spirit Today*, 2nd ed. (1964. Downers Grove, IL: InterVarsity, 1977).

[4] *Baptism in the Holy Spirit* (Philadelphia, PA: Westminster, 1970).

[5] See especially Paul Elbert's *The Lukan Gift of the Holy Spirit* (Canton, GA: Foundation for Pentecostal Scholarship, 2021). John Baker writes the following: "For while some Epistles, like Romans and Ephesians, are essentially didactic treatises, others are essentially narration of and comment upon the situations in the churches. 1 Corinthians itself is the most outstanding example of this, and the verse in question, 1 Corinthians 12:13, is not primarily a didactic, but an historical statement; it is declaration of what had happened to the believers in Corinth, rather than a direct declaration of what ought to happen to us" (*Baptized in One Spirit: The Meaning of 1 Corinthians 12:13* [Plainfield, NJ: Logos Books, 1967], 10); see also Roger Stronstad, *The Charismatic Theology of St. Luke*, 2nd ed. (1984; Grand Rapids: Baker, 2012), 5–14; William W. Menzies, "The Methodology of Pentecostal Theology: An Essay on Hermeneutics," in *Essays on Apostolic Themes: Studies in Honor of Howard M. Ervin* (Peabody, MA: Hendrickson, 1985), 1–14; Robert W. Graves, *Praying in the Spirit* (Tulsa: Empowered Life Academic-Harrison House, 2016), 205–16. See footnote at 98n40 below.

the Holy Spirit in empowering for witness is confused with conversion."[6] But as serious as this violation of scholarship is, it pales in significance to Kaiser's later mischaracterization of Larry W. Hurtado's position on tongues as the initial evidence of Spirit baptism. He quotes Hurtado approvingly when the latter confirms that the NT does not raise the question of the initial evidence of Spirit baptism. Then he chastises Hurtado for not thinking that this renders the doctrine invalid and for thinking that experience "can fill in the needed evidence here!" (30). Kaiser has grossly misread Hurtado, whose last clause of the quoted essay reads, ". . . the doctrine of 'initial evidence,' whatever its historic significance for institutionalized Pentecostalism, should be set aside as a sincere but misguided understanding of Scripture."[7] Was Kaiser so desperate to compare the supposed *experience-based* Pentecostal view of Spirit baptism to Evangelical rationalism that he totally misread Hurtado? Whatever the case, Kaiser turns Hurtado into a tremendous strawman, and he owes Hurtado an apology, since Hurtado seems to be on Kaiser's side. Hurtado is not a Pentecostal, though perhaps a Charismatic, who does not believe Luke intended to teach Theophilus anything about the relationship between tongues and Spirit baptism even though Luke, following contemporary Greco-Roman rhetorical conventions, strategically linked them in pivotal scenes that demonstrate the programmatic Christ sayings of Luke 24:45–47 and Acts 1:4–8. (See Elbert, footnote 5.)

In his response to Kaiser, Del Colle gently raises the question of the theological import of Kaiser's Evangelical doctrine of Spirit baptism, since it did not exist before the Holiness/Pentecostal movements (41). In other words, it was only because of the tacit Pentecostal challenge that Evangelicals formulated a counter-doctrine. (In fact, as a Pentecostal scholar-friend commented to me, this book would not exist if it were not for the Pentecostal movement.) Del Colle also questions Kaiser's use of a single scripture— 1 Corinthians 12:13a—whereby all other Spirit-baptism-related verses are interpreted (43).

Kaiser, taking his cue from Stott, uses this verse at least 14 times in structuring his Reformed position of Spirit baptism or rebutting the Pentecostal position. I was disappointed that Horton did not take him to task for

---

[6] *Mighty in Word and Deed: The Role of the Holy Spirit in Luke-Acts* (Peabody, MA: Hendrickson, 1991), 127.

[7] "Normal, but Not a Norm: 'Initial Evidence' and the New Testament," in *Initial Evidence: Historical and Biblical Perspectives on the Doctrine of Spirit Baptism*, ed. Gary B. McGee (Peabody, MA: Hendrickson, 1991), 200.

his heavy dependence upon a single verse.[8] His entire argument hinges upon a two-letter Greek word, the preposition *en*, which, according to him, must be translated *in* ("*in* one Spirit we were all baptized") and must be univocal in meaning with the other six non-Pauline occurrences. Furthermore, this Pauline *baptism in the Spirit*, once asserted, must be the one passage that dictates the meaning of the other six. Hence, the one-verse soteriology of Paul trumps the prophetic empowerment contexts of John the Baptist (in all the Gospels) and quoted by Jesus, who was in turn quoted by Peter (and all by Luke, Acts 1:4–5; 11:16). Is it legitimate that 1 Cor 12:13a is *translated* based on the other six occurrences, yet the other six are *interpreted* based on Paul's single verse? (Because of Kaiser's misuse of 1 Cor. 12:13a, I took a closer look at it and the other six verses that mention Spirit baptism; my findings are in the Excursus below.)

The chapter by Horton begins with nine pages of interesting Pentecostal history and personal anecdotes, but I question the propriety of that genre in this volume. Does it not reinforce the perceived Pentecostal shibboleth of placing experience above Scripture? Horton does cover the relevant Lukan passages, but much of it (at least 10 lengthy quotations) comes from his previously published works. One of his assertions will, no doubt, serve only as a distraction, i.e., that tongues are always foreign languages. He bases this on Acts 2, where tongues are understood as foreign languages, but that is the only place they are so identified, and the only place where their occurrence is logical, occurring before an *international gathering*. (On this matter, see chapter 13 below.)

Larry Hart capably represents the Charismatic view, which he considers a "dimensional perspective," as Spirit baptism is a metaphor "encompassing all the saving, sanctifying, and empowering dimensions of the Spirit's activity" (112). Evangelicals and Pentecostals are both right—"both the regenerational/indwelling and empowering dimensions of the Spirit's work are included in Spirit baptism" (118). Unfortunately, in this view, Spirit baptism becomes so many things that it becomes nothing and, ultimately, obscures the genius of Luke-Acts.

Ray Dunning's chapter representing the Wesleyan perspective was an eye-opener. I was unaware of the undercurrents of resentment that swirl in that tradition against the Holiness and Pentecostal movements. It appeared to me that, at every convenient place he could find, Dunning tried to distance Wesleyanism from these movements. God forbid that adherents of these movements use the sacred writings of Wesley to defend their errant

---

[8] If there is a non-Pentecostal doctrine more dependent on one verse of Scripture than that of the doctrine of Spirit baptism, I am not aware of it.

doctrines! Dunning caps off his presentation contra Pentecostalism by quoting C. H. Dodd and James S. Stewart in their assessments of the value of Paul's contribution to the understanding of the Spirit. "It saved Christian thought," writes Dodd, "from falling into a non-moral, half-magical conception of the supernatural in human experience" (228). According to Stewart, Paul saved Christianity from reverting to "the cruder conceptions of the Spirit, . . . in such phenomena as speaking in tongues. It was Paul who saved the nascent faith from that dangerous retrogression" (228). This is appalling—all the more so because its source is the tradition that emphasizes entire sanctification and perfect love!

Ralph Del Colle, a charismatic Catholic, displays exemplary knowledge of the history of the Pentecostal/Charismatic movement within Catholicism. He recounts the history and theology of early and later leaders such as the Ranaghans, Clark, O'Connor, Gelpi, Suenens, Baumert, and McDonnell. In reading Del Colle's contribution, Evangelicals and Pentecostals will experience something akin to culture shock, since, for the Catholic, it is not Scripture that is the touchstone for doctrine, but the church (i.e., the Catholic Church). In other words, the Catholic scarcely needs to bring exegetical concerns to the table. For Del Colle and these other Charismatic Catholic leaders, it becomes a matter of fitting their Pentecostal experience suitably into Catholic tradition. Nevertheless, Del Colle's presentation is performed with intelligence and graciousness.

Excursus on 1 Corinthians 12:13a

"For by [in] one Spirit we were all baptized into one body . . ." (NASB)

It wasn't without cause that Harold D. Hunter wrote in 1983 that "Protestants evaluating Pentecostal pneumatology most often view 1 Corinthians 12:13a as the first and last word on the issue of Spirit-baptism."[9] Based on their interpretations of this verse, scholars such as James Dunn, Dale Bruner, Anthony Hoekema, J. I. Packer, John Stott, Richard B. Gaffin, Jr.[10], and many others have declared that all Christians are Spirit-baptized.

---

[9] *Spirit-Baptism: A Pentecostal Alternative* (Lanham, MD: University Press of America, 1983), 39. (Hunter's book has since been updated and republished by Wipf and Stock, 2009 [without *Spirit Baptism* hyphenated]; further references will be to this edition).

[10] Gaffin, creating a whale of a red herring and a superb misdirection, calls this verse, "[T]he hard rock which shatters all constructions of Holy Spirit baptism as an additional, postconversion, second-blessing experience" (*Perspectives on Pentecost* [Grand Rapids: Baker, 1979], 31).

And there is a sense in which this is true, more on that later, but they believe that it is true based on the synonymous relationship of Paul's verse and the six other occurrences in Scripture where the Greek words *en pneumati* are used (Matt 3:11, Mark 1:8, Luke 3:16, John 1:33, Acts 1:5, and Acts 11:16). According to Stott, "The Greek expression is precisely the same in all its seven occurrences, and therefore *a priori*, as a sound principle of interpretation, it should be taken to refer to the same baptism experience in each verse."[11] He must be talking about the two words *en pneumati*; actually, I should write, *en . . . pneumati*, because Paul's verse inserts another word between the preposition *en* and its object *pneumati*. Well, so much for them being "precisely the same." Hoekema, a bit more careful, says that 1 Cor 12:13a "is virtually identical with that used in the Gospels and Acts, except that Paul adds the words *one* and *all*."[12] Here is how Hoekema's gambit fares:

1. Paul's clause contains 11 words, seven of which *do not occur* in any of the other six clauses (eight, if you consider that *kai* is not used in the same sense); the other six passages have an average of only seven words, which means *only four of the words in 12:13a appear in the other six clauses* (and two of those four words are of a different tense and person);
2. Of the 15 different words that are used in the other six verses, Paul matches only two of them *identically* (*en* and *pneumati*), and even then, not by order;
3. John the Baptist, who appears in the context of all the other passages, is conspicuously missing from Paul;
4. Two words that Paul uses ("one body") that are *critical* to his intent, and the non-Pentecostal view, do not occur in any of the other six verses;
5. Two of Paul's words that are common to all the verses are separated by another critical word, "one," transforming the critical phrase "in the Holy Spirit" in the six non-Pauline verses to "in one Spirit," which is balanced semantically by "in one body," a phrase totally foreign to the six;
6. The word "Holy" does not appear in Paul's passage though appearing in all six of the other passages, not that Paul didn't mean "Holy Spirit," but my point is that Paul, being aware of John the Baptist's prophecy from the Jesus tradition, as he no doubt would have been, had an ideal opportunity to link this passage to it and thus to Pentecost, but chose not to;[13]
7. Furthermore, neither is Jesus named as the baptizer in Paul's passage although he is named in all Gospel references and implied in the Acts references; "Jesus is the obvious activator in the first four passages and the

---

[11] *Baptism and Fullness*, 40.

[12] *Holy Spirit Baptism* (Grand Rapids: Eerdmans, 1972), 21.

[13] Hunter says it like this: "The first six references [i.e., those in the Gospels and Acts] have the complete πνεύματι ἁγίῳ [*Holy Spirit*] while Paul has simply ἑνὶ πνεύματι [*one Spirit*]," *Spirit Baptism*, 57.

implied activator in the next two, but the Pauline passage seems to place the Holy Spirit as the agent."[14]

8. The verb in Paul's verse ("were baptized") occurs in a tense and person not found in the six non-Pauline verses; additionally, in the Greek text "the prepositional phrase '*en* the one Spirit' precedes the verb *baptize*; in all the other passages it follows the verb (except Acts 1:5, where . . . it comes between *Spirit* and *Holy*.)"[15]

9. "The use of και πυρί [*and fire*] which appears in Matthew 3:11 and Luke 3:16 would seem appropriate with any of the first six references, but not the seventh [i.e., Paul's]."[16]

Hoekema's gambit falls short.

It is apparent from the foregoing discussion that the Evangelists and Paul were *not* describing identical Christian experiences, but I do not come to this conclusion merely because of the grammatical differences; these serve only as clues. The greater point is made not with grammar but with contexts, that is, Paul's and Luke's contexts. Few have written as pointedly about the contexts as Roger Stronstad and Howard Ervin:

> The term "baptized in the Holy Spirit" appears just seven times in the NT. Yet its value outweighs its limited number of references. Of the seven, one is found in Paul's first letter to the Corinthian Church. He writes, "for by one Spirit we were all baptized into one body" (12.13). This passage references initiation-incorporation (cf. 1 Cor 12.18). The four evangelists also report John the Baptist's prophecy regarding his successor who "will baptize in the Holy Spirit [two of the evangelists add:] and fire" (Matt 3.11–12; Mark 1.7–8; Luke 3.16–17; John 1.30–34). But Luke, and Luke alone, reports Jesus' reference to the Baptist's prophecy as the day of Pentecost approached (Acts 1.4–5) and Cornelius' reception of the Spirit as a fulfillment of the Baptist's prophecy (Acts 11.16). Thus, Matthew, Mark, John, and Paul each have one reference to being baptized in the Holy Spirit; yet Luke has three references to this experience [five if you include the implied references in Luke, 11:11–13 and 24:49 (cf. Acts 2:32–33)]. From these numbers one may infer that being baptized in the Holy Spirit is more important to Luke than to any other NT writer. As a corollary,

---

[14] Hunter, *Spirit Baptism*, 57. Hunter is not saying that Paul's passage isn't about conversion; to the contrary, he writes, "[T]he use of εἰς [*into*] with 1 Corinthians 12:13a rather clearly indicates that the Pauline reference is to one's entry into the body of Christ," 58.

[15] Anthony D. Palma, "Article G: Baptized by and in the Holy Spirit," 896 in *Life in the Spirit New Testament Commentary*, ed. French L. Arrington and Roger Stronstad (Grand Rapids: Zondervan, 1999), 895–96.

[16] Hunter, *Spirit Baptism*, 57.

one may also infer that the meaning of the term in Luke's narrative is the normative meaning. A further corollary is that Paul's use of the term in his letter to the Corinthians does not determine its meaning in Luke-Acts. One final observation is that each of Luke's three references to the term is interpreted in its immediate context (Luke 3.16–17/Acts 1.5/2.1–21; Acts 10.44–48/11.15–17).[17]

. . . in interpreting the baptismal metaphor, the phrase εἰς ἕν σῶμα, *into one body*, weighs in favor of Christian initiation. However, this is not the whole of the context, and contextual as well as hermeneutical considerations argue for an *equivocal* rather than a *univocal* sense in which baptism in the Spirit is to be understood here. The phrase cannot be conflated univocally into one sense in the NT. Contextual considerations, as these reflect the theology and literary style of the several authors, must be consulted. (The Lukan sense of the metaphor is not definitive of the Pauline usage.)[18]

---

[17] "On Being Baptized in the Holy Spirit: A Lukan Emphasis," in *Trajectories in the Book of Acts: Essays in Honor of John Wesley Wyckoff*, ed. Paul Alexander et al. (Eugene, OR: Wipf and Stock, 2010), 161.

[18] *Conversion-Initiation*, 101–2. Clark Pinnock, in a review of Michael Green's book *I Believe in the Holy Spirit*, adds the following to this discussion:

> It is so common in high calibre books on the Spirit by Dunn, Bruner, and now Green, to 'harmonize' Paul and Luke so that Luke gets painted with Paul's brush. If you read Luke by himself, and listen to him, it seems rather clear that the outpouring of the Spirit he has in mind is not brought into relation to *salvation*, as it is in Paul, but in relation to *service* and *witness*. . . . Therefore, Luke does not tie the coming of the Spirit to the salvation event. . . . Even non-charismatics like Green, sensitive and open as they are to the renewal, seem unable to grant that the pentecostals [*sic*] may understand Acts better than they do" (*HIS*, June 1976: 21, quoted in Stronstad, *Charismatic Theology* 12; Charles E. Hummel, *Fire in the Fireplace: Contemporary Charismatic Renewal* [Downers Grove: InterVarsity, 1978], 262n9, see also 136, and the 2nd edition of Hummel's book, *Fire in the Fireplace, Charismatic Renewal in the Nineties* [1993], 51–54, 246–47.)

Of course, this isn't to say that Paul was all soteriology and Luke all pneumatology. Frank Macchia speaks to that issue:

> Paul is also charismatic in his pneumatology, but his understanding of Spirit baptism is more intimately connected to faith, confession, and sealing through water baptism. Paul is prominently concerned with incorporation into Christ, by which believers become members of Christ's body and of one another (e.g., 1 Cor. 12:13). . . . Luke's Spirit baptism doctrine is "charismatic," having to do with the divine empowerment of the church as a living witness, while Paul's is primarily soteriological, having fundamentally to do with being in Christ. . . .
>
> Although Luke accents the participation in Spirit baptism that flows from faith, especially as visibly demonstrated, Paul focuses attention on the act of

In the Lukan text, John the Baptist's statement, later quoted by Jesus, is adequately explained by Jesus (through Luke). It occurs in Acts 1:8, where Theophilus learns that this baptism, yet to come to the disciple-believers, will be for *power to witness—elements not in view in 1 Cor. 12:13a.*

So, the Pentecostal can agree with the non-Pentecostal that the baptism of 12:13a incorporates the new believer into the body of Christ; the Pentecostal, with the turning of a blind eye to nuancing, can even agree that it is a "Spirit baptism";[19] where the Pentecostal would disagree would be in designating it the *same* Spirit baptism of which Luke (and Matthew, Mark, and John) wrote, for that Spirit baptism clearly occurs after[20] (or possibly simultaneously with) conversion and is repeatable (see Acts 2:4; 4:8, 31; 9:17; 13:9 [52?]) and has a manifestly different function. Whereas

---

Spirit baptism that leads to the attachment to Christ by faith (1 Cor. 12:13). Paul does not neglect the charismatic dimension of participation in the life of the Spirit. Luke does not omit the importance of faith and baptism in the reception of the missionary Spirit. But Paul's accent is on Spirit baptism as that which initiates us to faith in Christ as members of his body, while Luke highlights the power of the Spirit that proceeds from faith. (*Baptized in the Spirit: A Global Pentecostal Theology* [Grand Rapids: Zondervan, 2006], 15, 87.)

[19] For a discussion of the labelling, see Douglas A. Oss, "A Pentecostal/Charismatic View," 239–83, in *Are Miraculous Gifts for Today? Four Views*, ed. Wayne A. Grudem (Grand Rapids: Zondervan, 1996) 257, 259–60. Packer writes, "Doubtless some believers have benefited and others would benefit from a postconversion experience of inner enlargement, but this is not Spirit baptism in Paul's sense" (*Keep in Step with the Spirit* [Old Tappan, NJ: Revell, 1984], 203). Anthony C. Thiselton, on the supposition that his interpretation of 1 Cor 12:13 is certainly correct and the Pentecostals' clearly wrong, implores Pentecostals, for the sake of a fruitful dialogue, to abandon their use of "Spirit baptism" as a reference to their post-conversion experience. His bargaining chip is his admission that the Pentecostals' experience is a genuine *reality*, a *respected* experience; he doesn't question its *authenticity*. But he rejects the biblical terminology applied to it by Pentecostals—primarily based on his interpretation of 1 Cor 12:13 (*The Holy Spirit—In Biblical Teaching, through the Centuries, and Today* [Grand Rapids: Eerdmans, 2013], 338, 491–92; *The First Epistle to the Corinthians* [Grand Rapids: Eerdmans, 2000], 999). Given the strides of Pentecostal scholarship over the past fifty years, I'd say it's premature to capitulate.

[20] *Believers* are instructed by Jesus to pray for the Holy Spirit and are shown doing so (Luke 11:11–13; Acts 1:12–14; 2:1–4; 4:31). And John tells us that the world cannot receive him (14:17); as New Testament scholar Craig S. Keener concludes, "[D]elays can happen for whatever reason," (*Gift and Giver: The Holy Spirit for Today* [Grand Rapids: Baker Academic, 2001], 163). Although subsequence is a possibility, Luke depicts it as an aberration in the early church, and it is urgently addressed (see Acts 8 and 19)—*we should be as diligent.* See William P. Atkinson, *Baptism in the Spirit: Luke-Acts and the Dunn Debate* (Eugene, OR: Pickwick-Wipf and Stock, 2011), xii, 136–37.

Paul's "Spirit baptism" functions to incorporate the believer into the body of Christ, Luke's Spirit baptism moves the believer into the realm of prophetic witness and service (Acts 1:8).[21] (Although, I think we get a glimpse of this usage in Paul, often in conjunction with *charismata*, in Rom 1:11; 15:19; 1 Cor. 1:7; 2:4–5; Eph. 3:16; 5:17–19; Col. 1:11; 1 Thess 1:5; 1 Tim 4:14; 2 Tim 1:6–8, 12; 2:1–3.[22])

Baptized "in" or "by" the Holy Spirit

Before considering this issue, it might be best first to reiterate what Pentecostals and non-Pentecostals, *in general*, agree that Paul is saying in 1

---

[21] That all four Evangelists mention the role of Jesus as the Spirit-baptizer speaks to the authenticity and importance of this logion. But it does so much more. It does, after all, have a context, and in each context Jesus and his Spirit baptism are given the superior position to John and water baptism. Here is how the Gospel of John frames it:

> This all happened at Bethany on the other side of the Jordan, where John was baptizing. The next day John saw Jesus coming toward him and said, "Look, the Lamb of God, who takes away the sin of the world! This is the one I meant when I said, 'A man who comes after me has surpassed me because he was before me.' I myself did not know him, but the reason I came baptizing with water was that he might be revealed to Israel." Then John gave this testimony: "I saw the Spirit come down from heaven as a dove and remain on him. And I myself did not know him, but the one who sent me to baptize with water told me, 'The man on whom you see the Spirit come down and remain is the one who will baptize with the Holy Spirit.' I have seen and I testify that this is God's Chosen One." The next day John was there again with two of his disciples. When he saw Jesus passing by, he said, "Look, the Lamb of God." When the two disciples heard him say this, they followed Jesus. (John 1:28–37)

Note also John's promising statement about the Messiah: "He must increase; I must decrease" (John 3:30 BSB); Matthew recorded John saying, "[A]fter me comes one who is more powerful than I, whose sandals I am not worthy to carry" (5:11b). This logion contains all the language of, not only superiority but, abrogation, *unless* the two baptisms represent two aspects of spirituality, which we see in Peter's statement in Acts 2:38–39: "Repent and be baptized, every one of you, in the name of Jesus Christ for the forgiveness of your sins. And you will receive the gift of the Holy Spirit. The promise is for you and your children and for all who are far off—for all whom the Lord our God will call" (Acts 2:38–39). (For a compelling argument against the synchroneity of these two aspects of spirituality, see Paul Elbert's, "Acts 2:38 in Light of the Syntax of Imperative-Future Passive and Imperative-Present Participle Combinations," 43–54 in *Luke's Rhetorical Compositions: Essays in Lukan Studies* [Eugene, OR: Wipf and Stock, 2022]; for book-length works, see Roger Stronstad, *The Charismatic Theology of St. Luke*, and Robert P. Menzies *Empowered for Witness: The Spirit in Luke–Acts*, [Sheffield: Sheffield Academic, 1991].)

[22] See Robert P. Menzies, "Subsequence in the Pauline Epistles," *Pneuma* 39.3 (2017): 342–63.

Corinthians 12:13a.[23] Most Pentecostal and non-Pentecostal scholars would agree with Ben Witherington, III, that "There are no Christians without the Spirit. At conversion the Christian is united to the body by the Spirit and is given the Spirit to drink."[24] According to Atkinson, "Pentecostalism has always recognized that all Christians have the Spirit, even before their Spirit baptism," and according to his survey of the literature, "the overwhelming majority of written Pentecostal teaching throughout its history has made room for Paul's soteriological pneumatology."[25]

Commenting on this verse, French L. Arrington writes, "By the agency of the Spirit, we are plunged into Christ at the moment of conversion . . . . [W]hen we receive Christ we are incorporated into or united with the community of believers *by* the Holy Spirit. . . . This baptism of which Paul speaks in 1 Corinthians 12:13 is the spiritual experience by which the Spirit unites believers to Christ and to one another. . . . At that moment we are joined to Christ by the Holy Spirit, and God saves us 'by the washing of regeneration and renewing by the Holy Spirit' (Titus 3:5 [NASB])."[26]

Gordon Fee writes that Paul was "remind[ing] the Corinthians how it came about that they are one body (whether Jew or Greek etc.). And the answer is that *all* have received the Spirit—the *sine qua non* of Christian life and experience for Paul."[27] "Without the Spirit, there *is* no Christian life or faith (precisely what Gal. 3 and Romans 8 plead)."[28] Most might also agree with Fee when he writes that the *context* of 1 Cor 12:13 "makes it abundantly clear that it has nothing at all to do with the 'baptism of the Holy Spirit.'"[29] I'm not sure we all agree, but he also writes that "none of these

---

[23] I am speaking in general; there are varying Pentecostal interpretations. For example, Donald A. Johns sees this verse as a reference to initiation, but not initiation into the body of Christ; instead, he sees it as initiation into the charismatic ministry; after all, he reasons, that is the context ("Some New Directions in the Hermeneutics of Classical Pentecostalism's Doctrine of Initial Evidence," pages 145–67 [160–61] in *Initial Evidence*). As for the problem with "all" (*pantes*) in both clauses, see Ervin, 102, and John Rea, *The Holy Spirit in the Bible* (Altamonte Springs, FL: Creation House, 1990), 259.

[24] *Conflict and Community in Corinth: A Socio-Rhetorical Commentary on 1 and 2 Corinthians* (Grand Rapids: Eerdmans, 1995), 258.

[25] *Baptism in the Spirit*, 108, 107.

[26] *Encountering the Holy Spirit: Paths of Christian Growth and Service* (Cleveland, TN: Pathway Press, 2003), 101.

[27] Personal correspondence (USPS) to author July 9, 1982. Fee expresses the same sentiment in his commentary (*The First Epistle to the Corinthians*, rev. ed. [Grand Rapids: Eerdmans, 2014], 668).

[28] Personal correspondence (USPS) to author October 19, 1981.

[29] Ibid. The passage, Fee would say, is concerned with diversity in unity (*Corinthians*, 665–73).

texts [i.e., 1 Cor 12:13 and Acts 2:38] either support or refute the doctrine of a subsequent baptism for empowering."[30]

The focus of my reply to Kaiser, Stott, and others isn't to argue that Paul's *en* in 1 Cor 12:13a should be translated "by." That isn't necessary to maintain the integrity of the Pentecostal doctrine of Spirit baptism, see, for instance, Atkinson's *Baptism in the Spirit: Luke-Acts and the Dunn Debate*, where he takes the position that Paul is referring to a "baptism in the Spirit"; it just isn't synonymous with the Lukan references, due to the contexts.[31] But I do think that since the 1960's, coinciding with the publication of Stott's *Baptism and Fullness*, the debate over "in" or "by" has heated up enough that opinions of anti-Pentecostal scholars and non-Pentecostal commentators may eventually affect future translation committees regarding the choice of "in" or "by." For that reason, I am presenting here data in favor of "by" that I have collected:

Does the dative (with or without ἐν or πνεύματι) ever designate the agent of the verb's action? According to Robertson, BDAG, Nunn, BDF, Dana and Mantey, Smythe, Murray Harris, and others,[32] it does. Here's a sampling of their statements:

1. Nunn, in *The Elements of NT Greek* (8th ed.), concluded this about *en*: "In [the] N.T. [*en* is] also of the instrument and even of the agent" (125). In his *A Short Syntax of NT Greek*, he wrote of *en*, "In the N.T. *with* or *by* of the instrument or agent" (30).
2. In their section on cases, Dana and Mantey have a subsection titled "The Instrumental of Agency." Here they state that "Agency is expressed

---

[30] Ibid.

[31] Atkinson, *Baptism*, 93–100. Menzies agrees, "Paul clearly speaks of Spirit baptism as the means by which one is initiated into the body of Christ (1 Cor 12:13), and he offers a rich and full description of the work of the Spirit" ("Subsequence," 345); George M. Flattery comments: "With regard to 1 Corinthians 12:13, the translation 'by' one Spirit, rather than 'in' one Spirit, is more in harmony with the immediate context. *However, in the final analysis there is not much difference. It is the action of the Spirit that unites one with Christ*" (*A Biblical Theology of the Holy Spirit: Luke–Acts*, vol. 2 [Springfield, MO: Global University, 2009], 80, italics added.) If Thiselton's dictum, "every writer uses terminology in context-dependent ways that may modify a more usual meaning," has validity when looking at the writings of one author, which he is doing, how much more might it prove true when comparing the writings of different authors? (*Corinthians*, 1085)

[32] Thiselton opines that Rudolf Schnackenburg, "One of the most careful and meticulous writers on baptism in Paul . . . recognizes that ἐν here might mean either *with*, *by*, or even *for* (although for himself he chooses an instrumental translation) . . ." (997; see Schnackenburg, *Baptism in the Thought of St. Paul*, 22–24 and 83–86). In favor of "by one Spirit," Thiselton also cites Oepke, Moffatt, Cullmann, Cerfaux, and Flemington as supporting the instrumental use of ἐν (997).

occasionally in the NT by the instrumental [i.e., dative] case without the use of any preposition" (*A Manual Grammar of the Greek NT*, 91).

3. BDF states about *en*: "It is used for the simple instr[umental] . . . . but (1) also to designate a personal agent" (#219).

4. BDAG under *en* lists definition #6 as "marker of agency" (329).

5. Smythe, in *Greek Grammar*, writes the following about the instrumental dative: "The Greek dative, as representative of the lost instrumental case, denotes that *by which* or *with which* an action is done or accompanied" (#1503).

6. Murray Harris, though preferring "in" over "by," writes the following: "There is no doubt that ἐν πνεύματι can express the agency of the Spirit in Paul (Ro 2:29; 1Co 12:3 [2x]; 14:16; Eph 2:22; 3:5; 4:30) . . . ." (*Prepositions and Theology in the Greek New Testament* [Grand Rapids: Zondervan, 2012]), 231.

So, to the question *Does the dative (with or without* en*) ever designate the agent of the verb's action?* According to these Greek scholars, it does. Here are some NT examples that illustrate such use: Matt 6:1; 9:34; 12:24, 28; 23:5; Luke 2:27; 4:1; 15:17; 23:15; Acts 2:33; 5:31; 17:31; Rom 12:2; 1 Cor 6:2; Jas 3:7; 2 Pet 3:14. Here are some Pauline examples of the dative with *pneumati*, some with *en* also: Rom 2:29; 8:14; 15:16; 1 Cor 6:11; 12:3 (2x), 9 (2x); 14:2; 14:16; Gal 5:18; Eph 2:22; 3:5; 4:30; Phil 4:13.

In reference to *en*, Robertson said, "Fierce polemical battles have been waged over its usage, but the theological bearing of the preposition can come only from the context" (*A Short Grammar of the Greek NT*, 120). The next important question should be *Does the* context *of 1 Cor 12:13 allow the dative* en *to be interpreted as a dative of agency?* The cotexts of 12:13, i.e., 12:3 and 9, contain the datives of agency best rendered with "by." But it is verse 11 that is operative: "All these are the work of one and the same Spirit, and he gives them to each one, just as he determines." Stanley Horton, after considering the dative of agency use of *en* elsewhere in the New Testament and especially in Paul's writings, concludes: "Thus, 'by one Spirit' is the correct translation here and is in fact found in most English versions . . . ."[33] This verse unequivocally puts the Spirit in the agent position, with power to will and distribute, and I would argue that he is still in that position two verses later. This is grammatically justifiable, as Hunter states, "To designate Paul's use of the preposition as instrumental [i.e., dative of *agency*] rather than locative is to stand equally within the bounds of Pauline grammar . . ." (59). (Incidentally, the second occurrence in 1 Cor 12:9 also contains *heni* [*one*]: "by the *one* [*heni*] Spirit," as 12:13a echoes.)

---

[33] *1 & 2 Corinthians* (Springfield, MO: Logion Press-Gospel Publishing House, 1999), 119.

So, in the immediate Pauline cotexts, the preposition *en* with the dative *pneumati* is best rendered "by" in the four occurrences (i.e., 12:3[2x] and 9[2x]), indicating that the subject prepositional phrases in these verses function as datives of agency (this is possible because the Holy Spirit is a person; see Robertson, *A Grammar of the Greek NT in the Light of Historical Research*, 532[j]; Wenham, *The Elements of NT Greek*, 70; see Smythe, *Greek Grammar*, #1504). Since the Spirit is the agent and the body (*soma*) the incorporating location, this baptism is apparently an initiation-incorporation act performed by the Spirit, as in its Pauline semi-parallels in Romans 6:3 and Galatians 3:27.[34] If it isn't performed by the Holy Spirit, who is the baptizer? If the exegete makes it the elliptical "Jesus" (or divine passive)[35] then he is creating an exception to the utterance of John the Baptist (so highly depended upon) wherein the baptizer *is specifically stated to be Jesus* (or implied to be Jesus in the two Acts occurrences).

David Petts examined 1 Cor 12:13 closely. Here are his findings in his own words:

> Discussion on the use of *en* turns around whether it should be translated "in" or "by". That grammatically it can legitimately be translated either way no Greek scholar would deny for the preposition may carry an instrumental or locative force. The decision as to which translation to adopt must, therefore, be made on the grounds of a) the immediate context, and b) any use of the expression elsewhere in Paul's writings. In the event of there being little or no help from these sources an examination of c) the use of the preposition in a similar expression elsewhere in the NT might also help the decision. I would suggest that from a methodological point of view the order of priority must be a), then b), then c) as outlined above for the most probable

---

[34] Regarding the functional difference in these Spirit baptisms, Anthony Palma writes the following:

> This concept of being baptized into the body of Christ is mentioned in a slightly different way in Romans 6:3, which speaks about being "baptized into Christ Jesus," and in Galatians 3:27, which speaks about being "baptized into Christ." This baptism is therefore different from the baptism mentioned by John the Baptist, Jesus, and Peter in the Gospels and in Acts. According to John the Baptist, it is Jesus who baptizes in the Holy Spirit. According to Paul, it is the Holy Spirit who baptizes into Christ, or into the body of Christ. *If this distinction is not maintained, we have the strange idea that Christ baptizes into Christ. (The Holy Spirit: A Pentecostal Perspective* [Springfield, MO: Logion Press-Gospel Publishing House, 2001], 100–105, italics added.)

[35] As do Atkinson, *Baptism*, ("divine passive"="God"), 98, and Murray Harris ("viz. Jesus Christ"), *The New International Dictionary of New Testament Theology*, vol. 3 (Grand Rapids: Zondervan, 1975), 1210, and repeated in *Prepositions and Theology*, 231; also, Stott, *Baptism*, 42.

interpretation of Paul's intention.

Considering the immediate context first, then, it certainly appears that the translation "by" is well justified. In a list of gifts which are distributed to each person as the Spirit wills (v11), we are told that faith is given *en to auto pneumati* [*by the same Spirit*] (v9) and that gifts of healing are likewise given *en to heni pneumati* [*by the one Spirit*]. This use of *en* to mean "by" in the immediately preceding context must give considerable weight to the view that *en* should also be translated "by" in verse 13.

Concerning b) above, we do not find any use of *baptizein* with *en pneumati* elsewhere in Paul's writings, and so we must either accept from the immediate context that "by" is the best translation here or we must consider whether the use of the expression in the wider context of the NT as a whole gives us any grounds for a different interpretation. And this is precisely where the problem lies. For in all the (six) other references to *baptizein* with *en pneumati (hagio)* the baptism in question is "in" the Spirit as distinct from "in" water.

Now if we follow the methodology outlined above we would almost certainly reach the conclusion that a) outweighs c).[36]

Petts's conclusion is cogent; all the more so when we consider that all the other NT evidence boils down to one statement by John the Baptist, not six different sources (see next section).[37]

The word *eis* (*in/into*) heavily impacts the meaning of *en* in Paul's verse. These two prepositions, when *en* is used in its locative sense, are virtually synonymous (Robertson, *New Short Grammar of the Greek NT*, 255–56; Moule, *An Idiom Book of NT Greek*, 75[1]; Zerwick, *Biblical Greek*, 33 [#99, #101]; BDF, #218.[38] Quoting J. H. Moulton [*Prolegomena*, 62f.] and referencing 1 Cor 12:13, Swete writes that "there are in the N.T.

---

[36] "The Baptism in the Holy Spirit in Relation to Christian Initiation" (MTh Thesis, University of Nottingham, 1987), 78–79.

[37] Atkinson's rejoinder to Petts's argument is misguided, as it suffers from complexity bias and discounts too much the personhood of the Spirit.

[38] Simon J. Kistemaker writes the following:

> Most translators have adopted the reading *by* to reveal means or agency. They think that this interpretation is the better of the two, for it avoids the awkwardness of having two quite similar prepositional phrases in the same clause . . . . I prefer the translation *by*. [Regarding this passage and Galatians 3:27–28, he writes:] "Paul stresses the unity in Christ Jesus regardless of racial, cultural, social, and sexual differences. He states that all were baptized by one Spirit into Christ. (*1 Corinthians*, New Testament Commentary [Grand Rapids: Baker, 1993], 429, 431)

'very clear examples of εἰς encroaching on the domain of ἐν."[39]) Dunn and others argue for the locative dative use for *en* here. This creates an odd action for the elliptical subject to perform, i.e., Jesus (or God) baptizes the believer *in* or *into* (*en*) the Spirit but also *in* or *into* (*eis*) the body. This interpretation is awkward[40] and strained for two reasons: (1) it creates two *elements* of the baptismal rite; (the locative sense of *eis* is generally agreed upon; see the aforementioned similar use in Rom. 6:3 and Gal. 3:27); and (2) it requires the insertion of the elliptical baptizer. This interpretation requires more engineering than the verse can withstand. True, the divine passive is plentiful in the New Testament, but it veers away from the content of the critical six non-Pauline occurrences.[41]

If the scholars cited above are correct and *en* (locative) and *eis* are virtually synonymous, the awkwardness is obvious when both are translated identically: "*in* one Spirit we all were baptized *in* one body" or "*into* one Spirit we all were baptized *into* one body." The expressions, if both are considered locatives, being universally metaphoric and spatial, would sound as odd to Greek as English ears. Perhaps odder since in the Greek the two prepositional phrases are not separated by the verb; it comes at the end, thus: "in one Spirit in one body we were baptized."

The perceived irregularity, both auditory and logical, of using both *en* and *eis* in the locative sense has convinced many translators to opt for the *en* of agency, that is, "by." Anthony Palma collected the following data regarding "by" or "in" in 1 Cor 12:13a as it is translated in the various translations (I've added additional versions in brackets):

> A comparison of . . . major versions shows a decided preference even by non-Pentecostal scholars for the rendering *by*. The following have the word *by*: KJV, NKJV, NASB, NIV, RSV, Living Bible, TEV, The New Testament in Modern English [Beck, Cassirer, CSB, CEV, GNB, GNT, GWT, Hart, HCSB, ISV, Leg.SB, MLB, NCV, NLT,

---

[39] Henry Barclay Swete, *The Holy Spirit in the New Testament* (London: Macmillan, 1910; repr., Grand Rapids: Baker, 1976), 125n1.

[40] Michael Green calls the use of two locatives (*en* and *eis*) "very harsh" and says, "the instrumental use [of *en*] is highly likely here" (*I Believe in the Holy Spirit* [Grand Rapids: Eerdmans, 1975]), 141. Elsewhere, Green's exposition of 1 Cor 12:13 is conflicted to the point of contradiction. Although he favors the instrumental use, at one point he writes that the "final reference to baptism *in* the Holy Spirit [is] in 1 Corinthians 12:13," and on the same page writes, "[I]t is the one Spirit who baptises believers into the one body of Christ" (140–41, italics added). He navigates around any hints of Pentecostal theological alignment by claiming that all six of the non-Pauline uses of *en*, as well as the one Pauline, occur in soteriological contexts (139–40).

[41] Which is even more important if the exegete accepts Stott's and others' numerical argument (i.e., six-to-one).

Phillips, SEB, TNT, Williams, Wright]. The translation *in* appears in the following: ASV, NRSV, NEB, NAB [BSB, JB, D-RB, ERV, ESV, LSB, MSB, NET, NJB, REB, TNT, WEB, WNT]. (*Life in the Spirit*, 896)

Based on the translation version evidence, Stanley Horton reasonably concluded the following: "Clearly, it is not just Pentecostal hermeneutical bias that makes a distinction between the baptism *by* the Spirit, which incorporates believers into the body of Christ, and the baptism *in* the Holy Spirit, in which Christ is the Baptizer."[42]

The "Seven" Occurrences of en pneumati in the New Testament

Much has been written of the numerical occurrences of *en pneumati* (7x) and how the six occurrences[43] elsewhere in the New Testament should govern its translation in 1 Corinthians. But Howard M. Ervin makes this observation:

> It has been urged in favor of this view [i.e., the synonymy of all the occurrences] that the phrase "to baptize in the Holy Spirit" occurs seven times in the NT. Vis-à-vis the Corinthian passage, this constitutes a ratio of six to one. It would appear then that numerically this provides an overwhelming precedent in favor of the locative "in one Spirit" (12:13). Such a methodology is, however, fallacious since the six non-Pauline references are all directly related to the one utterance of John the Baptist. The comparison is, therefore, in the nature of a one to one ratio.[44]

New Testament scholar Gordon D. Fee ignores the point Ervin makes and bases his rejection of "by" at least partially on this fallacious numerical

---

[42] *1 & 2 Corinthians*, 119.

[43] Given the prominent position of Acts 1:4–5 and 8 as well as Luke 3:16 and its parallels in this discussion, it's difficult to understand why Thiselton says of 1 Cor 12:13, "This specific verse has particular importance within Pentecostal thought because it is the only verse in the NT which explicitly uses the phrase **baptized by** (or *in*) [**one**] **Spirit**" (998, brackets and bold Thistleton's). He questions whether the Pentecostal tradition "can gain any terminological support from the single passage in the NT which employs this term" (999). The Pentecostal tradition is not trying to do that; it looks to the predictions in the Gospels and their fulfillment in Acts—scriptures that are conspicuously missing from Thistleton's discussion.

[44] *Conversion-Initiation and the Baptism in the Holy Spirit* (Peabody, MA: Hendrickson, 1984), 99, 104n29. (Ervin credits me for bringing this to his attention; it was Anthony Palma who brought it to my attention in a 1980 interview at the Society for Pentecostal Studies conference in Tulsa.)

statistic.[45] Likewise, Thomas R. Schreiner, who, in his commentary, considers the references to the saying of John the Baptist as support for "in."[46] Dunn, in his classic non-Pentecostal work *Baptism in the Holy Spirit*, writes that the instrumental interpretation of *en* is "almost certainly to be rejected," and proceeds to "prove" it by using the six-against-one argument.[47] Frederick Dale Bruner, in his work *A Theology of the Holy Spirit*, claims that the instrumental translation of *en* "has no support in the New Testament grammar or texts"; he then proceeds to list the references to the Baptist's saying, and no others.[48]

Murray Harris's Six Reasons for Rejecting "by"

Murray Harris, a non-Pentecostal New Testament Greek scholar, has probably itemized as many or more grammatical reasons (six) not to translate *en* "by" in 1 Cor 12:13 than anyone. Some of his reasons have already been addressed above, but I would like to list his reasons and reply serially:

1. *Elsewhere* ὑπό *expresses personal agency with* βαπτίζεσθαι . . . .
    REPLY: 1. None of the six verses to which non-Pentecostals like to connect Paul's verse contain ὑπό even though, in their view, the agent (Jesus) is named or implied, so there is no support there for this argument. 2. This doesn't consider stylistic variances of genre and author. (This point is applicable to several of Harris's reasons against the instrumental "by.") 3. The Pauline corpus does not contain one instance where *Paul* uses ὑπό with βαπτίζεσθαι. 4. It is true that the Greek *can* distinguish clearly between the locative and the instrumental (agency), and it can do so with ὑπό. But this is not to say that it always does. ὑπό certainly isn't the only way the Greek can express agency. Robertson writes this about the instrumental dative: "But no usage of this case is more common than that of means. With things sometimes we call it means, with persons agent, though more often the agent is expressed by ὑπό" (532[j]). Robertson evidently believes that the instrumental dative *could* serve the same function as ὑπό, although ὑπό is the more prominent use for showing agency.

2. *There is no certain instance of an instrumental* ἐν *with* βαπτίζεσθαι. *In other examples of* ἐν πνεύματι *with* βαπτίζεσθαι, *the parallel with* (ἐν) ὕδατι *dictates that* ἐν *should mean "in" or "with," not "by [means of]"—denoting the "sphere" or "material" (Mt 3:11; Mk 1:8; Lk 3:16; Jn 1:33; Ac 1:5; 11:16), but not the agent.*

---

[45] *Corinthians*, 671, 671n196.

[46] *1 Corinthians: An Introduction and Commentary*, Tyndale New Testament Commentaries (Downers Grove, IL: InterVarsity, 2018), 263.

[47] Dunn, *Baptism*, 128.

[48] Bruner, *Theology*, 293–294n13.

REPLY: 1. No other instance of ἐν with πνεύματι also contains ἐις, a synonym. 2. ὕδατι may indeed dictate that in the referenced verses; however, ὕδατι does not occur in 1 Cor 12:13, and it is impossible for water, being an inanimate object, to act as an agent and baptize anyone, whereas the Holy Spirit is a person and capable of baptizing the believer. 3. This argument also assumes the validity of the numerical argument of six to one; when in reality, it is one to one.

3. *In the logia of John the Baptist regarding "Spirit baptism," it is always Jesus who is the baptizer, never the Spirit. Accordingly, in 1Co 12:13, the agent should be taken as implied (i.e., Jesus Christ).*
   REPLY: 1. This argument begs the question of the translation/interpretation of 12:13, including the consideration of the contexts, and, perhaps, assumes the Holy Spirit is incapable of baptizing the believer. 2. The logion of the Baptist points to Pentecost, whereas Paul's verse doesn't. 3. There is also a reliance here on the flawed numerical argument.

4. *In the one [other] place Paul uses ἐν with βαπτίζω (1Co 10:2), the preposition is local in sense ("In the cloud and in the sea").*
   REPLY: 1. Unlike the Holy Spirit (in 1 Cor 12:13), the cloud and the sea, as inanimate objects, are incapable of baptizing, so "by" would be illogical. 2. This passage of Scripture is an analogy in which Christians and their deliverer (Jesus) are compared to the Israelites and Moses. The cloud and the sea are more *symbolic* of baptism than the body of Christ into which believers are *genuinely* baptized (cf. Rom 6:3; Gal 3:27).[49]

5. *The following phrase, "and we were all given one and the same Spirit to imbibe," suggests an inward participation in the Spirit to which a preceding outward "immersion in the Spirit" would correspond. The Spirit is both around believers (v. 13a) and with them (v.13b; cf. Eph. 5:18).*
   REPLY: 1. This would indeed preach well! However, it creates the strange and unprecedented image of believers drinking themselves into the kingdom.[50] 2. This assumes a correspondence but does not prove one. I used to believe that this verse exhibited Semitic parallelism, but a closer look at the Greek dispels that belief, or at least the certainty of it. There are indeed two clauses, but they are interrupted by an eight-word parenthetical phrase; the first clause contains eleven words (nine if you disregard the introductory words) and two prepositional phrases and its supposed parallel clause contains five words and one prepositional phrase. Is this a case of parallelism? I think it may only be serial similarity. But the rhetoric is nice: every word

---

[49] The Israelites were not immersed into the sea (they walked on dry land, after all) or the clouds in a similar way that believers are immersed (incorporated) into the body of Christ. Paul's analogy is strained but understandable; it is not comparable to Paul's imagery in 12:13a.

[50] Ervin, *Conversion-Initiation*, 100.

of the last clause but one (the verb) is contained in the first clause. So, the correspondence may not be as certain as Harris supposes. (Incidentally, Harris is fudging a bit when he lengthens the second clause by adding "and the same" to his translation. Though justifiable, that's an *interpreted* meaning rather than a literal rendering.) 3. Thiselton notes that some scholars believe that the final verb should not be translated "drink" but "*drenched in, plunged in, saturated, imbued* or *submerged in*" (997).

6.   *The parallel* ἐν ἑνὶ πνεύματι *in Eph 2:18 cannot be an instrumental use of* ἐν, *since* δι' αὐτοῦ *(=Christ) precedes. However,* ἐν τῷ ἑνὶ πνεύματι *in 1Co 12:9 is undoubtedly instrumental in sense, in light of the preceding* διὰ τοῦ πνεύματος *(12:8; cf. vv. 7, 8b, 11).*
     REPLY: 1. The first comment is irrelevant. Even so, I will say that the translations are still split with several preferring "by" (e.g., NIV, BSB, BLB, KJV, NKJV, HCSB, ISV, MSB, WBT), indicating that the relationship between and within the two clauses is nebulous. 2. Harris's second comment is true, but what is he implying? Is he implying that if Paul had wanted to make the Spirit the agent in 12:13a, he would've used διὰ τοῦ πνεύματος? But he's already argued for ὑπό for that purpose (see #1 above). Also, Paul's instrumental phrase ἐν [. . .] πνεύματι occurs five times in 1 Cor 12; he uses διὰ only once, just prior to v. 13. Perhaps Paul felt that since he had used it a few lines above (12:8) that the reader/listener would understand. 3. "In verses 8 and 9, the word *en* is used interchangeably with the word *dia*, meaning 'through.' Whether by the Spirit or through the Spirit, the Spirit is clearly the agent."[51]

It is my opinion that if the data gathered from the grammar and the context are allowed to govern the interpretation of *en pneumati*, the dative of agency is the more plausible possibility. The facts, regarding the meaning of *en pneumati*, are certainly clear enough to disallow Packer's dogmatic position that "the distinction is linguistically baseless"[52] and disallow Baker's alignment with Stott in calling it "'special pleading,' linguistically and exegetically completely unwarranted . . . no justification."[53]

The Scriptures depict the Holy Spirit not only as a person but as the agent/activator in so many realms of spirituality. Here are several: He regenerates, teaches, directs, testifies, guides, warns, empowers, intercedes, inspires, comforts, sanctifies, convicts, reveals, frees, equips, sends, commands, restrains, anoints, adopts, unifies, distributes spiritual gifts, and cultivates spiritual fruit.[54] In another context in 1 Corinthians, Paul writes the

---

[51] Stanley M. Horton, *What the Bible Says about the Holy Spirit* (Springfield, MO: Gospel Publishing House, 1976), 215–16.

[52] *Keep in Step with the Spirit*, 203.

[53] Baker, *Baptized*, 11–12.

[54] Many of these are listed with scripture citations in Arrington, *Encountering*, 22.

following, using ἐν τῷ πνεύματι (*by the Spirit*) : "... you were washed, you were sanctified, you were justified in the name of the Lord Jesus Christ and *by the Spirit* of our God" (1 Cor. 6:11, italics added). I believe that non-Pentecostals would agree that the Spirit actively does these things. Why then would they deny that the Spirit might be the *agent* of the believer's baptizing (incorporation) into the body of Christ in 1 Cor 12:13? I hate to think that it is primarily to counter the Pentecostal doctrine of Spirit baptism, which, according to Fee,[55] has nothing to do with this verse.[56]

---

[55] See footnote 29 and its referent.
[56] Whether the interpretation favors the Pentecostal or non-Pentecostal view.

11

The Speaking in Tongues Controversy— A Narrative-Critical Response: A Review Article with Emphasis on Initial Evidence and Subsequence[1]

Unfortunately, as is the case with defending any topic, that topic by nature becomes the central focus of the discussion, to the exclusion of all other topics, even topics that may be of much greater importance. Readers usually understand this and indulge the author. I trust that this will be the case with the readers of this review, which, in the larger picture of the kingdom of God, salvation, and fallen humanity, is small indeed (unless many pages are spent explaining the connection, which cannot be done here). So let it be said here that more important than one's initial baptism in (filling with) the Holy Spirit with the evidence of speaking in tongues are the numerous

---

[1] Originally published in an earlier version in two parts in *The Pneuma Review* (October 10, 2005); available online here: http://pneumareview.com/the-speaking-in-tongues-controversy-a-narrative-critical-response-part-1/; (March 5, 2006): http://pneumareview.com/the-speaking-in-tongues-controversy-a-narrative-critical-response-part-2/.

Spirit-fillings—with or without tongues—along life's journey that embolden the believer to enter his or her mission field with power to share the gospel of the kingdom of God. But, of course, there must always be that initial step, and that is the subject of this review.

The thrust of Rick Walston's book *The Speaking in Tongues Controversy: The Initial, Physical Evidence of the Baptism in the Holy Spirit*[2] is that the two major distinctive doctrines of Pentecostal theology—the initial evidence of tongues and the separability/subsequence of Spirit-baptism—are wrong. In his own words, Walston is "attempting to lead the reader to the obvious conclusion that Luke does not intend to establish tongues-as-evidence as a doctrine or as a paradigm" (85).

Walston's endeavor to disprove these aspects of Pentecostal theology relies on several strategies. First, he attempts to show that whereas Pentecostals believe Luke's theology is predominantly pneumatological, it is in fact more soteriological. For Walston, this entails (1) accepting Acts 2:38–41 as the paradigmatic passage of Acts, (2) statistically comparing the occurrences of pneumatological and soteriological passages in Acts, and (3) defining the baptism in the Holy Spirit as a salvific event. Second, in a classic example of arguing from silence, he builds a massive construct upon what Luke does *not* say at opportune times; he then relates this to the hermeneutical principle of *authorial intent*.

Before examining Walston's success in developing his argumentation, it should be noted that the work, as a whole, is written in a mixed popular-academic style, complete with endnotes and bibliography. There is nothing wrong with this, if it is done correctly; we need writers who can translate biblical truths into popular language. However, in this case, there seems to have been a severe oversight of the most recent scholarship in the relevant fields. Walston's work would have been more balanced and forceful if he had interacted with and utilized key players in this discussion, such players as James Dunn, Howard Ervin, Craig Keener, Robert Menzies, and Max Turner, to name a few. These are missing from Walston's work. (There is a passage [47–48] referencing Dunn but only in that he was the stimulus of a response from a Pentecostal theologian.) Given that Walston's work was published in 2003 and the others earlier, the lack of engagement with these authors results in a misrepresentative product and leaves the reader with thoughts of unfair source selectivity. Furthermore, Walston's heavy reliance upon a single source to bolster his arguments, in this case one early work of Gordon D. Fee, leaving the work of other influential scholars who have spoken directly to this issue virtually unmentioned, is bewildering.

---

[2] Fairfax, VA: Xulon Press, 2003.

The Paradigmatic and Soteriological Nature of Acts 2:38–41

According to Walston, "[S]ince Peter proclaimed [in Acts 2:38] . . . that all who believed would receive the gift of the Holy Spirit, and since all of the three thousand on Pentecost received the Holy Spirit in the same fullness as the 120 had and just as Peter said would happen, then it cannot be denied that *a paradigm was established*. However, it is not the paradigm of baptism in the Holy Spirit with the evidence of speaking in tongues. Rather, the paradigm was (and continues to be) 'repent and accept Jesus and *automatically* receive the baptism in the Holy Spirit'" (138; emphasis his). The paradigm, having been "clearly explained" (79) by Peter became "the divinely established pattern" (77). "Perhaps the strongest argument for this is Acts 2:41: 'Those who accepted his message were baptized, and about three thousand were added to their number that day'" (125). Thus, for Walston, not only is Acts 2:38 paradigmatic, but it is illustrative of Luke's emphasis throughout Acts, which is "predominantly soteriological" (72–73).

In Walston's opinion, because the three thousand "accepted his [Peter's] message," "were baptized," and "were added to their number that day," clearly they received the gift of the Holy Spirit. "Logic demands (and Luke implies) that they did receive the 'gift of the Holy Spirit,'. . ." (125). Does it (and did he)? Walston rushes on to the subject of the absence of tongues in the passage, leaving the reader wondering *what logic?* and *what implications?* Only an uncritical reading of this passage, driven by an inordinately strong dependency upon a particular interpretation of Pauline literature (à la Fee), could lead to these conclusions.

In pursuing Luke's intent in Acts 2:38, first, consideration needs to be given to the grammatical construction of the verse. After all, if the Greek future ("will receive") *demands* an *immediate* consummation rather than allowing a dilatory (later) fulfillment, the argument is half over ("half" because Walston still must prove that tongues did not occur, or Luke's omission of them is implicative, and that the baptism in the Holy Spirit was the *cause of* and not *in addition to* salvation).

In a personal interview of NT scholar Paul Elbert, I asked his opinion about the following passage from Catholic scholar George T. Montague's *The Spirit and His Gifts* (New York: Paulist Press, 1976): "The future *lempsesthe* of Acts 2:38 is not a dilatory future but the future of unqualified promise, to be fulfilled immediately upon the conditions preceding," (53). Elbert responded:

> "He [Montague] has no basis to say that other than his opinion. Now it would be a fine thing if biblical scholars would start thinking that they had opinions instead of facts. That is an opinion. It might be so, but, on the other hand, it might not be so, because the indefinite use

73

of the future was widely used and there is no way to tell whether that is an indefinite future or a future that is right away. In fact, the whole weight of the sermon is that this will happen in the future. . . . Jesus would say, 'Seek and ye shall receive.' That is an indefinite future. He doesn't say *when* God would do it. And the indefinite in the promises of Jesus is very common. It was a very common way to talk . . . using the future tense. . . . Interesting thing is, if you go back and look at all the future tenses in Luke-Acts (especially the ones where the subject is to be acted upon) . . . you'll find that the . . . majority . . . are exactly these kind of futures—they're indefinite. God is going to do something, but they don't say when. In every case . . . that the future is used that involves an action of God, which it is in this case, in Acts 2:38c, . . . it is indefinite. It's never pinned down." (October 28, 1984)

Fourteen years later, Elbert would write the following about this verse:

Now, just as the disciples before them who have just experienced their first coming of the Lukan gift of the Spirit, Peter's hearers, meeting the salvific condition set forth, are prepared for their own promise of this gift. The two imperatives are followed by a future indicative, "and you shall receive the gift of the Holy Spirit. . . ." Grammatically, the general observation of Winer is apropos, "The future tense does not always indicate pure actual futurity, but sometimes possibility (as indeed the future and the possible are closely allied) and expresses what *can* or *should* or *must* take place." This indefinite tense indicates a time relatively future to the preceding imperatives, which set the qualifying ideas for the expected future event, but do not set the time for it. The tenses themselves certainly allow for, and normatively require in a predictive and gnomic future, the possibility for a separation in time between the immediate qualifying conditions and the future events. The immediate context from Lk 11:13; 24:47, 49 to Acts 1:14; 2:4, (1:8; 2:38c) simply predicts the expected reception of the gift to take place at a time and in a form designed by the Lord, anticipating its evangelistic use within a future occasion as the Lord directs.

Theophilus [to whom Luke and Acts were written], not being or needing to be a grammarian, would add two and two and get four. Luke does not intend to confront Theophilus with "weighty problems," problems that afflict interpreters who want to force Luke to be Paul and allow for no development or diversity in NT pneumatology. Rather Luke's case is clear and contains no hidden variables which Theophilus needs to detect before he can understand this narrative. Sensing that the whole story is Luke's vehicle for his understanding, I suggest that he would recall the pointed conditional lesson on persistent prayer set out in the context Luke provided for disciples with the first mention of the gift of the Holy Spirit at Luke 11:13 and now apply that lesson to the condition set out here. . . . If he would repent, seek forgiveness, call upon the Lord's name (become a convert via salvation which Jesus offers), and submit to baptism, then he too, through persistent prayer, would confidently expect the Lord to pour out upon him (2:33) the Lukan gift of the Holy Spirit.[3]

R. Menzies agrees, concluding that "the phrase 'and you will receive the gift of the Holy Spirit' (2.38) should be interpreted as a promise that the Spirit shall be 'imparted to those who are already converted and baptized.'"[4] (Having explored the interpretation of *lempsesthe* as dilatory, I recognize that the Pentecostal interpretation that the three thousand were baptized in the Spirit *and* spoke in tongues is also feasible. How this could happen without Luke's recording it is covered later.)

As I mentioned earlier, Walston places unsustainable weight upon the work of Gordon Fee. For that reason, he may appreciate this next point. Pre-dating the interview with Elbert, I corresponded with Fee and asked him the same question that I put before Elbert concerning the future tense of the Greek *lempsesthe*. He replied: "You will note that no good commentary (Cadbury-Lake, Haenchen, Bruce) even take[s] up Montague's questions. The question, by the way, is not what the Greek will allow (it will 'allow' either), but rather what did Luke intend his readers to understand by so reporting Peter's words" (October 19, 1981). So, even Fee agrees that, on a strictly grammatical basis, the future tense of "will receive" does not have to be interpreted as an *immediate* fulfillment. (Concerning the second part of Fee's statement, I would ask, *How can a reader get to Luke's intentions before settling on the possibilities that the language allows?*)

---

[3] Paul Elbert, "Towards an Understanding of Luke's Expectations for Theophilus Regarding the Lukan Gift of the Holy Spirit," *Pentecostal Mission at 2000: Issues Home and Abroad, Conference Papers of the 29th Annual Meeting of the Society for Pentecostal Studies, Northwest College, Kirkland, WA* (Lexington, KY: Society for Pentecostal Studies, 2000), 16–17, see 10–11, available in revised and expanded form as the monograph *The Lukan Gift of the Holy Spirit* (Canton, GA: Foundation for Pentecostal Scholarship, 2021), 64–67, 73–75; and Paul Elbert, "Luke's Fulfillment of Prophecy Theme: Introductory Exploration of Joel and the Last Days," Society for Pentecostal Studies Conference, Marquette University (March 2004), 18–22, available now as a chapter in *Luke's Rhetorical Compositions: Essays in Lukan Studies* (Eugene, OR: Wipf and Stock, 2022), 1–32. Elbert has also persuasively argued that all the imperative-future middle/passive combinations (as at Acts 2:38) in Luke-Acts and the Septuagint are intended in Greek thought to represent two temporally non-simultaneous verbal ideas or events, see "The Syntax of Imperative-Future Combinations and Imperative-Present Participle Combinations in Luke-Acts and Elsewhere," Society of Biblical Literature Conference, Gregorian University, Rome (July 2001), available now, in revised form, as a chapter in *Luke's Rhetorical Compositions*, 43–55.

[4] "Spirit of Prophecy," 64.

For Walston, Acts 2:38 is the Lukan *paradigm* or *pattern* for conversion. Here are the components: (1) repent, (2) be baptized in water in the name of Jesus Christ, (3) receive the gift of the Holy Spirit. Conditions 1 and 2 are not enough since the gift of the Holy Spirit is what saves (per Walston): "If one is a Christian, he has been baptized in the Holy Spirit; in fact, it is this gift of the Holy Spirit that separates him from the world and makes him a Christian" (135). "The dual idea that there are Christians who are 'spirit-filled' and Christians who are not 'spirit-filled' is an idea that is foreign to the New Testament. . . . One does not receive Christ and not receive the gift of (or baptism in) the Holy Spirit" (135). "The New Testament never makes the distinction between (1) getting saved and (2) being filled with the Holy Spirit as though they are two entirely different experiences" (139).[5] Practically speaking, does this mean that we are baptizing non-Christians? In Walston's world, it must mean this, for they are not Christians until they receive the gift of the Holy Spirit, and they cannot be Christians until they have fulfilled the conditions of the "divinely established pattern," which requires repentance and baptism before the promise of the gift can be realized.

If one repents, accepts Christ as his savior, is baptized in water, and then receives the gift of the Holy Spirit, what is the function of the gift? In the Pentecostal view, one need only follow Luke as he leads Theophilus (who stands in for all of us) through the narrative of Jesus's promise in Acts 1:8 to its fulfillment in 2:1–41 to see that the gift is not for one's personal salvation but is a prophetic empowerment for service and witness. In fact, as Roger Stronstad writes, "Peter restricts the eschatological gift of the Spirit to the penitent, the saved."[6] Eduard Schweizer agrees, "[T]he Spirit is imparted to those who are already converted and baptized."[7]

William and Robert Menzies argue forcefully against the view that Acts 2:38–39 is primarily soteriological:

---

[5] This statement is flatly contradicted by Luke, who describes Peter and Paul as experiencing the filling of the Spirit numerous times (Acts 2:4; 4:8, 31; 9:17; 13:9, 52?). Were they saved each time they were filled? Of course not. Then a person can be filled after he is saved, making the two experiences different and separate (see also Ephesians 5:18 where Paul exhorts *Christians* to be filled with the Spirit not drunk with wine).

[6] Roger Stronstad, *The Charismatic Theology of St. Luke*, 2nd ed. (1984; Grand Rapids: Baker, 2012), 57; see also Roger Stronstad, *The Prophethood of All Believers: A Study in Luke's Charismatic Theology* (Sheffield: Sheffield Academic Press, 1999), 68–70.

[7] Eduard Schweizer, "πνεῦμα, ktl." in *Theological Dictionary of the New Testament*, vol. 6, ed. Gerhard Kittel, trans. Geoffrey W. Bromiley (Grand Rapids: Eerdmans, 1968), 412.

In Joel's prophecy the Spirit comes as the source of prophetic inspiration, a point that again Luke highlights by altering the Greek text of
Joel by inserting the phrase "and they will prophesy" (Acts 2:18).
Another alteration, Luke's transformation of Joel's "slaves" into
"servants of God"—effected by his double insertion of "my" in Acts
2:18 . . .—highlights what is implicit in the Joel text: The gift of the
Spirit is given only to those who are members of the community of
salvation. Thus, Luke's explicit definitions (Luke 24:49; Acts 1:4–8)
and his use of the Joel citation indicate that "the promise" of the
Spirit, initially fulfilled at Pentecost (Acts 2:4), enables the disciples
to take up their prophetic vocation to the world.

Although the Lukan "promise" of the Spirit must be interpreted in
light of Joel's promise concerning the restoration of the Spirit of
prophecy, Acts 2:39 does include an additional element, insofar as
Luke extends the range of the promise envisioned to include the
promise of salvation offered in Joel 2:32 (as well as the promise of
the Spirit of prophecy in Joel 2:28). As Dunn notes, Acts 2:39 echoes
the language of Joel 2:32/Acts 2:21: "Everyone who calls on the name
of the Lord will be saved." In Acts 2:39 Luke extends the range of
"the promise" to include this salvific dimension because the audience
addressed is not disciples.

Yet we must not miss the fact that "the promise" of Acts 2:39 em-
braces more than the experience of conversion. Consistent with Luke
24:49; Acts 1:4; 2:33, the promised gift of the Spirit in Acts 2:39 refers to the promise of Joel 2:28, and thus it is a promise of prophetic
enabling granted to the repentant. The promise of Acts 2:39, like the
promise of Jesus in 1:8, points beyond "the restoration of the preserved of Israel": Salvation is offered (Joel 2:32), but the promise includes the renewal of Israel's prophetic vocation to be a light to the
nations (Joel 2:28). . . .

Acts 2:39 does not indicate that the Spirit comes as the source of
new covenant existence. Rather, it simply reminds us that the prophecy of Joel 2:28–32 includes two elements: the gift of the Spirit of
prophecy (v. 28) and the offer of salvation to those who call on the
name of the Lord (v. 32). Acts 2:39 refers to both, but it does not
suggest the two are identical. Indeed, this sort of equation runs counter to Luke's explicit statements (Luke 24:49; Acts 1:4–8), his use
and redaction of the Joel citation . . . , and the broader context of his
two-volume work. . . .

There is simply no evidence to support the notion that by referring
to Joel 2:28–29, Luke intended his readers to think of some com-
monly expected, all-embracing soteriological bestowal of the Spirit,
the details of which were pieced together from a variety of Old Testament texts. . . . [T]he most that can be gleaned from the text [of Acts

2:38] is that repentance and water baptism are the normal prerequisites for reception of the Spirit, which is promised to every believer.[8]

If Luke, as Walston believes, is setting up Acts 2:38 as the soteriological paradigm, *we should expect to find the paradigm illustrated somewhere in Acts.* This is what Walston believes, for he writes in another context that "Had Luke made a point of clearly, repetitiously, and consistently depicting throughout the book of Acts that all who were saved and filled with the Holy Spirit spoke in tongues, then there would be a paradigm (norm) that we would have to follow" (153). In an effort to demonstrate the preeminence of Luke's soteriological interest (evidently through *repetition* and *consistency*), Walston identifies twenty-six passages where Luke mentions people being saved. Here is how they compare to Walston's declared paradigm gleaned from Acts 2:38: (1) repentance is not mentioned in *any* of the passages, (2) water baptism is mentioned in only seven of them, (3) the gift of the Holy Spirit is mentioned in only five. Thus, using Walston's own methodology, *the statistical evidence does not support the claim that Acts 2:38 is a soteriological paradigm encoded with the non-Lukan concept of a soteriological Spirit-baptism.*

Luke did not write the summary verse of Acts 2:38 in a vacuum. On each side, it is couched with examples of believers who received the Spirit subsequent to conversion, i.e., Acts 2, 8, 9, and 19. As New Testament scholar Craig Keener has observed, "Luke apparently intends us to interpret his direct statement in Acts 2:38 and his narrative examples in light of each other."[9] It would be highly unusual if Luke did not expect his readers to interpret Acts 2:38 in light of the vivid examples and precedents throughout his work. (But I am getting ahead of myself; more on this in the section on authorial intent.)

---

[8] William W. and Robert P. Menzies, *Spirit and Power: Foundations of Pentecostal Experience* (Grand Rapids: Zondervan, 2000), 77–80; see also Robert P. Menzies, *Empowered for Witness*, 171, 182, 203–4; regarding Acts 2:38 and the timing of the receiving of the Spirit, see Elbert, *Rhetorical Compositions*, 43–54; Twelftree (*People of the Spirit*) writes that repentance and baptism is in "preparation" of receiving the Spirit (98), which is in God's "timing" (86).

[9] *Gift and Giver*, 158. Luke's readers learn in Acts 8 that the new Samaritan Christians "still need to 'receive' the Holy Spirit (8:15), although this is the same expression Acts 2:38 promised in response to conversion (10:47; 19:2). The promise was available upon conversion but apparently had not yet been appropriated. Whether the early Christians regarded this delay as normal or not—the apostles do seem to have been concerned about it—a delay is plainly in view. Even if abnormal, such a delay would count as evidence that *delays can happen*, for whatever reason" (*Gift and Giver*, 163; italics added).

The Soteriological vs. The Pneumatological

According to Walston, "Pentecostals have only minored on Lukan soteriology. . . . Classical Pentecostals have *minored* on what Luke *majored* on" (44). But, Walston continues, if Pentecostals would allow Scripture to speak for itself instead of interpreting it through their assumptions, it would become "obvious that Luke's intent is to establish the soteriological nature of the early church in conjunction with the preaching of the gospel and the infilling of the Holy Spirit" (85). Walston quotes Pentecostal scholars Roger Stronstad's *The Charismatic Theology of St. Luke* and Douglas Oss's contribution to *Are Miraculous Gifts for Today?* and Donald John's contribution to *Initial Evidence* a number of times in an attempt to demonstrate that Classical Pentecostals believe that Acts is, for the most part, a pneumatological, not soteriological, narrative (47–55).[10] (Interestingly, Fee sides with Stronstad and against Walston's view, writing, "I strongly agree with . . . Stronstad, on the 'charismatic nature' of Lukan theology. . . ."[11]) It is clear that Walston has misread the nuances of the Pentecostal argument. Luke records incidents of repentance, salvation, and conversion in Acts; these are soteriological elements and Pentecostals recognize them as such. *However, Walston fails to realize that Luke does not directly associate these elements with the Holy Spirit.* Thus, Luke's pneumatology does not include regeneration, as, for example, Paul's can be interpreted as including.[12] Walston's own list of twenty-six soteriological incidents in Acts is made up mainly of Luke simply saying, in various forms, that *the Lord added to their numbers* or *certain people believed.* This is the case in at least seventeen of the incidents, and in another five the Spirit is mentioned specifically because what is being described is the baptism in the Holy Spirit, not salvation! In none of Walston's twenty-six incidents of salvation does Luke describe the Spirit as being directly and explicitly active in the heart of the believer to effect regeneration. For these reasons, Pentecostals can validly say that although Luke speaks of salvation and regeneration in Acts, his focus is the Spirit in

---

[10] Douglas A. Oss, "A Pentecostal/Charismatic View," in *Are Miraculous Gifts for Today?* 239–283; Donald A. Johns, "Some New Directions in the Hermeneutics of Classical Pentecostalism's Doctrine of Initial Evidence," in *Initial Evidence*, 145–167.

[11] *Gospel and Spirit: Issues in New Testament Hermeneutics* (Peabody, MA: Hendrickson, 1991), 101.

[12] Menzies, *Spirit and Power*, 89; Robert P. Menzies, "Spirit-Baptism and Spiritual Gifts," in *Pentecostalism in Context: Essays in Honor of William W. Menzies*, ed. Wonsuk Ma and Robert P. Menzies (Sheffield: Sheffield Academic Press, 1997), 52–56. R. Menzies rightly believes that Luke's pneumatology "is missiological rather than soteriological in nature. . . . When the pentecostal gift of the Spirit is understood in soteriological terms, Luke's missiological focus and our expectation of it is lost" (*Pneuma* 43.3–4 [2021]: 440).

relation to the prophetic empowerment of believers for service and mission. (Are we not reminded of Luke's programmatic prophecy of Jesus's, "You shall be my witnesses. . . ."?)

As mentioned above, Walston presents statistical data that prove (for him) that Luke's intent was soteriological and not pneumatological. As proof of this, he presents twenty-six reports of conversion and notes that only three explicitly mention tongues. (He also uses these statistics to show that it was not Luke's intent to present tongues as the initial evidence of the baptism in the Holy Spirit. I address this below.) In my own survey of Acts, I discovered that Luke narrates seventy-five scenes in which charismatic activity is present (e.g., tongues, prophecy, visions, healings, miracles) compared to sixty-six scenes where soteriological activity is present. These seventy-five and sixty-six scenes usually overlap, with the charismatic activity (which is usually more detailed) leading to the, usually, very generalized salvific outcome, which is just as we should expect given the promise in Acts 1:8.[13] *Statistically (once again using Walston's methodology), Luke's intent (or emphasis) leans not toward the soteriological but toward the pneumatological.*

What do Pentecostal scholars actually believe about the soteriology of Acts? Based on Walston's assessment, they think Luke *minored* in soteriology. That may be so, but, as Walston admits, they haven't ignored it. Just so there is no mistake, here are a few comments. In Stronstad's work cited above, he writes that ". . . Acts is the story of the geographic advance of the gospel" (63); "The inaugural gift of the Holy Spirit on the day of Pentecost is a pivotal event in Luke's history-of-salvation theology" (49); and "[I]n the charismatic theology of St. Luke, the Holy Spirit plays a leading role on the stage of salvation history" (48). In a later work, he writes that Acts "is primarily about Christ, salvation and the Holy Spirit. . . . In Luke's theology, the day of Pentecost is a momentous and epochal episode in the forward movement of the history of salvation" (*Prophethood*, 27, 70). Finally, as though Stronstad had Walston's position in view, he penned the following:

> Since Luke-Acts is the story of the origin and spread of the gospel, and since the Spirit of prophecy is given to the penitent, it is historically and theologically impossible for there not to be a close relationship between salvation and the gift of the Spirit. But in spite of the close relationship between salvation and the gift of the Spirit, for Luke-Acts the *function* of the gift of the Spirit is not soteriological but prophetic. To confuse the close relationship between the two as

---

[13] Which is why Keener writes, "Luke's writings focus almost exclusively on prophetic empowerment" (*Gift and Giver*, 158).

meaning an identity of function is a serious methodological error and leads to a gross distortion of Luke's very clear and explicit pneumatology. (*Prophethood*, 122)

In a paper read at the 2004 Society for Pentecostal Studies Conference, Paul Elbert speaks of Luke as having "two main thematic experiential nexuses, the soteriological one and the gift of the Holy Spirit [i.e., the pneumatological] one" ("Luke's Fulfillment," 25). In the same work, he writes,

For Luke, the ministry of the earthly Jesus and of the heavenly Jesus are dynamically linked, the soteriological nexus of faith/repentance/ forgiveness/salvation in the ministry of the earthly Jesus in characters' lives (Prodigal Son, Woman with Ointment, Zaccheus) continues in characters' lives under the ministry of the heavenly Jesus (Ethiopian Eunuch, Sergius Paulus, Lydia, Philippian Jailer, Crispus). The former characters can be understood by Luke to fulfill prophetic announcements from heaven and from the Holy Spirit prompted revelation that Jesus is a Savior, with narrative coupling to that same component of Joel's prophecy (Acts 2:21). The latter characters can be similarly understood. And for Luke, the ministry of the heavenly Jesus also includes the outpouring of the gift of the Holy Spirit, fulfilling a programmatic prophecy by John the Baptist, teaching on prayer and known predictions by the earthly Jesus and His narrative predictions, as well as another component of Joel's prophecy (Acts 2:17a, 18). This ministry takes its literary place alongside the soteriological nexus in Lukan personification in another collection of experientially descriptive and delicately different phrases, namely the pneumatological nexus of Spirit-reception/Spirit-filling/Spirit-falling-upon/Spirit-outpouring. This latter pneumatological nexus of the Lukan gift of the Spirit is narratively connected . . . with distinctly noticeable and prominently placed promissory language. I argue that both the soteriological nexus and the pneumatological nexus are well illustrated by the expected examples and precedents and that both are contained in Luke's programmatic concept of ongoing prophetic fulfillment. I also suggest that prophetic fulfillment is understood by Luke as underpinning the missionary guidance portrayed in Acts. (6; also in *Luke's Rhetorical Compositions*, 6–7)

Robert Menzies explains the relationship between the Holy Spirit and conversion in Acts, writing, ". . . Luke always attributes forgiveness . . . , which is granted in response to faith/repentance, to Jesus. . . . Luke does not view the gift of the Spirit as a necessary element in conversion. In Luke's perspective, conversion centers on God's gracious act of forgiveness (e.g., Acts 5.31–32; 10.43). And, . . . in terms of human response, faith-repentance is the decisive element in conversion, for it forms the sole prerequisite for receiving the forgiveness of God (Lk. 5.20; 24.47; Acts 3.19; 5.31;

10.43; 13.38; 26.18)."[14] Elsewhere, Menzies rightly concludes that "the Spirit in Luke-Acts is *never* presented as a soteriological agent."[15]

James Shelton summarizes the Lukan data succinctly and accurately:

> Although Luke is not averse to associating the Holy Spirit with con-version, this is not his major pneumatological thrust. Some misunder-standing has arisen when the role of the Holy Spirit in empowering for witness is confused with conversion. . . . Luke associates the Holy Spirit with conversion to some degree, but he does not clearly de-scribe that role since his attention is centered on another major role of the Spirit: inspired witness.[16]

So, an examination of Walston's claim that Pentecostals have "mi-nored" on Lukan soteriology (re Acts) proves true. However, *his claim that Pentecostals have "minored" on what Luke "majored" on proves false.* Since Luke "majored" on pneumatology, the Pentecostal position aligns best with the material in Acts. Pentecostals recognize that Luke is communi-cating to Theophilus (and us) information about the prophetic-empower-ment available through the Spirit to accomplish the mission of Luke's pro-grammatic verse 1:8, i.e., Spirit-inspired disciples will spread the gospel.[17]

Defining the Baptism in the Holy Spirit

To refute the view that there is a spiritual experience beyond conversion known as *the baptism in (filling with) the Holy Spirit* and solidify a non-Pentecostal view of conversion-initiation, it is *absolutely necessary* that Luke's characters in these pneumatological narratives be defined as non-Christians, thus rendering the pneumatological activity soteriological (alt-hough this need not be a logical necessity since simultaneous events need not be identical events). Of the scholars who take this conversion-initiation view of Luke, James D. G. Dunn has written the most enduring presentation in his 1970 *Baptism in the Holy Spirit* (Philadelphia: Westminster Press).[18]

---

[14] *Empowered for Witness*, 217, 224.

[15] "The Spirit of Prophecy, Luke-Acts and Pentecostal Theology: A Response to Max Turner," *Journal of Pentecostal Theology* 15 (1999): 49–74 (53).

[16] *Mighty in Word and Deed: The Role of the Holy Spirit in Luke-Acts* (Peabody, MA: Hendrickson Publishers, 1991), 127, 148.

[17] If anyone is skeptical of the "and us" in this sentence, I recommend he study dis-cipleship as laid out in *The Kingdom Case against Cessationism*, for which I served as the editor.

[18] For critiques of Dunn's work see Howard M. Ervin, *Conversion-Initiation and the Baptism in the Holy Spirit: A Critique of James D. G. Dunn's* Baptism in the Holy Spirit (Peabody, MA: Hendrickson, 1984); Menzies, *Empowered for Witness*; Stronstad, *The Charismatic Theology of St. Luke* and *The Prophethood of All Believers: A Study in Luke's Charismatic Theology*; E. A. Russell, "'They believed Philip preaching,' (Acts

Interestingly, even Dunn believes that "Luke *intended* to portray 'speaking in tongues' as 'the initial physical evidence' of the outpouring of the Spirit."[19] Gordon Fee, once a Classical Pentecostal, in the 1980s (if not before) chose to camp with the Pauline charismatics. As mentioned earlier, Walston does not use Dunn or other reputable scholars to support his arguments, *with the lone exception of Fee*. Fee's work that Walston relies upon most is *Gospel and Spirit: Issues in New Testament Hermeneutics*; the actual chapters that Walston depends upon were first published in 1980 and 1985.[20]

8.12)," *Irish Biblical Studies* 1 (1979): 169–176; J. Giblet, "Baptism in the Holy Spirit in the Acts of the Apostles," *One in Christ* 10 (1974): 162–171; William P. Atkinson, *Baptism in the Spirit: Luke-Acts and the Dunn Debate* (Eugene, OR: Wipf & Stock-Pickwick Publications, 2011); David Petts, "The Baptism in the Holy Spirit in Relation to Christian Initiation," MTh thesis (University of Nottingham, 1987); Shelton, *Mighty in Word and Deed*; and Youngmo Cho, *Spirit and Kingdom in the Writings of Paul* (Milton Keynes, UK: Paternoster-Authentic Media, 2005). Although not specifically responses to Dunn, see also Gonzalo Haya-Prats, *Empowered Believers: The Holy Spirit in Acts* (1967. ET: Eugene, OR: Wipf and Stock, 2010) and Odette Mainville, *The Spirit in Luke-Acts* (1991. ET: Eugene, OR: Wipf and Stock, 2016).

[19] *Jesus and the Spirit: A Study of the Religious and Charismatic Experience of Jesus and the First Christians as Reflected in the New Testament* (London: SCM, 1975), 189–190 (italics his). Here is the full context from Dunn:

> It is a fair assumption that for Luke the Samaritan "Pentecost," like the first Christian Pentecost, was marked by ecstatic glossolalia. If so, then the fact is that in every case where Luke describes the giving of the Spirit it is accompanied and "evidenced" by glossolalia. The corollary is then not without force that Luke *intended* to portray "speaking in tongues" as "the initial physical evidence" of the outpouring of the Spirit. (190)

[20] For an assessment of Fee's earlier ideas see William W. and Robert P. Menzies, *Spirit and Power*, 109–118, and Menzies, *Empowered for Witness,* 237–39. Perhaps, it is apropos to bring attention to certain statements by Fee that relate to our discussion. In his article "Hermeneutics and Historical Precedent—A Major Problem in Pentecostal Hermeneutics" (in *Perspectives on the New Pentecostalism*, ed. Russell P. Spittler [Grand Rapids: Baker Book House, 1976], 118–32), Fee concludes by asserting that "a charismatic dimension was a normal phenomenon in the reception of the Spirit. . . . Speaking in tongues, if not normative, was a repeated expression of the charismatic dimension of the coming of the Spirit. . . . If the Pentecostal may not say one *must* speak in tongues, he may surely say, why *not* speak in tongues?" (131–32). Perhaps Walston would agree with these statements; I am not saying that he would not. (See also Fee's statement in footnote 31 below.) If one should ask, "Why tongues?" Keener replies that it "is not an arbitrary sign, but the one sign, of any Luke might have narrated, which most effectively communicates the purpose of baptism in the Spirit as an empowerment for universal mission" ("Why Does Luke Use Tongues," 183). In other words, tongues are emblematic for "the biblical task of cross-cultural, global evangelism" to which "glossolalia bears eloquent witness" (184). And if one asks, "Must I speak in tongues

Summarizing from Fee's earlier work, Walston writes, "Fee says that to be saved *is to be filled with the Spirit.* . . . Christians are filled with the Holy Spirit by virtue of being Christians" (129). "[I]f people are saved, they are as a matter of course, baptized in the Holy Spirit" (114). For Fee to arrive at these conclusions, he must explain away the clear language of Luke. Walston appears to accept Fee's assertions uncritically. He should at least press Fee to demonstrate why the extemporaneous and independently valuable discursive writings of Paul should be used to interpret the carefully and elegantly designed rhetoric of Luke.

Luke narrates at length four episodes where believers are specifically baptized in, filled with, or are recipients of the Holy Spirit for the first time:

(1) the 120 Jewish disciples (Acts 2)
(2) the Samaritans (Acts 8)
(3) the Gentiles (Acts 10)
(4) the Ephesians (Acts 19)

(1) Acts 2: Since Walston agrees, albeit inconsistently, that the 120 were saved before they received the gift of the Holy Spirit (141), it is not necessary to discuss this episode.[21]

(2) Acts 8: Walston presents no evidence to counter the obvious separability/subsequence illustrated in this passage. Briefly, in Samaria the evangelist (and deacon) Philip preached Jesus, the people believed, they were baptized in Jesus's name (v. 12, 16), *but* they did not receive the Holy Spirit in his prophetic-vocational role. The apostles in Jerusalem hear that the

---

when baptized in the Spirit?" Menzies replies, maybe not, but "why would we want to settle for anything less than the full apostolic experience?" (*Pentecost: This Story Is Our Story* [Springfield, MO: Gospel Publishing House, 2013], 100), and "Luke presents speaking in tongues as a powerful and edifying sign—a sign that reminds us of our calling as end-time prophets and that testifies to the majesty and exalted status of Jesus. . . . Speaking in tongues, as a special form of prophecy, marks the disciples of Jesus as the true heirs of Joel's prophecy [Joel 2:28–32/Acts 2:17–21] and validates their message" (*Speaking in Tongues*, 108); see also R. Menzies "The Spirit in Luke-Acts: Empowering Prophetic Witness," *Pneuma* 43.3–4 (2021): 432.

[21] See Timothy Laurito's *Speaking in Tongues: A Multidisciplinary Defense* (Eugene, OR: Wipf and Stock, 2021), 7–11; Graham H. Twelftree, *People of the Spirit: Exploring Luke's View of the Church* (Grand Rapids: Baker Academic, 2009), 16, 18, 21–22, 28–29, 75, 83; Howard M. Ervin, *Spirit Baptism: A Biblical Investigation* (Peabody, MA: Hendrickson, 1987), 14–21, or, in the older edition, *These Are Not Drunken, As Ye Suppose* (Plainfield, NJ: Logos, 1968), 25–33.

Samaritans have "received the word of God" (v. 14), so they send Peter and John, who, when they arrive, pray for them that they might receive the Holy Spirit (v. 17). After laying hands on them, they receive the Holy Spirit. Obviously, any attempt to explain away the separability/subsequence exhibited in this passage becomes fantastical. Menzies calls this passage "an insoluble problem for those who maintain that Luke establishes a necessary link between baptism/Christian initiation and the gift of the Spirit."[22] Non-Pentecostals usually claim that this is an exception (the exception that proves the rule, no less![23]). To the contrary, it firmly proves, experientially and soteriologically, the possibility that one can be saved without receiving the Spirit *as Luke describes it*, and it forever breaks the cause-effect link between Spirit-baptism and salvation.[24]

(3) Acts 10: Luke's narrative of the gentiles being baptized in the Holy Spirit is *the single precedent* that non-Pentecostal scholars have where the subjects of the narrative evidently are saved and baptized in the Holy Spirit simultaneously (note that it is still quite impossible to prove that the latter was the cause of the former). According to Walston, this passage "needs little argument" and provides "evidence beyond a reasonable doubt" (122). He admits, "The first outward evidence that they had been baptized in the Holy Spirit was that they spoke in tongues (10:46)" (122). But remember, he believes that the baptism in the Holy Spirit effects salvation. So, he explains, "[T]he first physical evidence that they had been *saved* was that they spoke in tongues (10:46)" (122, emphasis his). "[S]peaking in tongues was not just the initial, physical evidence of the baptism in the Holy Spirit; it was in fact the initial physical evidence of salvation . . ." (95). In Walston's view, Peter associates tongues with a salvation experience (87). But why would Peter do this? Luke doesn't portray Peter as having any experiences with unbelievers who, upon repenting, calling on the name of the Lord, and being baptized in the name of Jesus, receive salvation and tongues. On the other hand, Luke does portray Peter as having experienced, at Jerusalem then Samaria, *believers*—not non-believers—receiving a baptism in the Holy Spirit, evidenced by glossolalia.[25]

---

[22] Menzies, *Empowered for Witness*, 211, see also 204–13; Palma, *Holy Spirit*, 119; and J. L. Hall, "A Oneness Pentecostal Looks at Initial Evidence," in *Initial Evidence*, 178.

[23] "When four of our five biblical examples are 'exceptions,' however, one is tempted to question the validity of the 'rule'" (Keener, *Gift and Giver*, 162).

[24] See Atkinson, "Pentecostal Responses to Dunn's *Baptism in the Holy Spirit*: Luke-Acts," 118; see Keener's comments in footnote 9 above.

[25] That the Samaritans experienced glossolalia is the most reasonable conclusion (see Laurito, *Speaking in Tongues*, 11–17).

Although Luke does not, as in the other scenes, make clear the timing of the gentiles' moment of salvation in relation to the moment when they were baptized in the Holy Spirit, he does possibly imply that the gentiles were saved before they received the Spirit when he has Peter say, "They have received the Holy Spirit just as we have" (10:47). Walston agrees that the 120 at Jerusalem were saved before Pentecost (141). If then, the gentiles received the Holy Spirit just as they did, perhaps they were saved before they received this enduement of power, if not but by mere moments. Furthermore, using the interpretive principle of analogy of scripture, it is quite clear that the Jewish, Samaritan, and Ephesian episodes steer the reader to this conclusion.

Having said this, there is, it seems to me, a logical reason why God telescoped the gentile experience of salvation and the baptism in the Holy Spirit into one event (or one of very close proximity), and that is because there is no outward, immediately observable evidence of salvation, without which the Jews would have been more apt to dispute and deny that God had "granted the gentiles repentance unto life" (11:18). But if one must be saved to receive this gift evidenced by tongues, as in the Pentecostal view, tongues are *a fortiori* evidence that one has been saved.[26]

Of the four episodes involving the baptism in the Holy Spirit, this is the only one whose timing is ambiguous. Why make the possible exception, the rule?

(4) Acts 19: Quoting Fee, Walston argues that the *disciples* who are mentioned here "were obviously not Christians because the one essential ingredient [i.e., the Spirit] was missing" (*Gospel and Spirit*, 114). However, Luke's consistent terminology ("disciple" for *believer in Jesus* or *disciple of Jesus*) is insurmountable and reveals the speciousness of the anti-Pentecostal interpretation.[27] But if that isn't enough, these disciples, as Luke narrates the scene, are baptized in water (surely they are Christians by now), Paul then lays hands on them, and only *then* does the Holy Spirit come upon them (19:5–6). Obviously, the Holy Spirit comes upon them *after* they are saved.[28] Yes, many scholars believe they were not Christians when Paul

---

[26] See also Menzies, *Empowered*, 215–18; Johns, "Some New Directions," 163; Roger Stronstad, "On Being Baptized in the Holy Spirit: A Lukan Emphasis," in *Trajectories in the Book of Acts,* 180–83; and chapter 7 above.

[27] See also Elbert, "Towards," 19–25, or *The Lukan Gift of the Holy Spirit*, 81–102; Paul Elbert, "An Observation on Luke's Composition of Questions," *CBQ* 66.1 (January 2004): 107–8, or *Luke's Rhetorical Compositions*, 40–41; Palma, *Holy Spirit*, 128; Menzies, *Empowered for Witness*, 218–25.

[28] However, as Pentecostals, we would do well to remember these words from Oss: ". . . Pentecostals historically have emphasized that this experience is available from the

first met them, but as Keener says, "Nevertheless, they do not receive the Spirit in the Lukan sense at the exact moment of their fuller faith in Christ or their Christian baptism; they receive it afterward when Paul lays hands on them (19:6)" (*Gift and Giver*, 161).

Authorial Intent—The Doom of Pentecostal Theology?

For Walston, "Of all the arguments opposing the initial, physical evidence of the baptism in the Holy Spirit, that of *authorial intent* is, without a doubt, the most convincing . . ." (59). His methodology for proving this entails asking what he calls a "Guiding Question" of each incident where Luke describes someone experiencing salvation. That question is: "What *importance* does Luke give to tongues as evidence of the baptism in the Holy Spirit?" (61, 71). He then claims that there are twenty-six references in Acts of people being baptized in the Holy Spirit (126). (He can say this because he assumes he has proven that anytime someone is saved, he or she is baptized in the Holy Spirit; ergo, to be saved = to be baptized in the Holy Spirit. So, he writes, "[E]ven though Luke does not specifically mention the words 'baptism in the Holy Spirit,' this baptism nonetheless transpires when one becomes a Christian," 125.) Walston continues, "If Luke mentions the outward manifestation of tongues on only three of twenty-six soteriological occasions, with the number of people demonstrating this outward manifestation to be around 150 out of well over three thousand people, then the obvious question must follow, *How important could it have possibly been to Luke?*" (110). Thus, he reasons concerning the Jerusalem Pentecost and Acts 2:41, "It cannot be logically nor exegetically argued that all Christians who are baptized in the Holy Spirit should speak in tongues from a small sampling of only 120 out of 3,120 people" (126). And, "If it were as important an issue as Classical Pentecostals say it is, Luke would have used this three-thousand-person example to develop the concept. But, he does not" (71).

    Throughout his chapter on authorial intent, Walston mentions several places where Luke, if he had wished to show that speaking in tongues is the initial, physical evidence of the baptism in the Holy Spirit, could have done so, explicitly, and with great effect, e.g., the three thousand in 2:41, the Samaritans, the priests in 6:7, and Paul, but Luke is silent. Even if all of these believers did speak in tongues, the fact that Luke *does not mention it* is proof

---

moment the Holy Spirit indwells the believer, and their testimonies often speak of being both saved and baptized in the Holy Spirit all at once, while responding to an invitation for salvation," *Miraculous Gifts*, 242. After salvation is obtained, the baptism in the Holy Spirit is prioritized.

that tongues are not that important to Luke; thus, it was not Luke's "intent to convey tongues as the initial, physical evidence of the baptism in the Holy Spirit" (73). (Obviously, it wasn't Luke's intent *in these examples*, but these are not the only episodes in Luke's narrative, and they certainly aren't the most prototypical.)

Just as Walston uses Acts 2:38–41 as the *locus classicus* to prove that to be saved is to be baptized in the Holy Spirit (and vice versa), he also uses this passage as the *locus classicus* to prove that it is *not* Luke's intent to teach that tongues are the normative, initial evidence of the baptism in the Holy Spirit. After repeating his Guiding Question, he writes, "The issue is not, 'Did the three thousand speak in tongues?' The issue is, '*Why does Luke not make a point of saying that they did (or did not) speak in tongues?*'" Walston continues, "He does not mention it because it is not an issue. What Luke does take the time and space to describe is the soteriological outcome on this unique day" (71). Walston calls the incident with the three thousand a "paradigmatic gold mine" had Walston wanted to establish tongues as the evidence of Spirit-baptism (72).

Let's examine the scene that Walston is using—all of it, as Luke intended, not just a portion. The way Luke presents it to Theophilus, it begins at Acts 2:1 and runs *in real time* all the way to 2:39; then, Luke caps it off with the summary statement of v. 41 (the verses that follow in chapter two describe action occurring days afterward). The scene has two foci: (1) the coming of the Holy Spirit with its accompanying signs and (2) Peter's sermon and interaction with the crowd. Luke has already portrayed Jesus as telling the disciples to remain in Jerusalem until they are baptized in the Holy Spirit so that they will receive power to be his witnesses (1:5, 8). Since the disciples are already saved, this is a post-conversion empowerment, i.e., a pneumatological, not soteriological, experience. Acts 2:1–13 describes the fulfillment of Jesus's promise in detail. Luke ends with a question ("Whatever could this mean?"), segueing into Peter's sermon. Peter explains what it means by quoting the prophet Joel. Significantly, Peter quotes a primarily pneumatological portion of scripture.[29] To make this point clear, Peter edits

---

[29] So also Mainville:

> It is significant, also, that Luke refers to the text of Joel 2:28ff. to shed light on the event of Pentecost instead of the text of Ezek 36:26–27. Ezekiel's prophecy envisions the gift of the Spirit in view of a spiritual metamorphosis, which would render the human being capable of living according to God's plans. But for Luke, it is in regard to testimony that the Spirit of Pentecost is poured out (Luke 24:49; Acts 1:8). Therefore, it is the vow formulated by Joel that finds its fulfillment. The dimension conveyed by Ezekiel's text cannot, of course, simply be ousted, for the testimony of faith in Christ presupposes conversion. (*The Spirit in Luke-Acts*, 251; see also Haya-Prats, *Empowered Believers*, 10–11). More to the point of authorial intent,

Joel's prophecy, adding "and they shall prophesy" to verse 18. Because he is speaking to non-Christians, Peter includes Joel's statement that "whoever calls on the name of the Lord shall be saved" (2:21). Peter, next, goes into an explanation of Jesus of Nazareth, Lord and Messiah, who has poured out "this which you now see and hear," speaking of the promise of the Father or, more specifically, the accompanying *signs* of the promise (v. 33). Cut to the heart, the Jewish listeners ask Peter, "[W]hat shall we do?" (v. 37). Peter replies, "Repent, and let every one of you be baptized in the name of Jesus Christ for the remission of sins; and you shall receive the gift of the Holy Spirit. For the promise is to you and to your children, and to all who are afar off, as many as the Lord our God will call" (vv. 38–39). Finally, Luke concludes the scene, "Then those who gladly received his word were baptized; and that day about three thousand souls were added to them" (v. 41).

Now, back to Walston's question: *"Why does Luke not make a point of saying that they did (or did not) speak in tongues?"* Part of the answer to this question relates to Walston's (under)statement that "Luke is not a substandard communicator" (85). Luke is believed by many scholars to be the most eloquent, articulate, intentional, and educated writer of scripture. For that reason, we should not expect him to write in a coarse, unreflective, or tedious style. Stronstad writes, "Arguably, Luke-Acts is the most carefully designed book in all of biblical literature, certainly in the New Testament" (*Prophethood*, 14). According to Elbert, the writings of Luke exemplify the highly developed, conventional Greco-Roman narrative tradition, as illustrated in the teachings of Theon of Alexandria, a rhetorician and contemporary of Luke's:

> Luke is in accord with the instruction of Theon on this expected method of narrative persuasion via plausible examples and precedents serving to provide Christian expectation. Clarity, understandability, and vividness of examples and precedents are the narrative tools deemed important by Theon; it is unsurprising then that Luke employs such contemporary narrative technique. Lukan portrayal of

---

Robert Menzies responds to Fee, writing, "The question of Luke's intent, which looms so large in Fee's argument, is clearly subordinate to the more fundamental question outlined above [i.e., the prophetic-empowerment rather than soteriological character of Spirit-baptism, and its universal character]. For if my description of Luke's 'distinctive' pneumatology is accurate, then Luke's intent to teach a Spirit-baptism distinct from conversion for empowering is easily demonstrated. One need only establish that Luke's narrative was designed to encourage every Christian to receive the Pentecostal gift. And, since Luke highlights Pentecost as a fulfillment of Joel's prophecy concerning an outpouring of the Spirit upon 'all flesh' (Acts 2.17–21), this appears to be self-evident" (*Empowered*, 239).

interaction with, and of Christian expectation of, the divine is quite harmonious with Theonic characterization and personification.[30]

Peter's preaching in Acts 2:38–39 occurs in the latter part of the last narrative scene of the chapter; however, the result of his preaching—the salvation of the 3,000—occurs outside of the narrative flow in a summary fashion. The reader must fill in the blanks, and there are a lot of blanks. What will he fill in the blanks with? The Greco-Roman rhetorical devices of Luke's day required that the reader be provided vivid examples and precedents with which to fill in the blanks. The closest example would be Pentecost; the next example would be Samaria, then Caesarea, and Ephesus. It is quite apparent that Luke's examples, wielding prototypical significance, would guide the reader to extrapolate the features of these narrative scenes to the *undescribed* summary of 2:39. If he did this, he would have a clear picture of the 3,000, after their baptism in water, coming into a position to receive (if not receiving) the prophetic empowering of the Holy Spirit with the extraordinary, observable effect of glossolalia. (This would not occur all at once any more than 3,000 people would be baptized in water all at once. Picture that!)

Luke's refined architectonics in Acts does not require the tedious repetitions that our 21st-century minds may desire.[31] Even as Luke tells the

---

[30] Paul Elbert, "Paul of the Miletus Speech and 1 Thessalonians: Critique and Considerations," *ZNW* 95.3–4 (2004): 265n34, or *Luke's Rhetorical Compositions*, 124n34. For information about Aelius Theon of Alexandria and his potential narrative-rhetorical influence on the composition of narratives, see the "Introduction" in James R. Butts, *The 'Progymnasmata' of Theon: A New Text with Translation and Commentary* (Ann Arbor, MI: University Microfilm International, 1987), 1–95.

[31] Note that Fee believes that in the early church, "Glossolalia . . . has all the earmarks of being commonplace" ("Toward a Pauline Theology of Glossolalia," in *Pentecostalism in Context: Essays in Honor of William W. Menzies*, 30; see also his *Empowering Presence*, 585), and concludes that "Precisely because it was 'normal' in this sense [i.e., expected and recurring], it was the presupposition of life in the Spirit for them; *thus they felt no compulsion to talk about it at every turn*" (*Gospel and Spirit*, 102, italics added); J. Rodman Williams notes that "If both the reception of the Spirit and tongues were common knowledge and experience to Luke's readers (as I believe they were), *he scarcely needs to say so each time*. Incidentally, this same point may be made about belief in Christ and baptism in water. Often Luke specifically mentions water baptism in connection with faith in Jesus Christ . . . ; on other occasions he describes people coming to faith without reference to water baptism. . . . However, it is very likely that Luke would have the reader assume the occurrence of water baptism when it is not mentioned. Such baptism was doubtless common experience and practice in the early church," (*Renewal Theology: Salvation, the Holy Spirit, and Christian Living* [Grand Rapids: Zondervan, 1990], 2:210n7; italics added); see Palma, *Holy Spirit*, 157.

disciples that they would be his witnesses in Jerusalem, Judea and Samaria, and to the ends of the earth (the gentiles), rather than laboriously naming all the cities and regions, he deliberately chooses two of the most momentous occurrences of tongues to narrate for Theophilus—the first Jews and the first gentiles saved calling upon the name of the Lord Jesus Christ. Would not *these* be the "paradigmatic gold mines" in Luke's mind? The third occurrence, the Ephesian disciples, was probably narrated, in part, because of Paul's involvement (given Luke's propensity to give Peter and Paul equal time) and because it is the last scene in the Acts narrative with characters who are baptized in the Holy Spirit. (For us, it serves the additional purpose of disallowing the Lukan cessationist notion that Spirit-baptism is an apostolic-age or unique experience.[32]) Of these three occurrences, Donald Johns writes, "It is difficult to deny that speaking in tongues *did* accompany being baptized in the Spirit in three texts in Acts. It is a common storytelling technique the world over to tell things in groups of threes: three times should be enough to tell anything. The paradigmatic effect of these stories *should lead us to expect the same things in our own experience with the Spirit.* Actually, as we are drawn into the story, we should experience the Spirit along with

---

Although the conventional narrative style of Luke's day deemed repetitious accounts unnecessary, there is yet an additional reason why Luke does not associate tongues with many of the occurrences of salvation in Acts (other than the quite plausible explanation that the subjects were saved but not immediately filled, per the Samaritan precedent). In many cases where Luke notes soteriological activity in Acts, it is with great brevity (as Williams notes, even repentance and water baptism are seldom mentioned). The brief soteriological conclusion comes about because of the narrative's clear emphasis—pneumatological activity, e.g., 2:1–41, where only a couple of verses can be considered soteriological. But not all pneumatic activity is related to tongues; in fact, tongues may be a result of previous pneumatic activity just as salvation may come because of previous pneumatic activity. For Luke, then, the issue of disciples speaking in tongues when baptized in the Spirit is akin to the issue of salvation—both usually occur because of prior Spirit-inspired witness. Both are extremely important to Luke, but they are simply not his central focus, a focus which is, in fact, the *efficient cause* of the spreading of the gospel, i.e., the Spirit-inspired witness of each individual disciple. And, as I have said, this is just as we should expect since Luke has laid out the prophetic missionary program from chapter one: "But you will receive power when the Holy Spirit comes on you; and you will be my witnesses in Jerusalem, and in all Judea and Samaria, and to the ends of the earth" (v. 8).

[32] See also Ronald Kydd, *I'm Still There! A Reaffirmation of Tongues as the Initial Evidence of the Baptism in the Holy Spirit* (Toronto: Pentecostal Assemblies of Canada, 1977), 13.

Peter, Cornelius, and all the rest. By telling these stories, Luke shows that this is the way his world works" (163; see also 153–56; italics added).[33]

Rob Starner expressed similar findings:

> Narratologists have long noted that repeated narrative segments— from individual words to entire self-contained episodes—frequently reveal an author's intended themes or concerns. Likewise, biblical scholars have long regarded and utilized repetition as an interpretive clue. In fact, the narrative function is well noticed to have paradigmatic overtones as a recurrent theme in [Earl] Richard's[34] treatment of the Spirit-reception episodes in the book of Acts. Repetition in the book of Acts is an interpretive clue, suggesting that Luke understands a certain doctrine or practice to be normative for Christians. When something is reported multiple times and in varied contexts in this narrative, it is likely that there is something of eternal relevance being communicated.[35]

---

[33] W. and R. Menzies approach the issue of tongues as evidence through a synthesis of biblical and systematic theology; through the contributions of each they conclude that "1. Paul affirms that the private manifestation of tongues is edifying, desirable, and universally available. . . . 2. Luke affirms that the Pentecostal gift is intimately connected to inspired speech, of which tongues-speech is a prominent form, possessing a uniquely evidential character. 3. Therefore, when one receives the Pentecostal gift, one should expect to manifest tongues, and this manifestation of tongues is a uniquely demonstrative sign (evidence) that one has received the gift" (*Spirit and Power*, 130). Using this methodology, the Menzies eschew Pentecostal hermeneutics based on "biblical analogy or historical precedent. . . . Rather, drawing from the full scope of Luke's two-volume work, it [their argument] focuses on the nature of Luke's pneumatology and, from this framework, seeks to understand the character of the Pentecostal gift. The judgment that the gift is distinct from conversion is rooted in the gift's function: It provides power for witness, not justification before God or personal cleansing. The universal character of the gift established in Luke's narrative rather than historical precedent is the basis for its normative character" (*Spirit and Power*, 115). It is unfortunate that, at the time of their writing (1991), the Menzies were, ostensibly, unaware of the Greco-Roman narrative rhetorical convention that Luke uses (cf. *Empowered for Witness*, 237, 245–46), for it pushes the so-called historical occurrences of Spirit-baptism and tongues beyond the "naïve historical precedent" (*Empowered*, 239) argument. Of course, the two methodologies are not mutually exclusive but, rather, corroborative; they each answer questions that the other does not address. It will be interesting to watch over time their symbiotic development in the field of Pentecostal scholarship. Walston seems unaware of both methodologies, focusing only on the older argument based on the repetition of glossolalia in conjunction with Spirit-baptism (113–18).

[34] "Pentecost as a Recurrent Theme in Luke-Acts," in *New Views on Luke and Acts*, ed. Earl Richard (Collegeville, MN: Liturgical Press, 1990), 133–49.

[35] "Luke and Paul: Co-Laborers . . . and Collaborators?" in *Trajectories in the Book of Acts*, 236. See also Keener, *Gift and Giver*, 158, 212.

Starner concludes that "the Pentecostal doctrine of Spirit-baptism as an empowering work of Christ distinct from and subsequent to salvation and evidenced initially and physically by the phenomenon of *glossolalia* does not hang on the ability to establish Lukan intentionality . . ." (238–39). Nevertheless, he believes that "careful attention to the rhetorical features [of] Luke-Acts does in fact corroborate Lukan intentionality vis-à-vis the doctrine of Spirit-baptism" (239).

Oss writes along the same lines regarding *authorial intent*:

> Beyond the traditional Pentecostal interpretation of Acts, two specific insights from narratology have proven helpful in more recent years in determining Luke['s] intent: the idea of narrative as "narrative world" and narrative analogy. Both of these aspects of narratological analysis are ways of looking at "patterns" as evidence of an author's intent in creating a narrative.

> (i) Regarding the notion of "narrative world" in any historical narrative, the manner of retelling has a purpose: to inform a community about its heritage, identity, common experience, and essential qualities. The narrator at the same time is informing the community about the nature of its own world, how it ought to be structured, and in some instances how it ought not to be structured. Thus, in the case of biblical narrative, the accounts provide order to our "world" and are intended to tell how to live our lives, how we experience the Spirit's presence, etc. The author uses biblical "narrative world" to shape the believing community's world.

> (ii) The second useful perspective on authorial intent is provided by what Meir Sternberg calls "narrative analogy." This refers to a specific relationship among events in a narrative, inviting readers to read one story in terms of other similar stories. Thus one event provides "oblique commentary" on another. The narrator accomplishes this particular phenomenon through carefully developed patterns or "echoes." His repetition of similar or contrasting events establishes the points of comparison for the reader. Repeating themes, details, phrases, behaviors, etc., call the reader's attention to the analogy. The "echo effect" thus serves to control interpretation, adding emphasis and specifying communication of central meanings.

> The composition of Luke-Acts was surely not a haphazard process. The analogies, or echo effects, in the narrative are evident because of the careful crafting of the narrative by the author. He included details because they were central to his agenda. In the case of tongues and Spirit-baptism in Acts, it seems improbable that Luke was unaware of the echo he was creating. Rather, *he intentionally created the relationship between tongues and Spirit-baptism in his narrative, along with the specific function of tongues as evidence, in*

order to communicate that relationship to his readership as a pre-scribed paradigm [italics added].

(iii) A redemptive-historical approach to the IPE [Initial Physical Evidence] doctrine is a third more recent development in Pentecostal hermeneutics. Simply stated, in the Old Testament when the Spirit came upon the prophets, prophetic speech always accompanied the Spirit's anointing. Likewise in Acts, when the Spirit comes upon an individual for the first time, Spirit-prompted speech occurs, except that in Acts the utterance is in tongues. Another dimension of this redemptive-historical development pertains specifically to Acts 10:44–46, where tongues is more than evidence of an individual experience (although it is that). There glossolalia functions as evidence of the inclusion of Gentiles in the Spirit's anointing. Stated in principle, it is evidence that the Spirit's power is for *all* who come into the kingdom. (*Miraculous Gifts*, 261–63)

Elbert's research accents the 21st-century reader's need to understand the Greco-Roman narrative-rhetorical tradition if he is to appreciate the literary artistry of Luke and come to understand what Luke *intends* to teach Theophilus:

If Theophilus was a literary minded person, as Luke appears to be, a person educated in the Empire where rhetorical training was mandatory in the schools, he would naturally expect Luke to illustrate ongoing prophetic fulfillment by examples and precedents in characters' lives within the framework of the two scrolls (or papyrus codices) dedicated to him. Such an expectation on Theophilus' part would be quite consistent with the accepted rhetorical procedure of illustrating main points with examples and precedents in the traditional standards of narrative composition, as set out in the contemporary treatise of Theon. Theon's instructional effort builds on solid rhetorical tradition concerning the necessity and the quality of the expected examples and precedents. Any real thematic paradigm that fulfilled prophecy beyond narrative time would have to be illustrated by examples and precedents in order to be convincing within Graeco-Roman narrative-rhetorical culture. ("Luke's Fulfillment," 3–4, also *Luke's Rhetorical Compositions*, 3–4)

Inasmuch as we are all Theophiluses, it would serve us well to become familiar with the literary medium with which Luke communicates to Theophilus, and not assume that he uses a medium contemporary to ourselves.

Whereas the foregoing discourses address the issue of Luke's intention by examining the genre in which Luke wrote and thus have discerned a strong intentionality on Luke's part to present tongues as a signification of Spirit-baptism, others have questioned the presupposition within the *authorial intent* argument itself. Menzies writes the following of Fee's conclusions regarding intent and the early Pentecostals' use of "naïve appeals to historical precedent" (239):

> [W]e should be careful not to jump to the unwarranted conclusion that this judgment necessarily invalidates the doctrine of evidential tongues. Nevertheless, this is precisely the conclusion that is usually drawn. The reason is clearly articulated by Fee, who suggests that normative theology at this point must be grounded in Luke's 'primary intent' or 'intention to teach'. But surely this is overly restrictive. Not all questions of normative teaching are rooted directly in the intention of the author. [Larry] Hurtado [in *Initial Evidence*, 191–92] notes the oft-cited illustration of the doctrine of the Trinity, which is not taught explicitly in the New Testament but developed on the basis of inferences from biblical teaching. Is it not valid to inquire about the character of Luke's pneumatology, and then to wrestle with the implications which emerge from his pneumatology for our contemporary questions? Only 'the most severe form of biblicism' would deny the validity of this sort of exercise.
>
> An exclusive focus on an author's 'primary intent' or 'intention to teach' too often leads to a form of tunnel vision which ignores the implications of an individual text for the theological perspective of the author. . . . *[T]he value of a passage for assessing the theological perspective of a given author cannot be reduced to its 'primary intent'.* A passage must be understood in terms of its original setting and intention, but *the theological freight it carries may transcend its 'primary intent'.* Each piece of evidence must be taken seriously as we seek to reconstruct the theological perspective of the biblical author. . . .
>
> . . . This task of reconstruction cannot be limited to a survey of the 'primary intent' of isolated passages; rather, it calls for a careful analysis of the theological significance of the author's entire work. (*Empowered*, 246–48; italics added)

Stronstad echoes Menzies sentiments and develops an understanding of Luke's intent based on the Greco-Roman culture of which Luke and Theophilus were a part:

> It was once commonplace among interpreters to affirm that authorial intentionality, that is, the author's purpose for writing a document, is the essential criterion which governs the reader's understanding of the text. But the question of authorial intentionality is complicated by a variety of factors. These include whether the purpose is explicit or implicit and whether it is simple or complex—that is, whether there is one primary purpose, or a combination of primary, secondary and

even tertiary purposes. Consequently, several dangers attend the search to determine authorial intention. One danger is the all-too-common tendency toward reductionism, putting forward the claims of one purpose to the exclusion of all others. Another danger is to confuse the use to which the document, in whole or in part, might be put with the purpose of the document. The most insidious danger is to identify the interests and agenda of the interpreter as those of the author.

Though the question of Luke's purpose has proven to be problematic it is not a matter for despair. The most satisfactory answer to the question of Luke's purpose lies in the recognition that it is multiplex. This multiplex purpose not only has a historical dimension, as the reader would expect since the genre of Luke-Acts is historical narrative, but it also has both a didactic or instructional dimension and a theological dimension. Luke himself identifies this multiplex purpose, beginning with his prologue (Lk. 1.1–4). . . .

Using the genre, or medium of historical narrative, Luke teaches Theophilus and his extended audience in a variety of ways. These include . . . (1) proof of prophecy; (2) precedents and patterns. . . .

. . . For example, Peter's witness to Cornelius and his household (Acts 10.1–48) is the historical precedent which justifies the salvation of the Gentiles by grace apart from the works of the Law (Acts 15.6–11). This same episode also makes explicit the pattern for Spirit-baptism which Luke has earlier implied in his programmatic Pentecost narrative. . . . And so, by reporting the pouring out of the Spirit, first upon the disciples, and, subsequently, upon Cornelius and his household, and also by reporting Peter's statements which connect the latter gift of the Spirit to the former, Luke teaches that here is a pattern of Spirit-baptism. It is an inaugural reception of the Spirit of prophecy attested to by the sign of speaking in tongues.

(Prophethood, 22–25)

So, it would seem that the *authorial intent* argument posed against the biblical doctrine of initial evidence is not as impervious as Walston believes, having been found to be vulnerable on at least two critical fronts: (1) its deficiency in rhetorical technique recognition and (2) its assumed imperiousness, which subjects it to neutralization by *reductio ad absurdum,* i.e., if doctrine must be based on authorial intention, then the virgin birth and the trinity are out the window.[36]

---

[36] The discerning reader will not perceive these two reasons as contradictory but complementary. While narrative principles provide intentionality, intentionality is not necessary to establish doctrine.

Conclusion

Concerning his work, Walston writes, "This book argues that the *tongues-as-evidence position* cannot be biblically supported. In fact, I shall show that the main book, i.e., Acts—from which this Classical Pentecostal peculiarity is derived—does not teach this idea at all" (27). His attempt to show this fails because (1) he does not prove that the passages that explicitly mention Spirit-baptism (or its synonyms) are describing conversion rather than post-conversion experiences, (2) he wrongly extrapolates Spirit-baptism to every incident of repentance/conversion/salvation in Acts, (3) he misunderstands the nuances of the elements that make up pneumatology and, thus, misreads his Pentecostal sources, (4) he uncritically accepts Fee's unwarranted and, now, elderly conclusions concerning authorial intent and assumes intentionality is necessary to establish doctrine, and (5) he shows no knowledge of and thus does not interact with the Greco-Roman rhetorical narrative conventions and their vindication of the Pentecostal understanding of Acts. Furthermore, (6) all of Walston's assertions are pervaded by a sense of incompleteness due to his omission of current scholarship (and even Fee's other writings).[37]

---

[37] Six years after Walston's book, Graham H. Twelftree wrote a much more thoughtful and rigorous book that, in places, has the effect of diminishing tongues as the consistent evidence of initially receiving the Spirit (*People of the Spirit*); even so, he wrote that "the Spirit's coming was unavoidably obvious to bystanders, and this evidence involved ecstatic or supernatural manifestations, sometimes including tongues" (99). Some of Twelftree's conclusions are subject to the same rebuttal as Walston's, especially item 5 above. Twelftree's conclusions seem contradictory (or, perhaps, he thinks Luke is ambiguous). For example, he writes of the 120 at Pentecost, "The most natural reading is that Luke is taking the ability to speak in tongues to be the result and, by implication, evidence of being filled 'with' (*en*, 'in') the Spirit" (85), and of Cornelius's household, he writes, "[T]he evidence that they had been given the Holy Spirit was not something deduced from what they believed . . . but their speaking in tongues and praising God (10:46)" (90). Yet, he concludes later that "Luke did not think speaking in tongues was the initial evidence of the coming of the Spirit" (98); he bases that, just as Walston does, on the *absence* of Luke's mentioning of tongues (that is, silence) in certain events and, in Twelftree's case, the inclusion of other evidence such as prophecy and praise. He concludes this despite having already concluded, in the context of initiation, that "Luke expects his readers to see these [shorter] stories as shorthand accounts in which all the other elements can be assumed. . . . In short, we can almost certainly take the less detailed narratives to be sketches in outline of a fuller view that Luke's readers are expected to assume is required for becoming a Christian" (96). "Luke's longer stories of initiation are to be assumed in reading his shorter ones" (99; see also footnote 31 above). As for multiple evidences of Spirit baptism, such as joy, praise, and prophecy, Pentecostals do not hold that they cannot occur as evidence but that Luke does not describe them *consistently* as occurring, whereas he does describe tongues as occurring in the three fully narrated events of Spirit baptism in Acts 2, 10, and 19.

The last two decades have seen tremendous strides in Pentecostal scholarship. Healthy introspection is always good, but in the approximately 100-year history of the Pentecostal Movement, this, of all times, is not the time to capitulate or call for a compromise on the Pentecostal doctrines of subsequence/separability or initial evidence.[38] In our lifetime, the strength of the evidence for the validity of these doctrines has grown exponentially.[39] Perhaps their acceptance shall develop as have two other Pentecostal issues: *First*, at the beginning of the twentieth century, no serious NT scholar believed that all of the NT spiritual gifts were for the contemporary church; before the century's end, relatively few serious scholars believed in the cessation of any of the gifts; *second*, a mere fifty years ago, a consensus of scholars relegated Acts to the genre of history; today, its didacticism is clear.[40] If Pentecostal scholarship continues to develop as it has in the last

---

Furthermore, in what way can praise to God or joy be considered a sure sign and immediate evidence of Spirit baptism since they may occur for numerous reasons among various individuals and religious groups? (Note also R. Menzies statement: "The arrival of prophetic power has a visible, external sign: glossolalia. This is not to say that there are not other ways in which the Spirit's power and presence are made known to us. This is simply to affirm that Luke's narrative indicates that a visible, external sign does exist and that he and his readers would naturally expect to manifest this sign" ["Luke-Acts," 420].)

[38] Unless one calls these compromises: (1) a person does not have to speak in tongues to be saved, (2) tongues do not accompany *every* Spirit baptism, but certainly the *initial* Spirit baptism, as demonstrated in the Acts 2 and 10 prototypes, (3) Spirit baptism may be accompanied by other signs, such as joy, praise, bold prophetic witness.

[39] Regarding the former, Robert Menzies, in his summation after his consideration of the works of three non-Pentecostals favorable to Lukan independency, wrote the following: "This bodes well for the future of pentecostal theology in general and, more specifically, the pentecostal doctrine of subsequence" ("Subsequence," 348).

[40] See W. and R. Menzies, *Spirit and Power*, 37–45; Kydd, 7–11, 14–15; Elbert writes to the point, relating the didactic view of Luke-Acts to its contemporary genre, "Pentecostals' view of narrative and their application of its didactic intentions is entirely consistent with, and essentially the same as, how it was regarded in the Graeco-Roman world at the time Luke-Acts was written, where the narrative-rhetorical tradition was regarded as a means to persuade with clarity and plausibility, to set forth vivid examples and precedents, and to provide the reasons for why such actions occurred. Therefore, one may appropriately mention that the criticism or condemnation of using Luke's narrative to establish what Luke expects believers to pray for and what Luke expects God to do in answer to prayer—because Lukan characters who bear witness to Jesus also pray and receive the Lukan gift of the Holy Spirit—is, from the perspective of Pentecostal tradition, negative criticism that misunderstands Luke as having only strictly historical motives, not theological motives," ("*The Globalization of Pentecostalism*: A Review Article," *Trinity Journal* 23NS, no. 1 [Spring 2002]: 83–84, or *Essays in Biblical Studies*, 218–19.)

twenty years, by the end of the twenty-first century, is it possible that no serious NT scholar will deny the Pentecostal doctrines of subsequence/separability and initial evidence? Of all times in the history of the Pentecostal movement and New Testament scholarship, today is not the time to seek a *tertium quid* or an *aggiornamento*.

* * * * *

I conclude with some thoughts for non-Pentecostals to consider while pondering the viability of their position. Concerning the Pentecostal doctrine of *initial evidence*, the *non-Pentecostal* view would be more tenable

➤ if, in Luke's vivid descriptions of those who were specifically baptized in the Holy Spirit, only some of the participants, instead of *all*, spoke in tongues,

➤ if Luke's two major illustrations of Spirit baptisms were not representative of both classes of peoples that made up the whole human race,

➤ if Luke had not connected glossolalia with his first and last explicit report of the baptism in (filling with) the Holy Spirit,

➤ if Luke had not connected glossolalia with every illustration of an explicitly described baptizing in/filling with/receiving of the Holy Spirit; prophecy isn't a constant, neither is praising God or joy, *only* tongues,

➤ if Luke had not said that the gift of the Spirit was for all people and for all times,

➤ if Luke had not implied that observers could know immediately from external observation that someone had received the Holy Spirit,

➤ if Luke had not described the Jews as recognizing that God had accepted the gentiles based on the externally perceptible, repeated sign of glossolalia,

➤ if Luke had mentioned occurrences of glossolalia in non-Spirit-baptism (and its synonyms) contexts,

99

> ➤ if Paul's baptism and the Ephesian disciples' baptisms in the Holy Spirit had been administered by one of the twelve apostles,

> ➤ if Paul had not said that he desired that all would speak in tongues.

Concerning the Pentecostal doctrine of *subsequence/separability*, the non-Pentecostal view would be more tenable

> ➤ if the 120 had not been Christians,

> ➤ if the Samaritans had not been Christians,

> ➤ if Paul had not been a Christian,

> ➤ if the twelve Ephesians had not been Christians,

> ➤ if Luke had not instructed disciple-believers to pray for the Spirit,

> ➤ if Luke had not equated filling=gift=reception=baptism and then reported subsequent fillings of disciples who had already been filled,

> ➤ if Luke had not associated prophetic utterances and empowerment with the baptism in the Holy Spirit,

> ➤ if, instead of prophetic utterances, Luke had associated salvation terminology with every Spirit-baptism episode,

> ➤ if Luke had not used pneumatological language of the Septuagint ("filling"), relating it to OT believers, to describe the NT baptism in the Holy Spirit,

> ➤ if throughout the OT and NT the activity of the Holy Spirit related to human functionality had not been associated with giftings (usually prophetic) for *believers*,

➤ if Paul had not exhorted the Ephesian *believers* to be filled with
the Spirit not drunk with wine

12

Documenting Xenoglossy[1]

"I began to speak in tongues, glorifying God. I talked several languages, and it was clearly manifest when a new dialect was spoken."[2] Thus Agnes N. Ozman describes her xenoglossic[3] experience of New Year's Day 1901. Sarah E. Parham, wife of Charles Fox Parham who was a prominent early leader of 20th-century Pentecostalism, writes that Miss Ozman "began speaking in the Chinese language, and was unable to speak English for three days."[4]

From the dawn of modern-day Pentecostalism to the present, Pentecostal literature has asserted belief in and collected documentation of xenoglossy. In front of me lies Ralph Harris's *Spoken by the Spirit*,[5] a collection of "over 75 documented stories of 'other tongues.'" This book contains a mere sampling of the purported cases of xenoglossy.

---

[1] Originally published in *Paraclete* 21.2 (Spring 1987): 27–30.

[2] Sarah E. Parham, *The Life of Charles F. Parham* (Joplin, MO: Tri-State Printing Co., 1930), 66; quoted in Steve Durasoff's *Bright Wind of the Spirit* (Plainfield: Logos International, 1972), 57.

[3] Xenoglossy is a term used by some social scientists to indicate the phenomenon of a person speaking a language with which he or she has had no prior acquaintance. In this paper I am using xenoglossy in this sense.

[4] S. Parham, *Charles F. Parham*, 53; in Durasoff, *Bright Wind*, 57.

[5] (Springfield, MO: Gospel Publishing House, 1973), 1; see also *Global Witnesses to Pentecost*, ed. Jordan Daniel May (Cleveland, TN: CPT Press, 2013).

Despite the testimonies, some Christians as well as non-Christians reject these and other accounts. Generally, those who do form two groups: (1) antisupernaturalists and (2) non-Pentecostal supernaturalists.

The Antisupernaturalists

The antisupernaturalist position denies by definition the occurrence of xenoglossy. Such an occurrence would be miraculous and, for the antisupernaturalist, the miraculous is an impossibility. R. M. Anderson provides us with a concise exposition of this position:

> Simple xenoglossy—the ability to speak a language with which one has had absolutely no prior acquaintance—is, of course, utterly incredible. That scholars should have to deal seriously with this claim is a tribute to the abiding strength and contemporary resurgence of pre-scientific modes of thought.[6]

A major problem of the Anderson view is that it is unfalsifiable.[7] Absolutely no quantity or quality of proof of xenoglossy would be enough to convince the antisupernaturalist of its reality. Such a position has as its basis an insuperable premise (*the miraculous, by definition, is an impossibility*), thus creating an invincible position (*xenoglossy is an impossibility*; with the minor premise being *xenoglossy is miraculous*).

Antisupernaturalism in Practice

How does the antisupernaturalist's bias affect his conclusions when dealing with claims of xenoglossy? Though Anderson has implied that scientists should not have to deal seriously with such claims, some studies have been made. But it seems these studies were made to discredit the claims, thus throwing into question the validity of Anderson's objection. The ultimate finding of these investigations is a telling commentary on the bias of the investigators.

---

[6] *Vision of the Disinherited* (New York: Oxford University Press, 1975), 19.

[7] For critiques of the principle of falsification, see Norman Geisler's *Christian Apologetics* (Grand Rapids: Baker, 1976), 19, 24, and Os Guinness's *The Dust of Death* (Downers Grove, IL: InterVarsity Press, 1973), 339–45. Both men allow conditional credibility to the principle, the condition being the empirical nature of the statements or data under scrutiny. Briefly, the principle states that propositions, concepts, or data which are not susceptible to refutation (i.e., falsification) are ipso facto meaningless. To say that a proposition is unfalsifiable is not to say that it is so sure that it is beyond refutation. To the contrary, an unfalsifiable proposition is meaningless because ultimately it does not allow the presentation of evidence which would refute it.

Let us assume a reputable source claimed that a genuine case of xenoglossy had occurred. And assume that a team of antisupernaturalists were commissioned to verify the occurrence (though in reality it would be easier to believe they were commissioned to disprove the claim). What steps would the antisupernaturalist take to test the truth of this claim?

Allow me to construct a possible scenario.

First, a team of linguists would be brought in to verify that the utterance was indeed, let us say, French. Second, a team of investigators must verify that the speaker had at no time learned the language. Third, a team of investigators must verify that the speaker was never exposed to the language; the slightest exposure would indicate, to the antisupernaturalist, that cryptomnesia was apparent in the case.[8]

If after the investigation Christian xenoglossy seemed the most satisfactory answer, we still would not expect the antisupernaturalist to capitulate, since he considers the miraculous impossible and xenoglossy miraculous. Given the antisupernaturalist world view, it is more reasonable for him to believe that an error was made in the investigation than that the miraculous occurred.[9] In accordance with the principle of falsification this leaves the antisupernaturalist with a meaningless position.

The Non-Pentecostal Supernaturalists

As far as 20th-century Christian xenoglossy is concerned, the effect of the non-Pentecostal supernaturalist definition is tantamount to that of the antisupernaturalist. For both, Christian xenoglossic occurrences are impossibilities. Although the major premise of the antisupernaturalist position (the miraculous is an impossibility) differs in wording from the major premise of the non-Pentecostal position (the operation of the miraculous gifts of the Spirit is not for today), they both have the same effect: they preclude by definition the occurrence of xenoglossy.

As an exponent of this view, B. B. Warfield provides us with this example:

> [The miraculous gifts] were part of the credentials of the Apostles as the authoritative agents of God in founding the church. Their function thus confined them to distinctively the Apostolic Church, and they necessarily passed away with it. Of this we may make sure on the ground both

---

[8] Cryptomnesic xenoglossy occurs when one utters a known language which was learned subconsciously or subliminally. See Anderson, *Vision,* 19.

[9] See J. W. Montgomery's "The Reasonable Reality of the Resurrection," *Christianity Today* 94 (April 1980): 16–19, for a response to this kind of reasoning (although in another context).

of the principle and of fact; that is to say both under the guidance of the New Testament teaching as to their origin and nature, and on the credit of the testimony of later ages as to their cessation.[10]

As in the case of the antisupernaturalists, no amount of evidence can substantiate the occurrence of Christian xenoglossy to the satisfaction of the non-Pentecostal supernaturalist. The belief that xenoglossy was restricted to the Early Church and cannot occur today has the same effect as the antisupernaturalist position that the miraculous cannot occur. Once again, in accordance with the principle of falsification the position of the non-Pentecostal is as unfalsifiable and thus as meaningless as the antisupernaturalist position.

Non-Pentecostal Supernaturalism in Practice

The scenario to be constructed for the non-Pentecostal investigation of purported xenoglossy would not differ from the scenario constructed for the antisupernaturalists: first, the language experts' findings (to eliminate glossolalia); second, an investigation of the xenoglossic's language studies (to eliminate conscious or unconscious chicanery); third, a search of subconscious foreign language exposure (to eliminate cryptomnesic xenoglossy).[11]

At this point, the non-Pentecostal supernaturalist suggests another explanation: Somewhat paradoxically, he denies the possibility of Christian xenoglossy but allows Satanic xenoglossy. With the addition of this explanation, the non-Pentecostals complete their repertoire of denials. Their intent is clear: the occurrence of Christian xenoglossy is an unacceptable thesis and claims of such occurrences are to be explained in a variety of ways. The unscriptural premise of first-century cessation compels the denial of xenoglossy—at all costs. This has generated the unfalsifiable and thus

---

[10] *Counterfeit Miracles* (1918; repr. Edinburg: Banner of Truth Trust, 1972), 6.

[11] Admittedly, a scientific study by Pentecostals should also follow this procedure. However, though such a study may serve to confirm Pentecostal beliefs, it would be impractical for the Pentecostal to remain coldly aloof to eyewitness reports of xenoglossy while awaiting the results of a scientific investigation. Pentecostals need not share the skepticism of René Laurentin (*Catholic Pentecostalism*, trans. Matthew J. O'Connell [New York: Doubleday, 1977]), who writes, "People claim that it [xenoglossy] happens, but there is no proof. . . . [U]ntil there is strict proof of a miracle having occurred we are justified in falling back on one or another natural explanation of the alleged facts" (75). As sober a scholar as I. Howard Marshall has written, "It is difficult to set aside the evidence of modern people who have claimed to hear their own languages being spoken by persons with the gift tongues" (*The Acts of the Apostles* [Grand Rapids: Eerdmans, 1980], 69, 70). Pentecostals can comfortably share Marshall's sentiments.

meaningless position of the non-Pentecostal supernaturalist. (See footnote 7.)

Conclusion

Contrary to the position of those who deny miracles, miracles have oc-curred,[12] and some skeptics have been transformed into believers when con-fronted with the miraculous. According to the documentation of Harris, Christian xenoglossy has served as an impetus which compelled the skeptic to believe in Christ as Lord.[13] However, though we see in Scripture that a miracle was often a convincing agent, we should not be surprised if in spite of evident miracles some will not believe. Even in Jesus's ministry there were those who rejected the miraculous. John wrote: "But though he had done so many miracles before them, yet they believed not on him" (John 12:37). Although the biases of the first-century Jew and the 20th-century antisupernaturalist and non-Pentecostal supernaturalist differ, they obtain the same end whether by precept of "science" or so-called doctrine of Scrip-ture, they *a priori* deny the miracle of Christian xenoglossy.

---

[12] See Craig S. Keener, *Miracles: The Credibility of the New Testament Accounts* (Grand Rapids: Baker Academic, 2011).

[13] Harris, *Spoken*, 87, 88.

13

The Nature of Glossolalia—
Foreign or S/spirit Language?[1]

It is asserted by some that glossolalia in its New Testament occurrences was *always* either a foreign language or an angelic language.[2] It was intelligent,

---

[1] By designating the non-foreign language position "S/spirit language," I do not mean to imply that the adherents of the foreign language view do not consider foreign-language-glossolalia as *of the Spirit*. They certainly do. Gordon Fee, who would fall into the non-foreign language camp, uses this slash-spelling and explains it in his commentary *The First Epistle to the Corinthians*, NICNT (Grand Rapids: Eerdmans, 1987), 670. Basically, it is a hybrid construction of the awkwardly hyphenated "Holy Spirit-human spirit." The implication is that if either *Spirit* or *spirit* (S/spirit) is missing, authentic Christian glossolalia cannot occur—it is a joint exercise. In the words of Heidi Baker, "This transrational prayer of the heart requires that both the Divine Spirit and human spirit are active. The human spirit acts in humble obedience to the Holy Spirit. . . . [God] provides a transrational form of prayer for us because he is sensitive to our need to commune with him, and he is willing to commune with us" ("Pentecostal Experience: Towards a Reconstructive Theology of Glossolalia," [PhD diss., King's College, University of London, 1996], 224; quoted in Mark J. Cartledge, *Charismatic Glossolalia: An Empirical-Theological Study* [Burlington, VT: Ashgate Publishing Co.], 194.)

[2] For example, William G. MacDonald, "Biblical Glossolalia—Thesis Four," *Paraclete* 27.3 (Summer 1993): 32–43; unless otherwise noted, further quotations and parenthetical citations are to this article. Such occurrences are considered *xenoglossy* or *xenolalia*.

"proper meaningful speech" (38), having form and coherence (40), "latent in the mind of Christ [which is] within [the believer]" (42); so stated William G. MacDonald, speaking not only of New Testament believers but of contemporary Pentecostals as well, he being one himself. MacDonald rejects the idea that glossolalia may be something other than human (or angelic) languages.

The Supremacy of the Rational

It isn't difficult to trace the source of MacDonald's position. It goes something like this: God is intelligent; he created man with intelligence; glossolalia must, therefore, exhibit intelligence; this is achieved by identifying glossolalia with foreign languages. "After all," MacDonald writes, "God is not known for speaking nonsense" (34). "To deny the language nature of glossolalia is to impugn the intelligence of the Spirit of God . . ." (35). "His [Jesus's] gifts reflect His supreme intelligence as the 'Word of God'" (39). "Since He is a God of order and infinite intelligence, the content of the speech He inspires cannot but be meaningful and ordered" (71).[3] For this view, glossolalia must be a genuine foreign language; otherwise, it is "nonsensical babbling," "garbled babel," "garblalia," "ecstatic gushings of vocables," "garbage of garbled sound," "concatenation of nonsensical sounds," "stupid sounds," (38, 40), or as MacDonald stated 30 years earlier, "unintelligent babbling," "nonsense syllables," and "nonlinguistic sound hash" (18–19).[4] According to this view, glossolalic utterance is none of

---

[3] "Pentecostal Theology: A Classical Viewpoint," *Perspectives on the New Pentecostalism*, ed. Russell P. Spittler (Grand Rapids: Baker, 1976), 59–74.

[4] "Glossolalia in the New Testament," Springfield, MO: Gospel Publishing House, 1964 (originally published in the *Bulletin of the Evangelical Theological Society*, 7.2 [Spring] 1964: 59–68). MacDonald is fond of using pejoratively charged words to describe non-xenoglossic glossolalia. God is intelligent; He would never inspire gibberish. The very idea is offensive to the enlightened mind! Given MacDonald's emphasis on language, its form, coherence, order, signification, and reflection of intelligence, it is surprising to see him characterize a genuine foreign language as "Jabbering" ("Pentecostal Theology," 73) and "babble" (33). Perhaps advocates of the S/spirit language view should not take offense at MacDonald's descriptions of glossolalia after all; there can't be much difference between gibberish and jabbering. Of course, what MacDonald means is that the Assyrian language was "jabbering" to the ears of the Hebrews (see 1 Corinthians 14:21), just as Spanish may be "jabbering" to the ears of some North Americans. But more important: whether or not glossolalia is a foreign language, it is jabbering gibberish to the ears of those who do not understand it. And according to Paul, that includes all unbelievers (1 Corinthians 14:21–23), and even the believers must have it interpreted.

these things, but rather always an authentic foreign language.[5] That is the position of many first- and second-generation Pentecostals (dating from 1901). My position, also, is that glossolalia is none of these things, not because it is a foreign language but because it finds meaning in the mind of God and meaningfulness in that it was promised by the Father and bestowed through the Spirit and bears witness to the glorified Son.

I think I understand the logic of the foreign language view. But I accept neither the premises nor the conclusion because the premises are incomplete. Based on this inferred syllogism, all that is needed to overthrow the foreign language view and allow the S/spirit language view is the insertion in the premise that both God and man are more than intellect, i.e., God is Spirit and man has a spirit.

When logic reigned supreme in the waning years of the 19th century and the first half of the 20th century, the term *logical* became the shibboleth of evangelicalism. Unfortunately, while this component of rationalism excelled in defending the supernatural in general and the historic Christian faith in particular, it often profaned mystery in its headstrong mission to confirm the truth of Christianity through natural means.[6] This, I believe, is the mindset that gave us the foreign language view of glossolalia based on the intelligence of God. (That plus the longstanding interpretation of the Acts 2 occurrence of glossolalia, but more on that later.)

In their defense of the Pentecostal distinctive of glossolalia, some have, understandably, sought to clear its name by refuting the loudest, most offensive charge leveled. But they are a generation late. The charge of *gibberish!* is no longer leveled by serious critics. At the turn of the century, in Topeka, in Los Angeles, later in writings of Morgan, Ironside, Dixon, Anderson, and others,[7] *gibberish!* was a vehement, vicious, and frequent anti-Pentecostal charge. But the 1950s and '60s brought a cure to that, probably through greater familiarity (transdenominational inroads), the unbiased conclusions of new psychological studies, and the search for the sacred in or through more than simply the rational.

Ironically, in this attempt to defend glossolalia through the foreign language perspective, these advocates are unwittingly refuting it.[8] In their

---

[5] Here and further references to "foreign languages" in this context will include angelic languages.

[6] See Thomas Molnar, *The Pagan Temptation* (Grand Rapids: Eerdmans, 1987), 80–109.

[7] See author's updated and expanded *Praying in the Spirit* for documentation (1987; Tulsa: Empowered Life Academic-Harrison House, 2016), 19–20.

[8] On the basis of linguists and glossolalists being unable to prove that glossolalia is xenoglossy, Cyril Williams believes that Pentecostals who "insist that modern glossolalia is continuous with the phenomenon in the Early Church would be on stronger

fervor to build the case from rationalism, they are weakening the case for sacred mystery. In other words, *rationalism de-mythologizes the sacred mysterium of glossolalia.*[9]

Strange Bedfellows

I have argued elsewhere[10] that the anti-supernaturalism which denies every claim of xenoglossy no matter what the evidence is *a priori* impervious to any contrary datum and ergo unfalsifiable and thus worthless. Interestingly, MacDonald has created the Pentecostal equivalent of this position—all glossolalic utterances are foreign languages whether or not they are identifiable as such. According to MacDonald, *God's* "data base" of human languages is enormous (6,000 known living languages and thousands of others not known and still thousands more that have come and gone), while *our* "data base" of human languages is pitifully incomplete. In addition, there are angelic languages (1 Corinthians 13:1) that man could never know, "all the languages of all time in earth *and heaven*" (41; cf. 37; emphasis added).[11] Moreover, there is the possibility, so goes his argument, that God,

---

ground if they regarded the utterances at Pentecost not as manifestations of xenoglossia but of glossolalia as at Corinth" (*Tongues of the Spirit*, 36).

[9] Pentecostal scholar Janet Evert Powers, basing her arguments on science and theology, also believes that the foreign language position is self-destructive and "weights the argument in favor of the traditional cessationist view" ("Missionary Tongues?" *Journal of Pentecostal Theology* 17 [2000]: 46). First, "This view puts Pentecostals in the position of having to prove that modern glossolalia always involves the speaking of foreign languages. There is no way Pentecostals can do this, especially if the 'objective' criteria of scientific linguistics are used to determine the nature of the glossolalic utterances, since the existence of foreign language glossolalia has never been proven linguistically" (46). Second, the position "anchors the meaning of glossolalia in the historical manifestation at Pentecost and the initial empowering for witness. Tongues becomes [*sic*] a sign that the gospel would be preached to all nations and is unique to Pentecost. When tongues are understood as foreign languages, the emphasis falls on the message which is to be proclaimed. . . . Tongues are merely the prelude to Peter's sermon in Acts 2 and, if the gospel is not preached in tongues [and it wasn't, see Acts 2:14ff], but in the vernacular, tongues are no longer necessary" (47).

[10] "Documenting Xenoglossy," *Paraclete* 21.2 (Spring 1987): 27–30. (Chapter 12 in this volume.)

[11] To Paul, the "tongues of angels" terminology conveys the other-world nature of glossolalia. Biblical references to angels always depict them as speaking human languages, naturally, since their addressee (except in visionary passages) is human and would not understand any other language! To suppose that humans could literally speak the tongues of angels supposes that angels are basically human, with anatomical organs identical to the human tongue, teeth, lips, larynx, lungs, esophagus, nasal cavity, vocal chords, trachea, jaw, and every organ, bone, or membrane they are attached to and all

to preserve the element of faith, purposely thwarts the efforts of linguists in their attempt to identify glossolalia as foreign languages. It seems that no matter what rock they turn, the skeptic (or investigating professional linguist) will never hear glossolalia as a foreign language, which, in fact, seems to militate against one of MacDonald's points: "The significant . . . value of glossolalia in the world at large rests exclusively on its being identifiable language . . ." (41). In the end, MacDonald's argument, unfalsifiable as it is, is no more valid than that of the anti-supernaturalists whose presupposition *a priori* rules out the possibility of xenoglossy.

A Most Damaging Argument Ignored

MacDonald fails to address what I believe to be a valid linguistic argument and perhaps the most damaging non-exegetical argument to his case. After linguist William Samarin's analysis of multiple specimens of glossolalia, he concluded that the syllables of glossolalic utterances were invariably drawn from the same syllabic pool of the speakers' native tongues.[12] For example, a Pentecostal whose native language is void of meaningful clicks and whistles (such as English) does not incorporate those into his glossolalic utterances, whereas we should expect to find clicks and whistles within the glossolalic utterances of those Pentecostals who speak from a syllabic treasury that contains these sounds, and according to Samarin that is the case.[13]

---

each of them is attached to and so forth until you have the entire human anatomy *and more*, for lungs presuppose the heart and oxygen and so on. Since angels are not of this world and must assume the form and language of man when communicating with humans, it is highly unlikely that their method of communication in the heavenlies is human or even human-like. Obviously, Paul is speaking figuratively here, and MacDonald is mistaken in implying that glossolalic speech could literally be angelic speech. For Paul, "tongues of angels" (saving hyperbole) means an ethereal speech of sublime transcendence. (Various occurrences of tongues of angels in Jewish literature may rule out hyperbole in Paul's language here. See John C. Poirier, *The Tongues of Angels* [Tübingen, Germany: Mohr Siebeck, 2010]. This assumes that at least some of the given instances of or references to angeloglossy pre-date 1 Corinthians. See Max Turner, "Early Christian Experience and Theology of 'Tongues,'" 29.)

[12] *Tongues of Men and Angels* (New York: Macmillan, 1972) 83, 227. Although Samarin's work is not without bias, his conclusion here appears credible, and Pentecostal scholars should not dismiss it until the evidence so warrants. Concerning Samarin's charitable hypothesis of glossolalia as sacramental symbolism, although MacDonald sarcastically berates Samarin, he fails to controvert his evidence or replace it with a more credible conclusion.

[13] Although anecdotal and secondhand, a friend relayed to me years ago of an incident at a Full Gospel Business Men's Meeting (probably in Florida) of just such a glossolalic occurrence that was recognized by an attending missionary. This would counter Samarin's conclusions. Also, David Hilborn cites Michael T. Motley's research as

If this is true, I must ask, *Has God limited himself to granting to Pentecostal believers only xenoglossic utterances that can be formulated from their native pool of syllables?* Isn't this a curious limitation? Is it done to thwart those skeptical linguists? This smacks of special pleading.

The Limitations of Languages—Native or Foreign

Advocates of both sides of this issue admit this: Among other things, "tongues . . . radiate and release the praise pent up in one's heart . . ." ("Pentecostal Theology," 66). It seems MacDonald is implying that the native tongue, at times, is incapable of conveying the heart's feelings. But there is a problem here for the foreign language view. For example, if English is not capable of conveying my heart's praise, then it could never be used by a non-English speaker in a xenoglossic utterance. Or, if Spanish is insufficient for the Hispanic, how could it suffice for the German? If the S/spirit is held in bondage to the learned language, how would speaking in someone else's learned language convey the message?

Also, all human languages have their blasphemous curse words and have been used for wicked ends; some commentators have observed that new (*kainais*) languages (Mk. 16:17) are needed because we have perverted and stained the earthly languages. No language has escaped the influence of the fall. From this angle, it makes sense that our new language be just that—new in every sense (S/spiritual, not earthly) and unique to each Christian.[14]

The Exegetical Case

According to MacDonald, Acts 2:1–13 is an "impregnable fortress of Pentecostal fact," and this passage should be considered the *locus classicus* (the authoritative passage) for defining the nature of glossolalia (36). This first · occurrence[15] of glossolalia at the first Christian Pentecost in Jerusalem was "the defining moment" (37). It was "very special linguistically," "extraordinary," "unusual," (39) with a "uniquely international gathering" (38), yet,

---

indicating that the phonological patterning of glossolalia "more resembles that to be found in languages unfamiliar to the glossolalist (French and Russian) than in the glossolalist's native tongue (American English)" ("Glossolalia as Communication," 112n6). So, more research is needed in this area.

[14] "The word *kainais* denotes something that is new and entirely distinct in nature from the old" (Powers, 51).

[15] But, regarding the order of scriptural composition, note the words of Dale Moody: "First Corinthians, ch. 14, is primitive and primary, not Acts 2:6b–11, so the earliest passage, not the secondary, should control interpretation" (*Spirit of the Living God: What the Bible Says about the Spirit*, rev. ed. [Nashville: Broadman Press, 1976], 63.)

argues MacDonald, "the proper place to begin to understand glossolalia . . ." (42). This exhibits a curious logic.

MacDonald is right. Pentecost was unique; it was special; it was extraordinary; it was unusual; and it is the only recorded occurrence of glossolalia before an international audience—the importance of this last fact cannot be overstated since it appears to be the *raison d'être* for the speakers to speak ostensibly in a foreign language. These are the very reasons the Acts 2 passage should *not* serve as the *locus classicus* for interpreting all other occurrences of glossolalia. Interestingly, even though MacDonald argues that Pentecost is the *control* occurrence in reference to the *nature* of glossolalia and that all other occurrences—be they Lukan or Pauline—must melt to its mold,[16] he inconsistently jettisons other elements of the Jerusalem glossolalic experience so that the Caesarean, Corinthian, Ephesian, Samaritan, and the Pauline experiences might qualify as "repetitions" of Pentecost.[17] I am referring to the rushing wind and tongues of fire of the Jerusalem Pentecost. (And for the Corinthian experience, MacDonald must, *contra* Paul, jettison one element that was not needed at Pentecost, i.e., *interpretation*.) What is his rationale for doing this? He explains: "[N]owhere in Acts is it ever stated that these introductory heavenly (2:2) signs are ever repeated" ("Glossolalia," 7). So, repetition, evidently, is MacDonald's validating hermeneutical principle. May I raise the obvious question: *Where in Acts or elsewhere in the New Testament is it ever stated that glossolalia was ever again understood by the audience as it was understood by the Jerusalem audience?*[18] This (with wind and fire) is exactly what makes this

---

[16] Cf. Powers: "If we had only Acts 2 or 1 Cor. 12–14 [either one or the other but not both], we would have no difficulty determining the nature of tongues. The problem arises in trying to harmonize the two accounts. . . . In fact the only way that we could arrive at the conclusion that Paul had foreign languages in mind is to take the Acts 2 account as primary and forcibly conform Paul's description to it" (42, 49).

[17] Elsewhere MacDonald admits that the later occurrences of glossolalia in Acts were "*mutatis mutandis*" (i.e., given the necessary changes) repetitions of Pentecost ("Pentecostal Theology," 59). In other words, all the occurrences of glossolalia were not identical. Why can this concession by MacDonald not include the *nature* of glossolalia? It certainly includes the more obvious miracles of fire and wind.

[18] MacDonald evidently sees the problem here and desperately attempts to turn the single occurrence of glossolalia at Jerusalem into multiple witnesses when he writes, "What is stated once and then repeated twice, all within five verses, cannot be missed by one who scrutinizes the text. . . . In that triadic statement the full weight of the emphasis falls on the concept of 'languages'" (36). In his summary (41), he again tries to inflate the one event in Acts 2 to three (or four) witnesses with this citation: ". . . Acts 2:4, 6, 8, 11. . . ." Furthermore, he lists Acts 10 and 19 with these although there is no mention whatsoever in these verses that tongues were understood, or that they were

passage unique. If xenoglossy ever occurred again, Luke inexplicably neglected three or four prime opportunities to record it.

Inasmuch as MacDonald concedes that there are elements of Pentecost that are not repeated, namely, the tongues of fire, the rushing mighty
wind, and the divine obviation of interpretation (through xenoglossy), he
should be willing to admit that Pentecost in all its parts is not a paradigm,
not normative, and, thus, not the *locus classicus* for interpreting other scriptural references to glossolalia.

MacDonald also attempts to build an exegetical case for his view
through brief word studies of *dialektos, logoi, phonai,* and *glossai* (34). But
this isn't very helpful, for if glossolalia is a S/spirit "language," all references to its nature must necessarily be based upon *analogous* human languages. What other terms are the writers going to use? Just as writers of

---

dialektos, or that they were *heterais glōssais*, or that they were *phōnē* or *apophthengesthai*, defining terms of the Acts 2 occurrence *alone*.

As MacDonald wrongly attempts to wed Acts 10 and 19 with Acts 2, he similarly
tries to wed Luke's and Paul's use of "other languages" (*heterais glōssais*), quoting
Acts 2:4 and 1 Cor 14:21 (38). What he doesn't reveal to the reader is that the verse he
cites in 1 Corinthians is not a reference by Paul to Acts 2 glossolalia or Corinthian
glossolalia but to a learned foreign language—Assyrian, which was no doubt understood by the speakers, *contra* MacDonald who writes of the verse (as though it were
Acts 2:4), "In all cases the speaker's mind does not comprehend his glossolalic speech
(1 Cor 14:14)" (38). Sadly, this appears to be a deliberate attempt by MacDonald to
mislead the reader to believe that Luke's *heterais glōssais*, which appears to be miraculous, Spirit-inspired languages, is identical to Paul's *heteroglōssois*, which in its context is obviously *not* miraculous, Spirit-inspired languages but the learned human language of the Assyrians. Since MacDonald rightly asserts that glossolalia does not occur
in the OT (32) and his citation of 1 Cor 14:21 is Paul's reference to Isaiah 28:11, Mac-
Donald knows that this cannot "mirror" (38) Luke's use of "'other' (languages)."

One holding the foreign language view could respond that 1 Cor. 14:21, in fact,
proves MacDonald's main point: the Old Testament passage speaks of a foreign language and Paul compares glossolalia to it. However, this misses the point of Paul's
reference. The comparison is not made to define or explain the *nature* of glossolalia (for
the speakers had *learned* their Assyrian language); it is made to demonstrate the bar-
renness, even detriment (to the hearers), of misused glossolalia (see Graves, *Praying in
the Spirit*, 139–42). Paul also compares glossolalia to a foreign language in 1 Corinthians 14:10. But one does not compare identical things, but similar things. Tongues are
similar in appearances to foreign languages, but they are not foreign languages. Otherwise, Paul would be comparing foreign languages to foreign languages—a "redundant
exercise," according to Cyril Williams (*Tongues of the Spirit*, 31; affirmed by Gordon
D. Fee, *The First Epistle to the Corinthians* [Grand Rapids: Eerdmans, 1987], 598. This
is Williams's and Fee's argument; I do not know what they would say to the retort that
though both are foreign languages, one is learned and the other is supernatural—perhaps
that Paul appears to be making a direct comparison [*prima facie*] between foreign languages and tongues *in use*, not to the source, which would be once removed.)

Scripture had to use earthly terms to describe heaven, they had to use earthly terms to describe glossolalia. So, it should not be surprising to see some of the same terms used of natural speaking applied to S/spiritual speaking.[19]

---

[19] Having said this, it should be noted that there are certain terms used in relation to Acts 2's xenoglossic glossolalia that are never used of any other occurrence of glossolalia. Perhaps it is possible this is attributable to statistical probability. Though there may not be enough evidence to confirm a judgment either way, the following facts are noteworthy: (1) Paul never applied the following Acts 2 terms to his favorite term for *tongue(s)*, *glōssa/glōssai*: *dialektos*, *phōnē* , *apophthengesthai*, *heterais*, (2) in Acts 10 and 19, Luke did not apply *dialektos*, *phōnē* , *apophthengesthai*, or *heterais* to *glōssais*. Although *dialektos* does occur three more times in Acts, it is only in a context where it, *without a doubt*, refers to a learned human non-glossolalic foreign language (21:40; 22:2; 26:14), and he uses *phōnē* three times, but never applies it to *glōssa*. In Lukan and Pauline literature, these kindred terms are used only in a context where foreign languages are obvious. Powers believes that Paul *intentionally* avoided applying *glōssa* to foreign languages: "In 1 Cor. 14.10–11, Paul uses a completely different word [*phōnē*] for languages *to show that he is not referring to tongues*" (48; emphasis added).

MacDonald attempts to answer the problem raised by the omission of *heterais*, writing: "Whenever the terse expression 'speaking in tongues' is used, the elliptical *heterais* ('other') is to be understood, or there would be no distinction from ordinary speaking" (33). His support for this is Blass and Debrunner's use of [*heterais*] *glossais* as an illustration of adjectival ellipsis: "*glossais lalein* is properly *heterais gl. lalein*, as it is designated in the narrative where the phenomenon first appears (A 2:4)." Blass and Debrunner cite no research for further scrutiny or support; neither does MacDonald. It sounds possible, but it neglects the data listed in the previous paragraph. It would be much more believable if just once Paul would have used *heteros/heterai* with one of his seventeen uses of *glōssa/glōssai*; the one and only place that Paul does use *heteros* is in 1 Cor. 14:21, where it, without a doubt, refers to the language of the Assyrians. So, the only place that Paul uses *heteros* in conjunction with *glōssa* is in a non-glossolalic passage. Johannes Behm evidently thinks this is material; he writes in *TDNT*, "The words *heterai* (Ac. 2:4) and *kainai* (Mk. 16:17) are a further indication that the essence of the gift lies in the fact that it . . . implies the new and unusual. It thus seems most likely that the word *glōssa* has here [in 1 Corinthians] the sense of 'language' . . . , and that it is used as a 'technical expression for a peculiar language,' namely, the 'language of the Spirit,' a miraculous language which is used in heaven between God and the angels (1 C. 13:1) and to which man may attain in prayer as he is seized by the Spirit and caught up into heaven. . ." (1:726).

Williams, referring to this word study as the "etymological argument," writes that, taken in isolation, "it is not convincing. Paul employed *glōssais* for the tongues of angels (1 Cor. 13:1) while 'he who speaks in a tongue' (*glōssē*) is said to address God, not men, and furthermore no one understands him (1 Cor. 14:2). It is highly unlikely that tongues signify known languages in these contexts" (*Tongues of the Spirit*, 26).

MacDonald's only other lexical attempt to disprove the S/spirit language position is a reference to the word *battalogein* in Matthew 6:7. According to MacDonald, Paul and Luke had a word to use to designate the S/spirit language if it were not an authentic human language—*battalogein*, babble or vain repetitions. But this wouldn't work for two reasons: (1) *battalogein* was used relative to learned languages and pagan prayers—

This also speaks to MacDonald's charge that "Implicit in the rejection of 'tongues' as a 'language' is the commensurate rejection of 'the gift of interpretation' as genuine" (37). In defending the gift of interpretation (*hermēneia*), Francis A. Sullivan wrote that the word for *interpretation*

> could merely have been an apt word to describe what happened when one person spoke out in what sounded like a strange language, and another person gave the meaning of his utterance in plain Greek. It would be only natural to say that the second person "translated" what the first had said. But this would be true whether the "interpreter" actually understood the language that had been spoken, or whether he were given a prophetic insight into the sense of the message that had been spoken in tongues, without actually understanding the "tongue" as such. If the "tongue" sounded like a language, the interpretation of it into plain Greek would also have sounded like a translation and that, it seems to me, is all that the use of these words necessarily implies.[20]

Furthermore, if one assumes that glossolalia can at times be xenoglossy (such as at Pentecost), Luke's and Paul's terminology applied to xenoglossy would, by association, be applied to glossolalia (both, in fact, are glossolalia, but not all glossolalia is xenoglossy).

---

both the *learned* and the *pagan* elements would present problems of incongruity and association, and (2) there is no reason to believe that the S/spirit language produces a "garbled," "rushed loquacious speaking," as MacDonald defines *battalogein* (33). Furthermore, an authentic foreign language sounds like babble to hearers who do not understand it (see 1 Cor. 14:11 [*barbaros*], 23; Acts 2:13). MacDonald's argument here seems to erode his overall argument from the intelligence of God, for (1) if a foreign language can be classified as "garbled," "babble," and "nonsense" (34) and (2) glossolalia must be a foreign language, then glossolalia could be garbled, babble, and nonsense.

[20] "'Speaking in Tongues' in the New Testament and in the Modern Charismatic Renewal," *The Spirit of God in Christian Life*, ed. Edward Malatesta (New York: Paulist Press, 1977), 35. Williams is unconvinced by Gundry's and Davies's argument that the use of *hermēneuō* suggests that Paul is speaking of the translating of a foreign language. They do not take into consideration the different contexts of its usage—a fatal flaw, in Williams's opinion: "This seems to me a circular argument since appeal is made to normal usage 'in such a context' when this is precisely the object of inquiry. Philological evidence of the use of terms in their primary connotation elsewhere does not necessarily rule out a more technical usage in this context. St. Paul could employ the terms *glōssa* and *hermēneuō* to indicate a new kind of 'tongue' and a new kind of 'translating'" (*Tongues of the Spirit*, 26–27). See also Thiselton, "Interpretation of Tongues," 30.

MacDonald is a skilled wordsmith; his choice and arrangement of al-literative words are a delight to read and are surpassed only at times by his superior skills of hyperbole. For example, in speaking of Robert H. Gundry's exegetical defense of the foreign language view, he calls it "insu-perable," "rock solid hermeneutically" and, thus, "incapable of refutation" (43). Well, there must be reasons why the most well-studied scholars in the field of pneumatology, including Gordon D. Fee, J. Rodman Williams, and James D. G. Dunn, reject Gundry's conclusions.[21] I believe the foregoing discussion covers some of those reasons. (Actually, Gundry *has* been re-futed.[22] The foreign language view is simply impervious to the evidence.)

---

[21] In *Praying in the Spirit*, 137, I list 37 NT commentators who reject the foreign language view, from Henry Alford to Bernhard Weiss; others include Barrett, Blomberg, Bruce, Conzelmann, Garland, Grosheide, Hays, Kistemaker, Moffatt, L. Morris, Plummer, A. T. Robertson, and Thiselton.

[22] See Williams, *Tongues of the Spirit*, 25–45, and my *Praying in the Spirit*, 121–37 (which is expanded from the 1987 edition, 64–72). What follows are some additional reasons why the foreign language position appears weak and unconvincing: (1) If tongues were a foreign language, Christians (even pagans) could possibly exercise the gift of interpretation naturally, i.e., without having the gift of interpretation, yet Paul implies in 1 Corinthians 12–14 that this gift comes only to Christians and only through divine intervention. A special gift is required, not a special nationality. As George Bar-ton Cutten opined 97 years ago: "The only 'interpretation' of which he [Paul] spoke was one which proceeded from a charismatic privilege . . . ." (*Speaking in Tongues: Historically and Psychologically Considered* [New Haven, CT: Yale University Press, 1927], 27). (2) Paul never exhorts those with the gift of tongues to employ their gift as a sign to foreigners (as happened with Acts 2 xenoglossy). Instead, he enjoins them not to use the gift of tongues before foreigners but before the church and then only with the gift of interpretation. (3) Throughout 1 Corinthians 14, the Greek verb Paul used for *speak (lalein)* is used elsewhere to signify non-lexical vocalizations. The word may convey the idea of either speech or these other non-speech variations. So, also, the word for *tongue(s)*, *glōssa*; in the Septuagint, it is used to refer to languages but also to the non-lexical growl of a dog (Exod 11:7) and the stammering of a stutterer (Isa 32:4). (4) If tongues are genuine foreign languages, how is a congregation (or an individual with the gift of interpretation) to know whether an utterance in a foreign language is a man-ifestation of the gift of tongues or is a prophetic utterance spoken by someone who is of a different nationality (language)? (5) First Corinthians 14:14–15 contrasts *pneuma* (human spirit) and *nous* (mind), a contrast which may be seen to favor the S/spirit lan-guage view and reduce the importance of the mind or the rational in determining the nature of this gift. (6) For commentator James Moffatt, the phrase "speaking in a lan-guage" seems redundant. How else is one going to speak? The Pauline phrase (*lalein glōssais*) is not found in Acts 2—because they were heard speaking in "other" (*heterais*) languages, ostensibly foreign languages. This points to Behms's conclusion that *glōssa* alone, as used by Paul, had become a "technical expression" for the "language of the spirit" (see footnote 20 above). (7) Regarding Paul's warning in 1 Cor 14:23 that unbe-lievers would think the glossolalic Corinthians mad, if the tongues were foreign lan-guages, Sam Storms notes that Paul's conclusion regarding madness would not always

The Nature of Glossolalia

The nature of glossolalia can only be determined by examining all the scriptures related to the phenomenon. This means looking at the Acts 2 occurrence as well as all others.

We might start our quest by asking: *What is the origin of glossolalia?* All of the gospels prophesied that Jesus would baptize believers in the Holy Spirit (Matt 3:11; Mark 1:8; Luke 3:16; John 1:33). In Acts 1:5, Jesus instructs his followers to wait in Jerusalem for the baptism in the Holy Spirit, which is the gift his Father promised. Luke later documents the occurrences of glossolalia at Jerusalem, Caesarea, and Ephesus (Acts 2, 10, 19) as believers are baptized in the Holy Spirit. Even the gifts of the Spirit as recorded by Paul are in some manner bestowed by Jesus (Eph 4:7–11). Thus, we can conclude that the origin of glossolalia, whether by Spirit baptism (Lukan) or gift (Pauline) is Christocentric (but notice how beautifully the triune Godhead is interwoven in the experience). So, whichever glossolalia is—foreign language or S/spirit language—the heavenly Jesus is the author.

We might next ask: *Who gives the utterance?* According to Luke, the Spirit gave the believers the utterances (Acts 2:4); Paul agrees, the glossolalic utters mysteries by the S/spirit (1 Cor 14:2; cf. alternate NIV [1973] translation, which capitalizes Spirit[23]); his utterance is a manifestation of

---

hold true, for "if the tongues being spoken are languages known throughout the world at that time . . . . any unbeliever who knew the language being spoken would more likely conclude the person speaking was highly educated rather than out of his mind" (*The Language of Heaven* [Lake Mary, FL: Charisma House, 2019], 71). (8) In 1 Cor. 14:7–9, Paul compares glossolalia to inchoate, unstructured music (indistinctive notes) which listeners do not understand; according to the contrast, glossolalia lacks clear words (*logon*) (see David Hilborn, "Glossolalia as Communication," 113–14). (9) Finally, 1 Corinthians 14:2, "For anyone who speaks in a tongue *does not speak to men but to God. Indeed, no one understands him; he utters mysteries by the Spirit*" (italics added). You cannot get much clearer than this. Only one passage in all the New Testament offers an alternative—Acts 2, the exception, glossolalia that is miraculously understood by men—the first Pentecost: unique, special, extraordinary, unusual, and international in scope. (Its dissimilarity with Corinthian tongues may also be seen in its violation of Paul's injunction that two or, at the most, three should speak in tongues [1 Cor. 14:27–28] and 14:23 where Paul warns the Corinthians that strangers, who came into a meeting where all were speaking in tongues, would consider them mad. The utterance is a mystery to all men: "no one understands him," says Paul, neither Galileans, Parthians, Medes, nor Elamites. He "does not speak to men but to God," not to Romans, Cretans, or Arabs—quite the opposite of the first Pentecost (nationalities listed above are taken from Acts 2). (See *Praying in the Spirit*, 121–37, for citations and bibliographic documentation.)

[23] For justification see Fee, 656.

the Spirit (1 Cor 12:7). However, Paul adds an interesting datum in verse 14: "For if I pray in a tongue, *my spirit* prays . . ." (emphasis added). Thus, with this added datum, it is apparent that the nexus of the Holy Spirit with the believer's spirit creates a synergy, allowing Luke to write, without contradiction, that glossolalic speech is given by the Holy Spirit and Paul to write, the speech comes from the renewed human spirit, thus the justification of describing glossolalia as a "S/spirit" language and concluding that the S/spirit gives the utterance.

We might next ask: *What, if any, is the linguistic content of glossolalic speech?* Here is where the rub comes with those who hold to the foreign language view. They may even agree with my answers to the previous questions, but my answer to this question is what puts us in separate camps. But before we go there, I might mention one more area of agreement: Both camps believe that glossolalia is communication—one argues for human languages, the other, for S/spirit languages; both camps (for the most part) believe it is communication from man to God.

Now for the rub. One of MacDonald's main arguments against the S/spirit language position is based on the intelligence of God and the nonintelligence of S/spirit languages. MacDonald must assume that the Spirit is unable or unwilling to lexically encode utterances that are not known to the human family of languages. Instead, the Spirit can only communicate through languages invented by humans, arbitrarily (or intuitively) encoded by a fallen race. Unawares, MacDonald has steered his ship into anthropocentric waters, where man is the measure of all things, and man's language is the measure of all glossolalia. According to the foreign language view, even *in the Spirit* we must depend upon human languages to communicate to God. My study of the Scriptures leads me to believe that when the Spirit helps us pray, he isn't limited by the finite lexical inventory of human languages. So, what is the content of glossolalia? It is the Spirit of God working in connection with the spirit of man, encoding the utterances, thus creating a numinous, supra-rational language of the S/spirit, unlimited, untainted, unknown.[24]

---

[24] Cartledge, summing up H. Baker's position, writes of glossolalia: "It is indeed a means of communicating which transcends mere words. It is a means of communication by participation in the divine life and represents the divinizing communion of the Holy Spirit. Thus it is symbolic both of union and *theosis* [i.e., "participation in the divine life"] occurring mystically and ineffably by God's grace" (*Charismatic Glossolalia*, 189).

Conclusions

MacDonald writes, "There exists no good reason to deny that biblical glossolalia, as expressed today in continuity with NT faith in Jesus, is in any given instance either a living language or an ancient (but now defunct) language" (36). To the contrary, based on the foregoing discussion, I can think of three very good reasons for denying that biblical glossolalia is always a foreign language.

(1) *Scriptural*: You can't build a rock-solid case on one passage (Acts 2), which is admittedly unique. Every Pauline passage and every Lukan passage, save one, supports the S/spirit language view.

(2) *Scientific*: The linguistic evidence does not support the foreign language view, but, in fact, gives credence to the S/spirit language view.

(3) *Pastoral*: This is one area that has not been discussed. But I think it needs to be said that the foreign language view has drawbacks in *praxis* for two types of Christians: (a) those who are seeking the baptism in the Holy Spirit, and (b) those who are recent initiates.

> (a) According to the foreign language view, these believers will fluently speak in a foreign language. When these Christians are taught this, then this is what they expect—gracefully fluent syllables of an existing foreign language. And this is what they wait for . . . and wait . . . and wait . . . and wait. The foreign language view surpasses the innocuous; it is, in fact, an impediment to the free moving of the Spirit.

> (b) For those who have received the Holy Spirit and spoken with a broken speech that they suspect or detect was not a foreign language, the teaching of the foreign language view sometimes causes intense doubting, depression, and even recanting.

The collateral evidence from the fields of science and scripture clearly indicate that glossolalia is a non-xenoglossic, S/spirit language, excepting infrequent divine intervention such as may have occurred in Acts 2 (with an obvious reason—it was an international audience and a unique occurrence—the initial giving of the Holy Spirit to the church).[25] This view is the biblical view and as such does in no way denigrate the gift of glossolalia.

---

[25] I say "may have" here because there is evidence that it was an aural instead of a lingual miracle. (See *Praying in the Spirit*, 125–27.)

In fact, it lifts this communication that is the result of the interior *nexus* of the spirit of man and the Spirit of God beyond the earthly to the ethereal, the sublime, the sacred, where its meaning and meaningfulness rests not in the understanding of man, but in the mind of God.

14

Why Trusting the Message of the Bible Is Reasonable[1]

The Bible has a message. If that message is true, there can be no greater message, for it impacts the eternal destiny of every human being. So, it is incumbent upon every thinking person to consider the Bible's message and weigh whether it is true. The remainder of this chapter considers the reasons why I believe the message of the Bible is true. If I'm wrong, I've lost nothing (and may even have gained a greater ethic), but if you reject the message and you're wrong, you've lost everything. Please do not reject the message for the wrong reason (for example, it doesn't suit your lifestyle[2]), but base your decision on the evidence of the facts presented.

---

[1] A prior version of this chapter was originally published as an appendix to *The Gospel according to Angels* (Grand Rapids: Chosen-Baker, 1998); I later revised it and put it into tract form, but this chapter has been revised further.

[2] I agree with Blaise Pascal who wrote, "People almost invariably arrive at their beliefs not on the basis of proof but on the basis of what they find attractive." Don't be one of those people—study the evidence.

The Written Legacy

Most of us have played the game of "Gossip" or "Telephone" in which someone whispers something to one person, who must whisper it to another, until the message has gone around the room. Usually, the final words bear comically little resemblance to the initial utterance.[3] The Bible was written over a span of fifteen hundred years by forty or so authors. Until AD 1454 every Bible was hand-copied, which raises an important question: How reliable are copies of copies of copies? How do we know that the words in the Bible are anywhere close to what was originally written? How careful were the copyists?

The Old Testament
Jewish scribes selectively appointed copyists who painstakingly protected the integrity of the text. They handled it, according to F. F. Bruce,

> with the greatest imaginable reverence and devised a complicated system of safeguards against scribal slips. They counted, for example, the number of times each letter of the alphabet occurs in each book; they pointed out the middle letter of the Pentateuch [the first five books] and the middle letter of the whole Hebrew Bible, and made even more detailed calculations than these. "Everything countable seems to be counted," says Wheeler Robinson . . . and they made up mnemonics by which the various totals might be readily remembered.[4]

The Dead Sea Scrolls—The real test of the copying process came in 1947 with the discovery of the Dead Sea Scrolls, which included the book of Isaiah. Until then the earliest Old Testament manuscript dated from AD 900. The Dead Sea Isaiah scroll dated from circa BC 125—that is, one thousand years earlier than the oldest existing manuscript. A comparison of the two texts would test the skill and care of the copyists. Here is what it revealed:

---

[3] Craig Keener effectively refutes this argument posed by Bart Ehrman, writing that "the comparison [of scripture transmission to the game of Gossip] is problematic for the gospel tradition, which involved net (group) rather than chain (a single line of) transmission" (411). And he notes that "Kenneth Bailey, a NT scholar with four decades of experience in the Middle East, recounts observing the telephone game played with Middle Eastern students, who, 'to the amazement and dismay of the western guest,' transmitted the story 'almost intact'" (*Christobiography: Memory, History, and the Reliability of the Gospels* [Grand Rapids: Eerdmans, 2019], 412).

[4] F. F. Bruce quoted in Josh McDowell, *Evidence that Demands a Verdict* (San Bernardino, CA: Campus Crusade for Christ, 1972), 58.

126

Of the 166 words in Isaiah 53, there are only seventeen letters in question. Ten of these letters are simply a matter of spelling, which does not affect the sense. Four more letters are minor stylistic changes, such as conjunctions. The remaining three letters comprise the word "light," which is added in verse 11, and does not affect the meaning greatly. Furthermore, this word is supported by the LXX [3rd–2nd century BC Greek translation of the Hebrew] and IQ Isb [a second Dead Sea Isaiah scroll]. Thus, in one chapter of 166 words, there is only one word (three letters) in question after a thousand years of transmission—and this word does not significantly change the meaning of the passage.[5]

There is no reason to believe, given this evidence, that the Old Testament was corrupted by the continuous copying. Rather, it was preserved with an astonishing degree of faithfulness.

The New Testament

The evidence for the trustworthiness of the New Testament is likewise formidable, although the proof is of a different kind. The credibility of the New Testament is found in the eyewitness accounts, the proximity of the writings to the events, the age and quantity of existing manuscripts, and collateral witnesses.

The four Gospels and the gospel message of Paul were written by *eyewitnesses or contemporaries of Jesus*. They relate the events in Jesus's life and teachings and have been dated between AD 45 and 90. Just as important: their source documents would have been in existence for some time before that.[6] Some epistles of Paul date to within eighteen years of the crucifixion. (Paul was an anti-Christian Pharisee who prosecuted Christians until he had a radical encounter with the risen Jesus sometime between AD 31–34.[7]) Some scholars believe that James, the half-brother of Jesus, wrote his epistle within seventeen years of the crucifixion.

---

[5] Norman L. Geisler and William E. Nix, *A General Introduction to the Bible* (Chicago: Moody, 1968), 263.

[6] See F. F. Bruce, *The New Testament Documents: Are They Reliable?* 5th ed. (Downers Grove, IL: Inter-Varsity, 1960) and John A. T. Robinson, *Can We Trust the New Testament?* (Grand Rapids: Eerdmans, 1977).

[7] According to Gary R. Habermas, "[T]he pre-Pauline creedal tradition in 1 Corinthians 15:3–7, dates to A.D. 30! In other words, there never was a time when the message of Jesus' resurrection was not an integral part of the earliest apostolic proclamation. No less a scholar than James D. G. Dunn even states regarding this crucial text: 'This tradition, we can be entirely confident, was *formulated as tradition within months of Jesus' death*'" ("Tracing Jesus' Resurrection to Its Earliest Eyewitness Accounts," in *God Is Great, God Is Good: Why Believing in God Is Reasonable and Responsible*,

This close proximity to the actual events also rules out the possibility of it being *mere legend*.[8] Besides, if it were mere legend invented by admirers of Jesus, there is no way they would have written it the way they did, portraying Jesus consorting with despised tax collectors, lepers, and harlots, having Peter (*Saint* Peter!) curse and deny him and having credulous and scorned women first discover the empty tomb and behold the risen Lord, and, above all, they would not have him dying the despicable death of a common criminal on a Roman cross.[9] (But what a stunning mystery that the heinous death of the Son of God would turn the scandalous cross into a wondrous altar—an unimaginable story!) "His movement," writes Craig Keener, "had no reason to invent him, and certainly not his execution for treason as a 'king'; following someone so executed was itself deemed treasonous, so inventing such a narrative would be suicidal."[10]

The *oldest existing fragment* of the New Testament is known as the St. John's Fragment, which is dated AD 117–130. It was found not in Asia Minor, where John's Gospel is believed to have been penned, but in the sands of Egypt. Thus, when time is allowed for further copying and transporting, this papyrus fragment pushes the date of the gospel of John back to the century of the events described. (Other elements, internal to the

---

ed. William Lane Craig and Chad Meister (Downers Grove, IL: InterVarsity, 2009), 212.

[8] Craig S. Keener has written an excellent work (*Christobiography*) that scrupulously examines the biographic nature of the four Gospels and the importance and accuracy of "living memory" and the concept of sources, both written and oral, that were essential for the composition of the Gospels. His work also answers many questions regarding the narrative discrepancies that might exist between the Gospels. He concludes that the Gospels "were composed during the early empire, the period of greatest historiographic sensitivity among ancient biographers, [which] reinforces the likelihood that the Evangelists had significant interest in recounting genuine historical information about their biographee. That they speak about a figure within living memory suggests that they had substantial information available" (120). Regarding possible Egyptian, Persian, Greek, or Roman mythical origins of the historical Jesus, see Josh McDowell and Bill Wilson, *He Walked Among Us* (San Bernardino, CA: Here's Life, 1988), 175–97, A. L. Van Den Herik, *The Shortest Leap: The Rational Underpinnings of Faith in Jesus* (Bloomington, IN: West Bow Press-Thomas Nelson/Zondervan, 2020), 123–41, and Keener, *Christobiography*, 340–41; for possible legendary development in the four Gospels, see Van Den Herik, 351–67, and Peter Kreeft and Ronald K. Tacelli, *Handbook of Christian Apologetics* (Downers Grove, IL: InterVarsity, 1994), 189–97, and Keener, *Christobiography*, passim, but especially 120, 150, 240, 252, 365.

[9] See Peter J. Williams, *Can We Trust the Gospels?* (Wheaton, IL: Crossway, 2018), 31; regarding corruption through transmission, see page 94.

[10] *Christobiography*, 5.

letters of Paul, push the message of the gospel—the death and resurrection of Jesus—back to the year of Jesus's crucifixion.[11])

There exist more than *five thousand Greek manuscripts* containing all or parts of the New Testament. In addition, there are nine thousand early translations into the Latin, Syriac, and Coptic languages. With this multitude of manuscript evidence, scholars have been able to reconstruct the original words of the New Testament to an accuracy of 99 percent or better. The remaining one percent is made up of inconsequential variants.

In addition to manuscript evidence, there is *the witness of the early Church fathers*, some of whom lived in the same century as Jesus. The writings of these men, according to J. Harold Greenlee, are so chock-full of Scripture quotations that the New Testament "could virtually be reconstructed from them without the use of New Testament manuscripts."[12] Sir David Dalrymple set out to search the early fathers for every New Testament verse. He found all but eleven.[13]

Thus, there is no reason to believe that the New Testament we have today differs in substance from the original documents written in the first century. The transmission of God's divine message to humanity was, by the account of the manuscript evidence, successful.

The Formation of the Canon

Having said the above, lest the reader get the wrong idea that the Scriptures are the source of Christianity, let me say this: Scripture isn't necessary for the truth of Christianity to stand, for it simply attests to the reality that exists. The church did just fine for four hundred years without a fixed canon of Scripture. The *Spirit* to which the Scriptures later attested created and sustains the church, not the Scriptures. Even today there exist believers who do not have the Scriptures in their own languages and many others who are illiterate. But they do have the Spirit. The Spirit sustains them.

Before the Scriptures were written, the first-century church was guided by the canon of faith, a faith grounded in the eyewitness testimony of the Spirit-filled apostles. Eventually, this testimony began to be written down by the apostles or their associates. Paul's epistles came as early as AD 50, within eighteen years of the ministry of Jesus, then the Gospel of Mark, around AD 64, then Matthew, Luke, and John. These four Gospels were written in the first century, within the lifetime and scrutiny of living

---

[11] Habermas, "Tracing Jesus' Resurrection," 202–16.

[12] J. Harold Greenlee, *An Introduction to New Testament Textual Criticism* (Grand Rapids: Eerdmans, 1964), 54.

[13] Quoted in Geisler and Nix, *General Introduction*, 357.

witnesses. It was *the words of Christ* within the eyewitness Gospels that became the first Christian writings considered authoritative for the church.

There were many other Christian writings that competed for the church's acceptance, but though some were beneficial to the believer, eventually they were not accepted as part of the inspired canon. Either they did not pass the test of (1) apostolicity or, at least, proximity in time to and association with the apostles,[14] (2) universal acceptance by the churches[15], or (3) adherence to the teachings of Jesus or the accepted Gospels.[16]

There exists the notion that Roman Emperor Constantine fixed the Christian canon. He was no doubt influential and helped guide the church in the direction of a set New Testament canon, but at the time of his death (AD 337), even then the New Testament canon was not fixed. Others assert that the canon was set by church councils. True, church councils were influential, but it must be remembered that those council attendees represented their churches, so ultimately, it was the Spirit-led members of the churches who set the canon.[17] Interestingly, the churches did not always follow council decisions by the church hierarchy.[18]

---

[14] Which is why there are many pseudepigrapha, that is, books written soon after the apostles died but bearing the name of an apostle, for example, *Gospel of Peter, Apocalypse of Peter, Infancy Gospel of Thomas, Gospel of Philip*. The authors knew that giving their works such names would give the works immediate credibility. Lee M. McDonald is right to conclude that "the tendency for many in the church to write pseudonymous writings to insure their acceptance in the early church, says it is unlikely that any book of the NT would have been accepted by the ancient church if it had been *known* that the writing was pseudonymous" (*The Formation of the Christian Biblical Canon* [Peabody, MA: Hendrickson, 1995], 232; see also 290.) Regarding the value that the apocrypha and pseudepigrapha might add to the fixed canon, McDonald believes that "there are no other ancient documents which are on the whole *more* reliable in informing the church's faith than our present biblical canon" (257; see also xix). In distinguishing the historical veracity between the Gospels and the apocrypha, Keener writes that "Most apocryphal gospels also stem from the heyday of ancient novels, the late second and early third centuries. Because of their date and novelistic features, these later Gospels are recognized by the majority of scholars as novels, not biographies. There is moreover in them (as opposed to Matthew, Mark, Luke, and John) little indication of Judean or Galilean elements or other signs of earlier tradition" (*Christobiography*, 59).

[15] In the words of McDonald, "The writings that did not survive in the church did not meet the needs of the greater church" (*Formation*, 246).

[16] Craig L. Blomberg, *Can We Still Believe the Bible?* (Grand Rapids: Brazos Press-Baker, 2014), 58–64; see also, McDonald, *Formation*, 228–49.

[17] McDonald, *Formation*, 172, 182–89, 208; Blomberg, *Believe*, 67–68.

[18] McDonald, *Formation*, 252.

The Legacy of Fulfilled Prophecies

Although it is necessary to have a trustworthy copy of God's written reve-lation, reconstructing the original words of a document does not prove that the document is, in fact, inspired by God. How do we get to that point? One way, I believe, is to show that the document contains predictive proph-ecies beyond the pale of human knowledge and coincidence.

Peter W. Stoner, former chairman of the Departments of Mathemat-ics and Astronomy of Pasadena City College, applied the laws of probabil-ity to eleven Old Testament prophecies and concluded that "the probability of these eleven prophecies coming true, if written in human wisdom, is . . . 1 in 5.76 x 10^{59}."[19]

Stoner also applied the principles of probability to eight messianic prophecies of the Old Testament that Jesus fulfilled. The eight prophetic predictions, he concluded, had only one chance in 10^{17} of being fulfilled in one man. Stoner used the following illustration to show the probability of this happening:

> Suppose that we take 10^{17} silver dollars and lay them on the face of Texas. They will cover all of the state two feet deep. Now mark one of these silver dollars and stir the whole mass thoroughly, all over the state. Blindfold a man and tell him that he can travel as far as he wishes, but he must pick up one silver dollar and say that this is the right one. What chance would he have of getting the right one? Just the same chance that the prophets would have had of writing these eight prophecies and having them all come true in any one man, from their day to the present, providing they wrote them in their own wis-dom.[20]

But there are more than eight messianic prophecies fulfilled in Christ. Stoner went on to calculate the chances of any one man's fulfilling 48 prophecies to be 1 in 10^{157}. But there are as many as 300 fulfilled messianic prophecies![21] This proof must be reckoned with by anyone who chooses to deny the supernatural character of the Bible.

The Legacy of the Church

That the church even exists points to the reliability of the Scriptures. For one thing, the existence of the church cannot be disputed. Obviously it is here now; indisputably it has not always existed. Historical and archeolog-ical evidence for the church indicates that it emerged onto the scene in first-

---

[19] Peter W. Stoner, *Science Speaks*, 3rd ed. (Chicago: Moody, 1969), 95.
[20] Ibid., 107.
[21] Ibid., 108.

century Judea. In 1945 a burial chamber in Jerusalem yielded two inscriptions on ossuaries ("caskets" for bones). These inscriptions are prayers to Jesus and date to between AD 40 and 50; one even alludes to a resurrected life.[22] No sufficient impetus for the church's origin and growth, other than the New Testament account, has ever been proven.

The church arose as a persecuted minority Jewish sect. All twelve of its founding apostles were persecuted, and all but one were martyred for their faith. Hundreds of other followers chose martyrdom rather than deny their faith in the resurrected Jesus. As for the obvious rebuttal that many people have died for mistaken beliefs, McDowell and Wilson have made this reply in reference to the eleven disciples:

> Yes, a lot of people have died for a lie, but they thought it was the truth. Now if the resurrection didn't take place (i.e., was false), the disciples knew it. I find no way to demonstrate that they could have been deceived. Therefore these eleven men not only died for a lie— here is the catch—but they knew it was a lie. It would be hard to find eleven people in history who died for a lie, knowing it was a lie.[23]

To say that the New Testament documents were mistaken or false means that the early martyrs chose to die for what they knew was untrue. The picture the gospels draw of the post-crucifixion disciples as a frightened, cowardly little huddle hardly looks like a group of men who would challenge the formidable power of the Jewish authorities, much less the unmatched might of the Roman Empire. Furthermore, to suggest that the disciples lied about Jesus goes head-on against the moral teachings of their Teacher.

Their very purpose for following Jesus would prevent them from fabricating an untruthful story about him. This strengthens the conclusion that their accounts of Jesus's words and deeds as recorded in the New Testament are true.

The Legacy of Changed Lives

One of the two remaining evidences has, more than anything else, changed the shape of our world. It is the evidence of people whose lives were transformed by the power of the gospel.

---

[22] Colin Chapman, *The Case for Christianity*, 1983 ed. (Grand Rapids: Eerdmans, 1981), 231; see also, Randall Price with H. Wayne House, *Zondervan Handbook of Biblical Archaeology* (Grand Rapids: Zondervan, 2017), 329.

[23] McDowell and Wilson, *He Walked Among Us*, 119.

There exists within each human a component of being that biblical writers refer to as the spirit or soul.[24] It sets humans apart from animals. The spirit of a man or woman is the nonmaterial, eternal component of each human being. Since it is often viewed as the core of human personality and the seat of human emotions, it is viewed spatially as an interior component. Thus, it is often viewed figuratively as "the heart."

The heart is the human component that can be in a communicative relationship with the spiritual. When we reach out to God or "hear" his voice, we do so through our spirits. Saint Augustine referred to this longing of the soul when he said of God, "Thou madest us for Thyself, and our heart is restless, until it repose in Thee."[25] Another writer, perhaps Blaise Pascal, the seventeenth-century mathematician, physicist, and philosopher, expressed a similar sentiment when he said that within the heart of every human is a God-shaped vacuum.

The condition of the soul affects the attitude and behavior of the individual. If this were not so, personal spiritual renewal or regeneration would be imperceptible to those around us. But attitude and behavior changes are usually apparent in someone who has had such a transformational religious experience. Christian history is full of individuals who have made 180-degree turns in their lives. Don't take my word for it. Ask any Christian—many have had such a life-changing experience. Prostitutes have become virtuous; thieves have stopped stealing; the greedy have become generous; the chemically dependent have been liberated; adulterers and homosexuals have become chaste; murderers have melted in repentance and become lovers of human life as forgiveness is granted through the death of Jesus, who took our place on the cross, creating a community of The Forgiven.

The list goes on, but I think you get the point. The gospel message, the good news of Jesus's death and resurrection on behalf of sinful men and women, has the power—through the Holy Spirit—to transform the soul and connect it to the presentness of the kingdom of God, which is exactly what the Bible claims, making *each person* a wanted and needed member of the body of Christ, without which the whole faith community is lacking.

The Legacy of the Greatest Ethic

The final evidence we will look at that supports the reliability of the message of the Bible is the evidence of the gospel itself, which has the capacity

---

[24] I use the two terms interchangeably in this section.

[25] *The Confessions of Saint Augustine*, trans. Edward B. Pusey (New York: Modern Library, 1949), 3.

more than anything else to change the world for the better. I am not aware of the teachings of any greater ethic than Jesus's ethic of love. If it were applied by every individual alive, we would live in the long-imagined utopia—one large community filled with love and respect, each person integrally belonging and each person striving to serve the other.

Here are some of Jesus's teachings on love:

➢ "Love the Lord your God with all your heart and with all your soul and with all your mind. This is the first and greatest commandment. And the second is like it: Love your neighbor as yourself" (Matt 22:37–39).

➢ "Greater love has no one than this, that he lay down his life for his friends" (John 15:13).

➢ "This is my command: Love each other" (John 15:17).

➢ "Do to others as you would have them do to you" (Luke 6:31).

➢ "Give to the one who asks you, and do not turn away from the one who wants to borrow from you" (Matt 5:42).

But Jesus does not stop here. He extends his ethic of love to include even those who do not show love in return.

➢ "Do not resist an evil person. If someone strikes you on the right cheek, turn to him the other also" (Matt 5:39).

➢ "You have heard that it was said, 'Love your neighbor and hate your enemy.' But I tell you: Love your enemies and pray for those who persecute you" (Matt 5:43–44).

This is the ethic of the Bible, whether or not it is practiced by all or any who call themselves *Christians*, and the truth of this teaching resonates within the heart of every human being. You might call this a *numinous* verification of the message of the Scriptures.

So strong is this ethic that some have argued that even if there were no God, and thus no good, to follow the ethic would still be admirable. Simone Weil writes,

> If we put obedience to God above everything else, unreservedly, with the following thought: "Suppose God is real, then our gain is total—even though we fall into nothingness at the moment of death; suppose the word 'God' stands only for illusions, then we have still lost nothing because on this assumption there is absolutely nothing good, and consequently nothing to lose; we have even gained . . . because we have left aside the illusory goods which exist but are not good for the

sake of something which (on this assumption) does not exist but which if it did exist, would be the only good. . . ."

If one follows this rule of life, then no revelation at the moment of death can cause any regrets; because if chance or the devil govern all worlds we would still have no regrets for having lived this way.[26]

Two thousand years ago, in a world of war, cruelty, and barbarism, in cultures that knew nothing but death, decimation, and destruction, where might made right and the weak were doomed, there emerged from an obscure corner of the world, out of the mouth of a Jewish carpenter, a new paradigm: *Love your enemies, go the extra mile, turn the other cheek.* How could a paradigm of peace, humility, and self-sacrifice overtake the age-old paradigm of brute force? Can a rabbit chase a lion from his den? But there is no power in self-sacrifice . . . *unless it is followed by resurrection.* This became the power that no army could match, no tyrant defeat, no entrenched paradigm suppress.

To sum up, the evidence for the trustworthiness of the Bible's message includes:

1. The reliability of the copying process
2. The proximity of the writers and their writings to the events described
3. The age of the extant manuscripts
4. The quantity of early manuscripts
5. The fulfilled prophecies in the Old and New Testaments
6. The origin and explosive growth of the early Church
7. The motivation for martyrdom of Christians who were contemporaries of Jesus
8. The unlikelihood of the early Christians adhering to the moral teachings of Jesus and at the same time propagating a distortion of him
9. The lives of those changed by the power of the gospel
10. The power of Jesus's ethic of love to transform the world

"This is love: not that we loved God, but that he loved us and sent his Son as an atoning sacrifice for our sins."

—John the Apostle,
witness to the resurrection,
circa AD 98, Ephesus, Greece.[27]

---

[26] Simone Weil, *Gateway to God*, ed. David Raper (1952; Glasgow: Fontana Books-William Collins Sons, 1974), 44–45.

[27] 1 John 4:10.

15

Bonus Chapter #1

On Exhibit: Autograph of Jesus[1]

The story is told of how Pablo Picasso, considered by many to be the greatest artist of the twentieth century, summoned a carpenter into his home to construct some furnishings. Instead of telling the carpenter how he wanted them constructed, he took out a piece of paper and made a sketch. When the carpenter agreed to take the job, Picasso asked how much it would cost. The man, looking at the sketch, handed it back to Picasso, saying, "Just put your signature right here."

Before Picasso signed his sketch it wasn't worth two cents. But the moment he penned the name Picasso on it, its value jumped several hundred dollars, at least.

The world places great value on the names of prominent men and women. The autographs of famous people are sought by many and treasured by all. According to Charles Hamilton, one of the world's leading appraisers

---

[1] Originally published in the *Church of God Evangel* (September 24, 1979): 22.

of autographs, the signature of Julius Caesar is valued at 2 million dollars. The six known signatures of William Shakespeare are valued at 1.5 million dollars each. The highest priced autograph of an American is that of Button Gwinnett ($250,000), one of three Georgians to sign the Declaration of Independence.

There is no way to estimate the value of the signature of Jesus, even if such an autograph did exist. But whatever the estimation, as highly as Jesus is revered, ink and parchment could never surpass the value of the softest whisper of that name.

For at the name of Jesus, blinded eyes have been opened and maimed limbs have stretched forth with new life.

At the name of Jesus, the drunken alcoholic and the stoned drug addict have found release from cruel bondage; the wracked soul of the homosexual has been redeemed and his heart filled with peace and joy. At the name of Jesus, the lonely have found an eternal companion and the grief stricken have found a comforter.

From the East to the West, through nearly two millennia, millions have bowed at that name and found a peace beyond understanding. They have passed from darkness into light. Having pleaded guilty, they were declared innocent. For the guilt was placed on another: His name was Jesus.

The Bible bears witness to the value of the name of Jesus: "Wherefore God also hath highly exalted him, and given him a name which is above every name: That at the name of Jesus every knee should bow, of things in heaven, and things in earth, and things under the earth; And that every tongue should confess that Jesus Christ is Lord, to the glory of God the Father" (Philippians 2:9–11 KJV). In his letter to the Ephesians, Paul writes that Jesus is above "every name that is named, not only in this world, but also in that which is to come" (Ephesians 1:21 KJV).

Jesus left us no signatures. Perhaps He knew we would make idols of such things. "In their hearts," He thought, "there will I engrave my name." And so it is; on every heart that is His has He written His name. There, on exhibit . . . for all to see.

16

Bonus Chapter #2: A True Story

The Wings of the Wind[1]

The prefabricated, one-story apartment buildings were laid out like Quonset huts. Evidently, they were built quickly and cheaply for employees of the Bell Bomber plant in Marietta, Georgia, which assembled airplanes for World War II. We lived on Wings Avenue. The militaristic names of the streets wouldn't register with me for many years to come: Patton Circle, Victory Drive, Aviation Road, Wings Avenue—a leader, the goal, the means, and an individual component.

But the war was fourteen years past, and the Bell Bomber plant had been renamed Lockheed. The apartments, well, they became part of America's public housing effort. Many still housed the employees of the plant, usually young blue-collar workers. By nature, this led to the inevitable: a

---

[1] Originally published in *Stepping Stones: Across the Stream of Time*, ed. Dick Byrum (Marietta, GA: Cherokee Christian Writers' Group, 2003), 76–79.

neighborhood chock-full of kids. My parents contributed, too: there were four of us boys. I was the second.

When the third child came along in 1957, we packed up, kissed 615 Wings Avenue goodbye and moved directly across the alley to 609 Wings Avenue, a three-bedroom apartment on the end of the building. Not many diapers later, Mama was pregnant again, and in 1958, our family of six was complete.

Mama raised us boys while Daddy worked at Lockheed, when he wasn't laid off, that is. Daddy was a good worker, but he was a better drinker. There were a number of pubs, taverns, bars, and, as my mama called them—beer joints—all within a mile or two of our house, and they were all on Daddy's radar screen. Come Friday night and all day Saturday, the siren call of the closest beer joint was more than Daddy, a former sailor, could stand. Sundays were a bit tamer, with blue laws and all, though boot-leggers *could* be found. I was in the car on more than one occasion when Daddy paid a discreet visit to a house near Blackjack Mountain. He'd al-ways get back in the car with an additional lump in his pocket.

Our house, being the five-room apartment it was, wasn't good for keeping secrets or hiding feelings. One windy, fall Saturday there was a charge in the air and fire in Mama's eyes. It wasn't a day for throwing rocks at your older brother, who might end up in the house complaining to Mama. It was a day to get lost, to blend into the walls if you had to come inside, to hang your head and cower like a whipped dog if you had to pass through a room full of hackle-raising electricity.

Daddy was nowhere around. That was the problem. He was, as Mama was apt to say, "Down at some beer joint drinking up the rent and the gro-ceries." She would have to go looking for him to get what was left of his paycheck so she could feed us the next week. She had an idea that he was at the Dixie Inn, a restaurant and bar on Fairground Street, not far from Lockheed and within walking distance of our house. Mama got my older brother and me into the house and told us to stay in and watch our younger brothers until she got back.

"Sure, Mama. Yes ma'am." Electricity demanded compliance.

She got into our 1940 faded blue Dodge. It had replaced the brand new 1955 Chevrolet that Daddy had let go back to the bank. It wasn't more than thirty minutes when we heard the Dodge crunching gravel in a parking area beside the house. Mama was back. She got out and walked hurriedly into the house. The fire in her eyes had subsided. She had found Daddy and he had given her a twenty-dollar bill. I'm sure she gave him a lot more. But things were going to be okay. There would be food on the table next week.

In the absence of fire and electricity, I was beginning to breathe normally when Mama rushed into the living room then the kitchen then back into her bedroom. She scurried from room to room a second time. The fire in her eyes was replaced with despair. She dumped the contents of her purse on her bed and raked her hands through it. The twenty-dollar bill was gone.

In her fury, as she left the Dixie Inn, she had put the bill in her lap. By the time she got home, she had forgotten that she had put it there instead of in her purse. When she realized what she had done, she ran out to the car and searched inside and around it. The wind was whipping leaves under the car and down the street. I knew if she had dropped that bill outside, it was long gone by now.

Mama walked slowly back toward the house, her gaze darting left and right, clinging to a quickly fading hope. In the house, she sat on the sofa, her hands cupped over her face in desperate prayer, calling on the Spirit our Pentecostal preacher so often talked about. She batted her eyes, fighting back useless tears. Reaching down, she picked up the newspaper and began tearing it. She walked back outside, got in the car, and closed the door. From the porch, I watched her as she opened the car door. Beneath the high-sitting body of the Dodge, I saw one foot touch the ground then the other. Then I saw a small piece of newspaper fall to the ground at her feet.

The wind quickly caught the piece of paper and drove it out of the parking lot and into Wings Avenue. It danced on its corners across the street and into a neighbor's yard, my mother right behind it. It tumbled through the grass of one, two, three, four neighbors and came to rest against the apartment wall. Not two feet away, pasted by the wind against the base of the wall, was the twenty-dollar bill. My mother danced across the street and back home. There would, after all, be food on the table next week.

* * * * *

A decade or so later, I learned that the Greek word for "wind" could also be translated "Spirit." How appropriate, I thought.

17

Bonus Chapter #3: A Short Story

The Altar[1]

They lived behind the county work camp, the farmer and his wife. They had no children, but the forty-eight they claimed—the forty-eight behind the fence, through the barbed wire, up whitewashed boards, through the bars, in the windows. These were the children they never had.

The guards turned them down at first. They would say, "You're not related. Can't let you in. We got rules, you know. We'd lose our jobs if we let you in." Nevertheless, they came. Every month they came. Every holiday they came—Easter, Thanksgiving, Christmas. After all, their children were there, inside.

"But I'm their mother," Martha would say with a gentle smile, her gray hair in a bun and the scent of freshly baked biscuits wafting from her

---

[1] Originally published in *The Plus Years* (Gospel Publishing House; Spring 2007): 1–3, 6–7. It won the 1st Place Award for Fiction Writing 2006–2007 at the Southern Christian Writers Conference.

covered basket. Her husband, John, would be right behind her with an arm-load of homemade gifts, nothing expensive, but made with a father's love. John had a warm, leathery face, eyes of honest blue, a smile that had a long friendship with God. John and Martha would come and talk to the guards in hopes of getting a glimpse of their children. But if not, they knew they'd see them one day—when their children were released. They always came by the house just to say, *hello*, but would stay till after supper—Mom and Dad saw to that. Then Dad would give them a lift to the bus stop in his '39 Ford pick-up. On the way, he mostly talked about Jesus and how He changed his wicked life and gave him a life worth living, abundant life, like a gushing well of joy inside. He prayed with each child at the bus stop. Some would pray for forgiveness and a new life. And those that received, he could tell, and he'd lead them into the baptism in the Holy Spirit, just like in the book of Acts.

The Christmas of '47, two years after John and Martha started coming, the warden relented and granted them visitation privileges, conceding that they had a relationship with some of the prisoners that was stronger than the inmates' relationship with their real mom and dad.

John and Martha's house behind the prison was a small, wood frame house, but as the sun dropped to the horizon, the house cast a giant silhouette upon the work camp. From the back of their house, they had a perfect view of their children. They could see every window. And every prisoner could see John and Martha's house and see into the kitchen and living room as Mom and Dad threw back the curtains as if to say, *Join us at the table* or *around the fire*. At Christmas time, John would cut a tree, and he and Martha would trim it in the evening when their children could watch. They always decked it with forty-eight ornaments—and concluded the ceremony with a brief dance, a hug, a kiss, a bow to their audience, and a wave of their arms as though saying, *Come on home, boys.*

The view was also important because every day, as sure as the seasons, John and Martha would walk out back where John had fashioned a wooden altar, and they would kneel in prayer. Those prisoners who watched, and all would watch sooner or later, could see them laboring in prayer. John would lift his arm and point his finger toward the prison. He was pointing to the window of the children they were about to pray for.

There were twenty-four windows, two prisoners per window. John would point at each one. To show which prisoner in the window they were praying for, John would hold his arm out level, with the palm of his hand first toward the ground. This meant they were praying for the prisoner who slept in the bottom bunk; then palm up, for the top bunk inmate.

As evening fell and twilight cloaked the altar, Martha would pull a candle out of her apron pocket, light it, and set it on her end of the altar. Soon, John would pull a candle out of his trouser pocket and place a gentle arm across Martha's shoulder as he touched his candlewick to hers. He would place his candle on the other end of the altar and the two would continue praying, . . . pointing and praying.

They had been praying like this for seven south Georgia winters, seven sweltering summers, ever since the commissioner built the county work camp behind them. At first, some of the prisoners would stand at their windows and laugh—months later, many would return to weep. Still today, the new prisoners react much the same way.

But as sure as the sun rose and the sun set, the Browns prayed.

From out the windows, between the bars, down the whitewashed boards, through the barbed wire, as the sun passes over the Browns' house, beds squeak in unison as men arise, shuffle to the window, and watch for the screen door to slowly open as Mr. Brown emerges from the shadows and walks to the altar and kneels. Mrs. Brown follows and kneels, ready to join him in prayer as he points to the left end of the building.

It was at such a time, one lazy July evening, that Mr. Brown stepped out the door and began walking to the altar, and then, stopped with a jolt. His hands grabbed his chest, he fell to his knees and onto his face. As he did, forty-eight shadowy faces looked on in disbelief. For a moment, no one moved, they just looked down upon Mr. Brown. "Get up," they began to plead under their breath. Suddenly, pandemonium broke loose as forty-eight men began shouting to the guards.

"It's Mr. Brown! He's had a heart attack! Help him! Call an ambulance!"

Several guards jumped to windows. One ran to a telephone and dialed the town clinic.

The prisoners returned to the windows to watch. Mrs. Brown was just coming out the door. She had no idea that anything was wrong. The prisoners felt a twinge of guilt, being privy to this hallowed information before Mrs. Brown. When she saw her husband on the ground, she moved quickly to him and kneeled. The prisoners watched as she gently turned him over and put her ear to his chest. She stood and ran back inside. The prisoners watched her through the living room window as she picked up the phone. Soon her lips began to move. They watched as she hung up the phone, held a well-worn handkerchief to her face, and returned to Dad.

She kneeled beside him again and began to pray. Her trembling hand brushed a silver tuft off his rough brow; she positioned herself to cradle his head in her lap, upon the apron that had prepared so many meals for him and witnessed so many prayers. Gently she stroked his head, looked toward heaven, and dabbed her eyes with her handkerchief.

In the prison, men were praying; some were kneeling beside their beds; some were standing beside their windows. And down the rugged faces of prisoners, tears coursed new trails.

The sound of the siren brought all the men back to the windows. A cloud of red dust snaked behind the ambulance approaching in the distance. The prisoners watched the eerie silent movements of the driver and his assistant as Mr. Brown was gently lifted inside the ambulance and driven away.

At eight o'clock that night, a guard brought the news—Mr. Brown had died. It spread quickly through the building. The muffled sounds of weeping could be heard long into the night. And it became a night without the usual chatter, a solemn night.

For three days the prisoners kept a vigilant watch over the locked and darkened house. The word was that Mrs. Brown was spending some time with her sister. On the fourth day, a car pulled into the driveway and Mrs. Brown got out carrying a small overnight bag. She had indeed spent some time with her sister, who went into the house with her and kept her company for almost an hour. Then she left Mrs. Brown alone in the house.

Many of the prisoners wondered if this would be the end of the altar, the end of the candles, the end of the prayers. Perhaps the altar would bring back painful memories, ever reminding her of the loss of Mr. Brown. How would she hold up without him?

He's gone, she thought. *Why couldn't I have gone with him? How can I live without him?*

"John, I miss you so!" she cried out. "Who will watch over me like you did? Who will care for me like you? I want so much to be with you."

But he was with God, and God had decided that she should stay a while longer on this earth.

She picked up her apron, tied it around her waist, and walked to the back door. A buzz went through the prison when the screen door opened and she walked toward the altar. Smiles and tears were mixed on forty-eight faces as she knelt. She lifted her trembling hand and pointed to the left end of the building and started to pray, but stopped in a gush of tears and collapsed onto the altar. Prisoners grabbed bars in empathy, as though to catch

146

her and hold her in their arms. Muffled tones were heard through the halls. "Mama," it sounded like.

"God, you know I don't feel like praying," she sobbed. "I need someone to pray for me. Who will pray for me now, . . . now that John is gone?"

As she cried, she took a candle out of her apron, lit it, and placed it upon the altar. Lifting her head, through her tears she noticed something change in the distance. Wiping her eyes, she looked at the prison. Her heart leapt as twenty-four windows were alit by the flickering of forty-eight flames. And she knew who would be praying for her

Bonus Chapter #4: A Short Story

Worn Carpet[1]

Margaret hadn't seen her mother, Claire, in nine years, and this would be the last time she would—as she lay in her casket. She almost let the chance go by but decided at the last minute to go, impulsively, as she did most things. She slammed the car door and began the two-hour trip, giving her plenty of time to ponder their fractured relationship. *Would mother have attended my funeral if it was me in a coffin?* she wondered. *Probably not.* The betrayal had cut deeply, wedging them asunder.

Standing before the open casket, Margaret stared down at her mother. *She looks at peace*, she thought. *I'm not surprised. You stole all the peace I*

---

[1] This short story won the 1st Place Award of the 2010 annual contest of the Christian Authors Guild.

had. You abandoned your only child and grandson when we needed you more than ever. A shiver crawled up her spine and she jerked her elbows to her sides; she tried to compose herself. She gazed through tearless eyes, but no amount of staring sparked any good memories. Her mind had feverishly erased all those just after her mother cut her and her three-year-old son, Chad, loose.

It would be a Christian funeral, as she knew it would be. Her mother claimed to be a believer, which made her betrayal all the more bewildering to Margaret. She just assumed that Claire was the world's biggest hypocrite. *It was just lip service*, she thought. How else was she to understand her mother's rejection? It was the only explanation that made sense—all her church-going and Bible reading was just a façade.

Someone squeezed her elbow. "Margaret?"

She turned. It was her mother's sister. "Hi, Dorothy."

"How have you been? And how's Chad? How old is he now, twelve?"

"We're doing okay. Chad's in the sixth grade." Margaret didn't feel much like talking.

"It's so good to see you. How long's it been, now?" Dorothy was from Opelika, a couple hundred miles away, over the state line, so they rarely saw each other. Margaret wasn't sure how much Dorothy knew about the rift, and she didn't want to air it here, so she kept her words short.

"A good while, I guess."

Dorothy put her arm around Margaret's waist and leaned over the casket. "She looks like herself, doesn't she?" Dorothy tilted her head as she continued to admire her sister's face. "Yes. I think she'd be proud if she knew she looked like herself." Dorothy leaned a little closer. "Oh, look. Isn't that the necklace you gave her? She just loved that necklace."

Margaret looked closer. She hadn't noticed it before. The heart-shaped locket was hidden by a pleat in the blouse. It was the necklace that she had given to her mother years ago.

"Yes," she said. "I gave that to her on Mother's Day, when I was in the ninth grade."

Dorothy reached down and picked up the locket. "I wonder if she still has your picture in it." Her hand trembled with palsy, but she was able to pry a thumbnail into the locket and open it.

"Well, look here. It is your picture . . . and Chad's, too."

Margaret's forehead wrinkled. "What?" She looked closer. In one half of the locket was a picture of her, with her flaming red hair, and in the other half was a three-year-old Chad. She was confused. *Why would she be wearing that, after disowning us?* Margaret wondered. *Someone who didn't know her must have told the mortician to put it on her. But why are our pictures still in it?*

Margaret walked out of the room and down the hall toward the office. Mr. Willoughby, the portly owner and mortician, was waddling out of his office when he saw her striding his way.

"Hello," he said, with a polite nod.

"Hi. I'm Claire Morton's daughter, Margaret."

He reached out his doughy hands and gently sandwiched her hand between them. "I'm so sorry about your mother." He patted the back of her hand. "Listen, if there's anything I can do for you, you just let me know."

"Well, there is one thing. I was wondering who instructed you on what to dress her in."

"Oh, I hope everything's okay. If it's not, I'm happy to fix it." Mr. Willoughby nervously pinched a fold of fat beneath his chin.

"Everything's fine. I was just wondering."

He visibly exhaled. "You had me going there for a minute. I thought I'd done something wrong." He invited her into his office.

"Mrs. Morgan, the pastor's wife, brought everything in. Even your mother's handwritten instructions. She was very meticulous, you know, your mother." His plump fingers fumbled through some papers on his desk. "They're here somewhere. Here, here they are." He handed her a sheet of paper.

Margaret looked at the familiar handwriting. Under "What to Wear," she found it: "Jewelry: Gold heart-shaped locket necklace with picture of Margaret and Chad." Her brow pinched up. "I don't understand," she whispered.

"Beg your pardon?" Mr. Willoughby said.

"Oh, nothing. I was just thinking out loud." She handed the paper back to him. He waved it off.

"You keep it. I'm finished with it." He looked at his watch. "You know, Pastor Morgan was looking for you earlier. He wanted to talk to you before you left. Something about your mother's estate, I believe. But the service is fixin' to start now. Will you be around afterwards?"

"Yes. I'll find him."

When the service was over, Margaret and Pastor Morgan talked. He gave her a large envelope full of various legal documents and keys, including a copy of her mother's will. She had left everything to Margaret, who thought that was strange, given their shattered relationship. She figured her mother would have left everything to the church, her last act of hypocrisy to shore up her façade.

Before Margaret started the long trip back home, she decided to go by the house. *Might as well*, she thought. *May save me a trip later*. Acorns crunched and popped under her tires as she pulled into the familiar driveway. Familiar, even though it had been nine years since she last pulled in.

She and Chad stopped by after court, when the divorce from Adam, her womanizing husband, was finalized. She needed someone's shoulder to lean on, maybe cry on. She thought she could depend on her mother, even though her mother hated the idea of divorce and tried to convince them both to try Christian counseling before giving up. But Margaret was headstrong and unforgiving. Three-year-old Chad jumped from stepping stone to stepping stone leading to the front door, leaping over the green moss between the stones.

"Come on, Chad," Margaret said, jerking on his arm. The court proceedings had frayed her nerves. She tasted blood from her lip where she clamped down on it in court to keep from coming uncorked during the opposing attorney's spiel.

Margaret opened the door. "Mama," she called. She walked into the living room. "Mama." She noticed something different about the room. She couldn't believe what she was seeing. All their pictures were missing. Pictures of her and Adam and Chad had all been taken off of the walls. All of their pictures on the shelves and tables were gone, too. She had heard about this kind of shunning by extreme religious sects, but never did she think her mother would do this. *We've been disowned*, she thought. *No. Worse. It was as though we had never lived.*

Margaret grabbed Chad and ran out the door. She choked back the sobs and vowed never again to talk to her mother. She spent the next nine years ignoring her. Ignoring her calls. Ignoring her cards and letters. Even. her knocks on their door.

Margaret retrieved the key to the front door from the envelope and stuck it in the lock. She hesitated, took a breath, turned the key, and walked in. An earthy scent from her mother's many plants brought back childhood memories she thought she had erased. But when she entered the living room, a calloused fist squeezed her heart again—the pictures were still missing. Hurt and hatred flared up again like blazing fire.

She hurried out of the living room and made her way to the nearest bedroom. The hinges squeaked as she pushed the door open. She stopped in the doorway, staring straight ahead. Her eyes began blinking rapidly, as though to beat away a thought. On the opposite side of the room, her mother had fashioned a prayer altar. On the altar were . . . all the pictures . . .

arranged as objects of prayer. That fist was at her heart again, crushing it, but for a different reason. She staggered to the altar and crumpled to the floor. Her knees fell into two depressions worn into the carpet. She began to cry, scream and cry, her lungs burning and heaving. Tears of remorse fell to the altar, finding stains of older tears. Margaret slumped over and buried her head into her folded arms.

"What have I done? What have I done?" echoed through the house. Then a choked cry, "Mama, oh, Mama."

19

Bonus Chapter #5: A Story

Never Carry a Whistling Bear to Church[1]

The pause in the minister's sermon and the stillness of the sanctuary served only to accent the shrill whistle. Before the echo diminished, my head and eyes had darted to my two-year-old son, Michael, who was squeezing his rubber teddy bear. You know the kind, the ones with the two-way whistles—squeeze in and it whistles, let go and it whistles again.

I snatched the toy from Michael, breathing somewhat easier as I strangled the thing. Looking up, I found several people glaring at me. The obviously rattled minister glossed over the incident with some remark about a joyful noise. I slumped into my seat, my face flushed.

As inconspicuously as possible, I tried to catch my wife's attention, hoping for some sympathy. She was seated on the other side of Michael and, to my chagrin, had inched her way down the pew from us.

---

[1] This story was originally published in *Moody Monthly* (February 1983: 93–94) and later reprinted in *Christian Parenting Today* (March/April 1994): 38–39.

Traitor, I thought.

Several minutes passed, giving me time to recover my senses. There I was, a grown man, visiting a new church, with a rubber teddy bear compressed between my hands. I could sit through the sermon squeezing teddy and risk the chance of losing my grip, or . . . .

I know. I'll pry the whistle out and be done with it. Then it occurred to me how whistling teddy bears are made these days—safety regulations don't allow for easily removable parts.

Teddy had not inhaled yet and my brain whirred frantically as Debbie continued to creep down the pew. Noticing that she left her purse behind, I figured I could stuff the toy inside. Trying to be inconspicuous again, I stretched out my leg to hook the strap of her purse with my foot.

Just a little farther, I consoled myself. Then suddenly . . . a seam in my trousers ripped.

I froze. Through the corner of my eye, I could see my wife's red face. She was struggling to suppress a burst of laughter. I could hear her choking back the tears. For a moment, I didn't move a muscle.

What am I going to do?

Aided by the expansion in my trousers, I slipped my foot through the strap and eventually drew the bag within reach. I placed the purse between my knees and unzipped it, thrusting teddy inside and pulling the zipper up to my wrist.

Slowly, I told myself. *Release it slowly.*

Then I discovered how impossible it is to stifle a whistling teddy. No matter how slowly I moved, it would not be denied. I froze again.

Now I was in an even worse predicament. Before, I could squeeze the toy as tightly as I wished. But since air had seeped in, I had to measure my grip—not too hard, not too soft.

This is ridiculous, I thought. I'll take the blasted bear outside and be done with it. I didn't care anymore about what the people behind me would think.

Determined this was the thing to do, I reached down to unzip the bag, but the zipper wouldn't budge. It was jammed! There I was—a grown man sitting in church with a rip in my pants, a teddy bear in my fist, and my hand stuck in a woman's pocketbook.

Have mercy! my heart cried. *What next?*

I finally got up and walked down the aisle with my wife's purse dangling from the end of my arm. Reaching the vestibule, I asked one of the more friendly looking ushers, "Which way to the restroom?"

He smiled, looked at the purse and said, "Which one?"

I tried to hide my discomfort. Then a shrill squeak from the bag left the ushers in tears.

I backed my way into the men's room and placed the bag on the vanity. Releasing my grip on teddy allowed him to inhale. I sighed with relief.

20

Bonus Chapter #6: A True Story

Confession[1]

I was only thirteen when I first lifted alcohol to my lips. By the time I was eighteen, I had seen the inside of several different jails, some more than once. I was headed down a wide road straight to hell.

You may be astounded by my next statement, but it is the truth. The police did the best thing for me anyone had ever done when they caught me and jailed me one cold February night. It may astound you even more to know that this time they booked me on three counts—all felonies! Yet, I rejoice!

I stayed in jail a week. But I prepared to stay longer. After all, my bond was set at $5,000, and I knew no one who would or could post that

---

[1] This is a redacted version of my testimony that appeared in *Christ for All* (November–December 1977): 4–5, under the title of "Ministering with Love." The youth version, "Confession," appeared in *HiCall* (February 4, 1973): 4–5 and was reprinted in *Encounter* 3.36 (May 5, 1974): 8.

much for me. So, I spent seven long days thinking. How did I get myself into such a mess? Why did I agree to drive a friend around and wait on him while he broke into several places? The only answer I could come up with was: Alcohol.

I was drunk the night of the crimes. And besides this, I was broke. That made being drunk twice as bad. So, I agreed to drive my buddy around and wait on him while he attempted to get us some money. What a fool alcohol made of me! But nothing to do now but wait . . . and hope that the judge would be lenient.

At the end of my seventh day in jail I heard the jailer call out a name. I didn't pay much attention. Why should I? I was in for keeps. Then I heard the name again. That was my name. What could he want with me? He unlocked the door. I asked him what he wanted, and he said I was going home!

The first person I saw as I stepped onto the ground floor was the preacher! You have never seen anyone as embarrassed as I was. But there he stood—the minister of the church I began attending when I was ten, the pastor of First Assembly where my mother had been a member for several years. Talk about embarrassment! He and the Sunday school superintendent had signed my bond.

He did not preach to me that night (to my surprise). He took me straight home, but he did say he wanted to see me Sunday evening before church started. I agreed, of course. Sunday night came, and I met him in his office. There he talked to me about Jesus Christ. At my age I knew all I wanted to know about Jesus—and that was very little. I walked out of his office that Sunday evening just as far away from God as I was the night I was locked up.

Yet, when I pleaded guilty in court one day in March, I did not hesitate to accept the money that man of God offered to loan me to pay my fine. The fine? Three hundred dollars and five years' probation. I knew what it would mean if I got into trouble again—revocation of probation and five years' imprisonment.

For four months I didn't touch one drop of alcohol. But then one warm June day, I took a drink and another and another and another. From that day forward I went downhill. From alcohol I went to pills, from pills I went to marijuana. After marijuana I experimented with amphetamines orally and via mainline injection. I stopped short of self-destruction. Something made me realize what I was doing to myself. I know now that mysterious something was the Holy Spirit dealing with me as a result of the prayers offered for me from the hearts of those dedicated Christians at the Assemblies of God church. I kicked drugs and the alcohol. It seemed too easy to be true; that, I know, also was because of prayer.

All the time these prayers were being answered, I was thinking about that Sunday night the preacher talked to me about Jesus Christ. I asked myself the same question Pontius Pilate had once asked, "What shall I do then with Jesus which is called Christ?" I came to the point where I could no longer just think about this man Jesus. I had to find Him. I had to find out who He was and why He was. It wasn't long before I found Him! I discovered who He was and why He was. He is more than I ever imagined. I rejoice with Solomon in that "He is altogether lovely!"

Now you know why I rejoice for being caught that cold February night. God turned what I thought was the greatest misfortune into the greatest fortune.

The transformation from my old life of misery, pain, and sin into a new life of joy, riches, and real life—it's only a sample of what God can do working through people sensitive to his Spirit, through the power of the Holy Spirit, changing lives others consider hopeless, bringing them new life in Christ.

The youth version ends with this paragraph:

Since that day [of accepting Christ] I have no longer needed to worry about my past record, for now that I belong to Jesus, I know nothing less than *goodness* and *mercy* will follow me into eternity.

"So then, if anyone is in Christ, he is a new creation; what is old has passed away—look, what is new has come!" (2 Cor 5:17 NET)

Bibliography

Augustine. *The Confessions of Saint Augustine*. trans. Edward B. Pusey. New York: Modern Library, 1949.

Anderson, Robert. *Spirit Manifestations and "The Gift of Tongues."* Wilmington, DE: Cross Publishing, n.d.

Anderson, Robert Mapes. *Vision of the Disinherited: The Making of American Pentecostalism*. New York: Oxford, 1979.

Arndt, W. F., F. W. Gingrich, and Walter Bauer. *A Greek-English Lexicon of the New Testament*. Chicago: University of Chicago, 1957.

Arrington, French L. *Encountering the Holy Spirit: Paths of Christian Growth and Service.* Cleveland, TN: Pathway Press, 2003.

Arrington, French L., and Roger Stronstad *Life in the Spirit New Testament Commentary*. Grand Rapids: Zondervan, 1999.

Atkinson, William P. "Pentecostal Responses to Dunn's *Baptism in the Holy Spirit*: Luke-Acts." *Journal of Pentecostal Theology* 6 (1995): 49–72.

———. *Baptism in the Spirit: Luke-Acts and the Dunn Debate.* Eugene, OR: Pickwick-Wipf and Stock, 2011.

Baker, Heidi. "Pentecostal Experience: Towards a Reconstructive Theology of Glossolalia." PhD diss. King's College, University of London, 1996.

Baker, John. *Baptized in One Spirit: The Meaning of 1 Corinthians 12:13*. Plainfield, NJ: Logos Books, 1967.

Banks, William. *Questions You Have Always Wanted to Ask About Tongues But . . . .* Chattanooga, TN: AMG Publishers, 1978.

Bauman, Louis S. *The Tongues Movement*. Rev. ed. Winona Lake, IN: BMH Books, 1963.

Bauer, Walter, Frederick William Danker, W. F. Arndt, and F. W. Gingrich. *A Greek-English Lexicon of the New Testament*. 3rd ed. Chicago: University of Chicago, 2000.

Baxter, Ronald E. *The Charismatic Gift of Tongues*. Grand Rapids: Kregel, 1981.

Berkhof, Hendrikus, *The Doctrine of the Holy Spirit: The Annie Kinkead Warfield Lectures, 1963–1964*. Richmond, VA: John Knox, 1964.

Blass, F., A. Debrunner, and Robert W. Funk. *A Greek Grammar of the New Testament and Other Early Christian Literature*. Chicago: University of Chicago, 1961.

Blomberg, Craig L. *NIV Application Commentary: 1 Corinthians*. Grand Rapids: Zondervan, 1995.

———. *Can We Still Believe the Bible?* Grand Rapids: Brazos Press-Baker, 2014.

Brand, Chad Owen, ed. *Perspectives on Spirit Baptism: Five Views*. Nashville, TN: Broadman & Holman, 2004.

Bruce, F. F. *The New Testament Documents: Are They Reliable?* 5th ed. Downers Grove, IL: Inter-Varsity, 1960.

———. *The Book of the Acts*, NICNT. Repr., Grand Rapids: Eerdmans, 1981.

Brumback, Carl. *"What Meaneth This?" A Pentecostal Answer to a Pentecostal Question*. Springfield, MO: Gospel Publishing House, 1947.

Bruner, Frederick Dale. *A Theology of the Holy Spirit: The Pentecostal Experience and the New Testament Witness*. Grand Rapids: Eerdmans, 1970.

Bundrick, David. "Ye Need Not That Any Man Teach You." *Paraclete* (Fall 1981): 17.

Bunn, John T. "Glossolalia in Historical Perspective." Pages 36–47 in *Speaking in Tongues: Let's Talk About It*. Edited by Watson E. Mills. Waco, TX: Word Books, 1973.

Burdick, Donald W. *Tongues: To Speak or Not To Speak*. Chicago: Moody Press, 1969.

Butts, James R. *The 'Progymnasmata' of Theon: A New Text with Translation and Commentary*. Ann Arbor, MI: University Microfilm International, 1987.

Carson, D. A. *Showing the Spirit: A Theological Exposition of 1 Corinthians 12–14*. Grand Rapids: Baker, 1987.

Carter, Charles Webb. *The Person and Work of the Holy Spirit: A Wesleyan Perspective*. Grand Rapids: Baker, 1974.

Cartledge, Mark J. *Charismatic Glossolalia: An Empirical-Theological Study*. Burlington, VT: Ashgate Publishing Co., 2002.

Cartledge, Mark J., ed. *Speaking in Tongues: Multi-Disciplinary Perspectives*. Paternoster, 2006. Repr., Eugene, OR: Wipf and Stock, 2012.

Chantry, Walter J. *Signs of the Apostles: Observations on Pentecostalism Old and New*. Rev. ed. Edinburgh, UK: Banner of Truth, 1976.

Chapman, Colin. *The Case for Christianity*. 1983 ed. Grand Rapids: Eerdmans, 1981.

Cho, Youngmo. *Spirit and Kingdom in the Writings of Luke and Paul: An Attempt to Reconcile These Concepts*. Milton Keynes, UK: Authentic Media-Paternoster, 2005.

Conzelmann, Hans. *1 Corinthians: A Commentary on the First Epistle to the Corinthians*. Hermeneia. Translated by James W. Leitch. Philadelphia: Fortress Press, 1975.

Cooke, Ronald. *Do Miracles Then Continue?* Hollidaysburg, PA: Manahath Press, 1981.

Coppes, Leonard J. *Whatever Happened to Biblical Tongues?* Phillipsburg, NJ: Pilgrim Publishing, 1977.

Criswell, W. A. *The Baptism, Filling and Gifts of the Holy Spirit*. Grand Rapids: Zondervan, 1966.

Dana, H. E., and Julius R. Mantey. *A Manual Grammar of the Greek New Testament*. Toronto: Macmillan, 1927.

DeHaan, Richard W. *The Charismatic Controversy*. Grand Rapids: Radio Bible Class, 1978.

———. *The Holy Spirit and You*. Grand Rapids: Radio Bible Class, 1973.

DeHaan, M. R. *Pentecost and After*. Grand Rapids: Zondervan, 1964.

Dillow, Joseph. *Speaking in Tongues*. Grand Rapids: Zondervan, 1975.

Dunn, James D. G. *Baptism in the Holy Spirit: A Re-examination of the New Testament Teaching of the Gift of the Holy Spirit in Relation to Pentecostalism Today*. Philadelphia: Westminster, 1970.

———. *Jesus and the Spirit: A Study of the Religious and Charismatic Experience of Jesus and the First Christians as Reflected in the New Testament*. Philadelphia: Westminster, 1975.

Durasoff, Steve. *Bright Wind of the Spirit: Pentecostalism Today*. Plainfield, NJ: Logos International, 1972.

Elbert, Paul. "Towards an Understanding of Luke's Expectations for Theophilus Regarding the Lukan Gift of the Holy Spirit." Paper presented at the annual meeting of the Society for Pentecostal Studies. Kirkland, WA, March 16–18, 2000.

———. "*The Globalization of Pentecostalism*: A Review Article." *Trinity Journal* 23 (Spring 2002): 81–101.

———. "Luke's Fulfillment of Prophecy Theme: Introductory Exploration of Joel and the Last Days." Society for Pentecostal Studies Conference. Marquette University, Milwaukee, WI, March 2004.

———. "Paul of the Miletus Speech and 1 Thessalonians: Critique and Considerations." *ZNW* 95/3–4 (2004): 258–268.

————. "Acts 2:38 in Light of the Syntax of Imperative-Future Passive and Imperative-Present Participle Combinations." *The Catholic Biblical Quarterly* 75 (2013): 94–107.

————. "Face to Face: Then or Now? An Exegesis of First Corinthians 13:8–13." Pages 493–520 in *Strangers to Fire: When Tradition Trumps Scripture*. Edited by Robert W. Graves. Tulsa: Empowered Life Academic-Harrison House, 2014.

————. *The Lukan Gift of the Holy Spirit: Understanding Luke's Expectations for Theophilus*. Canton, GA: The Foundation for Pentecostal Scholarship, 2021.

————. *Essays in Biblical Studies: New and Penetrating Ideas on the Work of the Holy Spirit*. Canton, GA: The Foundation for Pentecostal Scholarship, 2021.

————. *Luke's Rhetorical Compositions: Essays in Lukan Studies*. Eugene, OR: Wipf and Stock, 2022.

Epp, Theodore H., and John I. Paton. *The Use and Abuse of Tongues*. Lincoln, NE: Back to the Bible, 1963.

Ervin, Howard M. *These Are Not Drunken as Ye Suppose*. Plainfield, NJ: Logos International, 1968.

————. *Conversion-Initiation and the Baptism in the Holy Spirit: A Critique of James D. G. Dunn's* Baptism in the Holy Spirit. Peabody, MA: Hendrickson Publishers, 1984.

————. *Spirit Baptism: A Biblical Investigation*. Peabody, MA: Hendrickson, 1987.

Fee, Gordon D. "Hermeneutics and Historical Precedent—A Major Problem in Pentecostal Hermeneutics." Pages 118–32 in *Perspectives on the New Pentecostalism*. Edited by Russell P. Spittler. Grand Rapids: Baker Book House, 1976.

————. *The First Epistle to the Corinthians*. NICNT. Grand Rapids: Eerdmans, 1987.

————. *God's Empowering Presence: The Holy Spirit in the Letters of Paul*. Peabody, MA: Hendrickson, 1994.

————. "Toward a Pauline Theology of Glossolalia." Pages 24–37 in *Pentecostalism in Context: Essays in Honor of William W. Menzies*. Edited by Wonsuk Ma and Robert P. Menzies. Sheffield, England: Sheffield Academic Press, 1997.

Flattery, George M. *A Biblical Theology of the Holy Spirit: Luke–Acts*. Vol. 2. Springfield, MO: Global University, 2009.

Flower, Joseph R. "The Purpose of Prophetic Utterance." *Paraclete,* 6.1 (Winter 1972): 22–25.

Gaffin, Richard B., Jr. *Perspectives on Pentecost: Studies in New Testament Teaching on the Gifts of the Holy Spirit.* Grand Rapids: Baker, 1979.

Gardiner, George E. *The Corinthian Catastrophe.* Grand Rapids: Kregel, 1974.

Gee, Donald. *Concerning Spiritual Gifts.* Rev. ed. Springfield, MO: Gospel Publishing House, 1972.

Geisler, Norman. *Christian Apologetics.* Grand Rapids: Baker, 1976.

Geisler, Norman L. and William E. Nix. *A General Introduction to the Bible.* Chicago: Moody, 1968.

Giblet, J. "Baptism in the Holy Spirit in the Acts of the Apostles." *One in Christ* 10 (1974): 162–171.

Graves, Robert W. "Confession." *HiCall* (February 4, 1973): 4–5.

———. "Ministering with Love." *Christ for All* (November–December 1977): 4–5.

———. "On Exhibit: Autograph of Jesus." *Church of God Evangel* (September 24, 1979): 22.

———. "Never Carry a Whistling Bear to Church." *Moody Monthly* (February 1983): 93–94.

———. "Tongues Shall Cease: A Critical Survey of the Supposed Cessation of the Charismata." *Paraclete* 17.4 (Fall 1983): 20–28.

———. "The Jerusalem Council and the Gentile Pentecost." *Paraclete* 18.1 (Winter 1984): 4–8.

———. "Preaching—the Spirit and Human Dimensions. *Advance* (August 1986): 6.

———. "Documenting Xenoglossy." *Paraclete* 21.2 (Spring 1987): 27–30.

———. "A Good Word from the Critics." *Paraclete* 21.3 (Summer 1987): 22–25.

———. "Praying in Tongues." *Paraclete* (Fall 1986): 14–15.

———. "The Pentecostal Baptism and a Good Word from the Critics." *Paraclete* (Summer 1987: 22–25.

———. "The Forgotten Baptism." *Pentecostal Evangel* (24 May 1987): 6–7.

———. "Use of *gar* in Acts 10:46." *Paraclete* 22.2 (Spring 1988): 15–18.

———. *The Gospel according to Angels.* Grand Rapids: Chosen-Baker, 1998.

————. "The Wings of the Wind." Pages 76–79 in *Stepping Stones: Across the Stream of Time*. Edited by Dick Byrum. Marietta, GA: Cherokee Christian Writers' Group, 2003.

————. *"The Speaking in Tongues Controversy*—A Narrative-Critical Response: Part 1 of 2." *The Pneuma Review* 8.4 (Fall 2005): 7–23.

————. "The Johannine Anointing: Focusing on Truth." *Pneuma Review* 8.1 (Winter 2005): 6–9.

————. *"The Speaking in Tongues Controversy*—A Narrative-Critical Response: Part 2 of 2." *The Pneuma Review* 9.1 (Winter 2006): 6–18.

————. "The Altar." *The Plus Years*. Gospel Publishing House. (Spring 2007): 1–3, 6–7.

————. "Why Not Acts?" *Pentecostal Evangel* (April 7, 2011): 14–16.

————. "A Review of *Perspectives on Spirit Baptism: Five Views.*" *Pneuma Review* (August 8, 2014): http://pneumareview.com/perspectives-on-spirit-baptism-five-views/.

————. *Praying in the Spirit*. Rev. and enl. ed. Tulsa: Empowered Life Academic-Harrison House, 2016.

Graves, Robert W., ed. *Strangers to Fire: When Tradition Trumps Scripture*. Tulsa: Empowered Life Academic-Harrison House, 2014.

————. *The Kingdom Case against Cessationism: Embracing the Power of the Kingdom.* Canton, GA: The Foundation for Pentecostal Scholarship, 2022.

Green, Michael. *I Believe in the Holy Spirit*. Grand Rapids: Eerdmans, 1975.

Greenlee, J. Harold. *An Introduction to New Testament Textual Criticism*. Grand Rapids: Eerdmans, 1964.

Gromacki, Robert Glenn. *The Modern Tongues Movement*. Rev. ed. Nutley, NJ: Presbyterian and Reformed, 1972.

Grudem, Wayne A. *Are Miraculous Gifts for Today?* Grand Rapids: Zondervan, 1996.

Guinness, Os *The Dust of Death*. Downers Grove, IL: InterVarsity Press, 1973.

Gundry, Robert H. "'Ecstatic Utterance' (NEB)?" *Journal of Theological Studies* 17 (1966): 299–307.

Gustafson, Robert R. *Authors of Confusion*. Tampa, FL: Grace Publishing, 1971.

Habermas, Gary R. "Tracing Jesus' Resurrection to Its Earliest Eyewitness Accounts." Pages 202–16 in *God Is Great, God Is Good: Why*

Believing in God Is Reasonable and Responsible. Edited by William Lane Craig and Chad Meister. Downers Grove, IL: InterVarsity, 2009.

Haenchen, Ernst. *The Acts of the Apostles: A Commentary*. Translated by Bernard Noble et al. Philadelphia: Westminster, 1971.

Hall, J. L. "A Oneness Pentecostal Looks at Initial Evidence." Pages 168–88 in *Initial Evidence: Historical and Biblical Perspectives on the Pentecostal Doctrine of Spirit Baptism*. Edited by Gary B. McGee. Peabody, MA: Hendrickson Publishers, 1991.

Harris, Murray. Appendix. III Special Problems: A. Prepositions with *baptizō*. Pages 1207–1211 in *The New International Dictionary of New Testament Theology*. Vol. 3. Edited by Lothar Coenen et al. Grand Rapids: Zondervan, 1975.

———. *Prepositions and Theology in the Greek New Testament*. Grand Rapids: Zondervan, 2012.

Harris, Ralph W., ed. *Spoken by the Spirit: Documented Accounts of "Other Tongues" From Arabic to Zulu*. Springfield, MO: Gospel Publishing House, 1973.

Haya-Prats, Gonzalo. *Empowered Believers: The Holy Spirit in the Book of Acts*. Translated by Scott A. Ellington. Edited by Paul Elbert. Eugene, OR: Cascade Books-Wipf and Stock, 2011.

Henry, Carl F. H. *God, Revelation and Authority*. 4 vols. Waco, TX: Word Books, 1979.

———. "Evangelicals: Out of the Closet but Going Nowhere?" *Christianity Today* (January 4, 1980): 16–22.

Hilborn, David. "Glossolalia as Communication: A Linguistic-Pragmatic Perspective." Pages 111–46 in *Speaking in Tongues: Multi-Disciplinary Perspectives*. Edited by Mark J. Cartledge. Paternoster, 2006. Repr., Eugene, OR: Wipf and Stock, 2012.

Hitt, Russell T. *The New Wave of Pentecostalism: A Second Look*. Reprinted from *Eternity* July 1963:1–8.

Hoekema, Anthony A. *What about Tongue-Speaking?* Grand Rapids: Eerdmans, 1966.

———. *Holy Spirit Baptism*. Grand Rapids: Eerdmans, 1972.

Horton, Stanley M. *What the Bible Says About the Holy Spirit*. Springfield, MO: Gospel Publishing House, 1976.

———. *1 & 2 Corinthians*. Springfield, MO: Logion Press-Gospel Publishing House, 1999.

Horton, Wade H., ed. *The Glossolalia Phenomenon*. Cleveland, TN: Pathway Press, 1966.

Hummel, Charles G. *Fire in the Fireplace: Contemporary Charismatic Renewal*. Downers Grove, IL: InterVarsity Press, 1978.

———. *Fire in the Fireplace*: *Charismatic Renewal in the Nineties*. Downers Grove, IL: InterVarsity Press, 1993.

Hunter, Harold D. *Spirit-Baptism: A Pentecostal Alternative*. New York: Univ. Press of America, 1983. Rev. Eugene, OR: Wipf and Stock, 2009.

Hurtado, Larry W. "Why Pentecostals Need the Bible." *Paraclete* 6.1 (Winter 1972): 20–21.

———. "Normal, but Not a Norm: 'Initial Evidence' and the New Testament." Pages 189–201 in *Initial Evidence: Historical and Biblical Perspectives on the Doctrine of Spirit Baptism*. Edited by Gary B. McGee. Peabody, MA: Hendrickson, 1991.

Johns, Donald A. "Some New Directions in the Hermeneutics of Classical Pentecostalism's Doctrine of Initial Evidence." Pages 145–67 in *Initial Evidence: Historical and Biblical Perspectives on the Pentecostal Doctrine of Spirit Baptism*. Edited by Gary McGee. Springfield, MO: Hendrickson, 1991.

Judisch, Douglas. *An Evaluation of Claims to the Charismatic Gifts*. Grand Rapids: Baker, 1978.

Keener, Craig S. *Gift and Giver: The Holy Spirit for Today*. Grand Rapids: Baker Academic-Baker, 2001.

———. "Why Does Luke Use Tongues as a Sign of the Spirit's Empowerment." *JPT* 15.2 (2007): 177–84.

———. *Miracles: The Credibility of the New Testament Accounts*. Grand Rapids: Baker Academic, 2011.

———. *Christobiography: Memory, History, and the Reliability of the Gospels*. Grand Rapids: Eerdmans, 2019.

Kildahl, John P. *The Psychology of Speaking in Tongues*. New York: Harper and Row, 1972.

Kistemaker, Simon J. *1 Corinthians: Exposition of the First Epistle to the Corinthians*. Grand Rapids: Baker Academic-Baker, 1993.

Kittel, Gerhard, and G. Friedrich, eds. *Theological Dictionary of the New Testament*. Translated by G. Bromiley. 10 vols. Grand Rapids: Eerdmans, 1968.

Kreeft, Peter, and Ronald K. Tacelli. *Handbook of Christian Apologetics.* Downers Grove, IL: InterVarsity, 1994.

Kydd, Ronald A. N. *I'm Still There! A Reaffirmation of Tongues as the Initial Evidence of the Baptism in the Holy Spirit.* Toronto: Pentecostal Assemblies of Canada, 1977.

———. *Charismatic Gifts in the Early Church.* Peabody, MA: Hendrickson, 1984.

Lampe, G. W. H. *God As Spirit: The Bampton Lectures, 1976.* Oxford, UK: Clarendon Press, 1977.

Laurentin, René. *Catholic Pentecostalism.* Translated by Matthew J. O'Connell. Garden City, NY: Doubleday, 1977.

Laurito, Timothy. *Speaking in Tongues: A Multidisciplinary Defense.* Eugene, OR: Wipf and Stock, 2021.

Lovekin, A. A., "Glossolalia: A Critical Study of Alleged Origins, the New Testament and the Early Church." MA Thesis, University of the South, 1962.

Ma, Wonsuk and Robert P. Menzies, ed. *Pentecostalism in Context: Essays in Honor of William W. Menzies.* Sheffield, England: Sheffield Academic Press, 1997.

MacArthur, John F., Jr. *The Charismatics: A Doctrinal Perspective.* Grand Rapids: Zondervan, 1978.

Macchia, Frank D. *Baptized in the Spirit: A Global Pentecostal Theology.* Grand Rapids: Zondervan, 2006.

———. "Groans Too Deep for Words: Towards a Theology of Tongues as Initial Evidence." http://www.apts.edu/ajps/98-2/98/2-macchia.htm.

MacDonald, William G. *Glossolalia in the New Testament.* Springfield, MO: Gospel Publishing House, 1964.

———. "Pentecostal Theology: A Classical Viewpoint." Pages 59–74 in *Perspectives on the New Pentecostalism.* Edited by Russell P. Spittler. Grand Rapids: Baker, 1976.

———. "Biblical Glossolalia—Thesis Four." *Paraclete* 27.3 (Summer 1993): 32–43.

Mainville, Odette. *The Spirit in Luke-Acts.* Translated by Suzanne Spolarich. Eugene, OR: Wipf and Stock, 2016.

Malatesta, Edward, ed. *The Spirit of God in Christian Life.* New York: Paulist Press, 1977.

Marshall, I. Howard. *The Acts of the Apostles.* TNTC. 1980. Repr. Grand Rapids: Eerdmans, 1983.

May, Jordan Daniel, ed. *Global Witnesses to Pentecost*. Cleveland, TN: CPT Press, 2013.

McDonald, Lee Martin. *The Formation of the Christian Biblical Canon.* Peabody. Rev. and enl. ed. MA: Hendrickson, 1995.

McDowell, Josh. *Evidence that Demands a Verdict*. San Bernardino, CA: Campus Crusade for Christ, 1972.

McDowell, Josh, and Bill Wilson. *He Walked Among Us*. San Bernardino, CA: Here's Life, 1988.

McNair, Jim. *Experiencing the Holy Spirit: Truths That Can Transform Your Life*. Minneapolis, MN: Bethany Fellowship, 1977.

Menzies, Robert P. *Empowered for Witness: The Spirit in Luke-Acts*. Sheffield, England: Sheffield Academic Press, 1994.

———. "Spirit-Baptism and Spiritual Gifts." Pages 48–59 in *Pentecostalism in Context: Essays in Honor of William W. Menzies*. Edited by Wonsuk Ma and Robert P. Menzies. Sheffield: Sheffield Academic Press, 1997, 52–56.

———. "The Spirit of Prophecy, Luke-Acts and Pentecostal Theology: A Response to Max Turner." *Journal of Pentecostal Theology* 15 (1999): 49–74.

———. *Pentecost: This Story Is Our Story*. Springfield, MO: Gospel Publishing House, 2013.

———. *Speaking in Tongues: Jesus and the Apostolic Church as Models for the Church Today*. Cleveland, TN: CPT Press, 2016.

———. "Subsequence in the Pauline Epistles." *Pneuma* 39.3 (2017): 342–63.

———. "The Spirit in Luke-Acts: Empowering Prophetic Witness." *Pneuma* 43.3–4 (2021): 408–41.

Menzies, William W. "The Methodology of Pentecostal Theology: An Essay on Hermeneutics." Pages 1–14 in *Essays on Apostolic Themes: Studies in Honor of Howard M. Ervin*. Edited by Paul Elbert. Peabody, MA: Hendrickson, 1985.

Menzies, William W., and Robert P. Menzies. *Spirit and Power: Foundations of Pentecostal Experience*. Grand Rapids: Zondervan, 2000.

Mills, Watson E., ed. *Speaking in Tongues: Let's Talk about It*. Waco, TX: Word Books, 1973.

Moffatt, James. *The First Epistle of Paul to the Corinthians*. London: Hodder and Stoughton, 1938.

Molnar, Thomas. *The Pagan Temptation*. Grand Rapids: Eerdmans, 1987.

Montague, George T. *The Holy Spirit: Growth of a Biblical Tradition.* New York: Paulist Press, 1976.

Montgomery, John Warwick. "The Reasonable Reality of the Resurrection." *Christianity Today* 94 (April 4, 1980): 16–19.

Moody, Dale. *Spirit of the Living God: What the Bible Says about the Spirit.* Rev. ed. Nashville, TN: Broadman Press, 1976.

Moon, J. K. "The Holy Spirit in Preaching." *Paraclete* (Fall 1977): 22–25.

Nunn, H. P. V. *The Elements of NT Greek.* 8th ed. 1914. Repr., Cambridge, UK, Cambridge University Press, 1958.

———. *A Short Syntax of NT Greek.* 1912. Repr. Cambridge, UK, Cambridge University Press, 1977.

Oss, Douglas A. "A Pentecostal/Charismatic View." Pages 239–83 in *Are Miraculous Gifts for Today?* Edited by Wayne A. Grudem. Grand Rapids: Zondervan, 1996; "Response to Richard B. Gaffin, Jr.," 86–93.

Packer, J. I. *Keep in Step with the Spirit.* Old Tappan, NJ: Fleming H. Revell, 1984.

Palma, Anthony D. *The Holy Spirit: A Pentecostal Perspective.* Springfield, MO: Logion Press-Gospel Publishing House, 2001.

———. "Article G: Baptized by and in the Holy Spirit." Pages 895–96 in *Life in the Spirit New Testament Commentary.* Edited by French L. Arrington and Roger Stronstad. Grand Rapids: Zondervan, 1999.

Parham, Sarah E. *The Life of Charles F. Parham.* Joplin, MO: Tri-State Printing Co., 1930.

Parnell, Chris W. *Understanding Tongues-Speaking.* Nashville, TN: Broadman Press, n.d.

Pentecost, J. Dwight. *The Divine Comforter: The Person and Work of the Holy Spirit.* Repr., Chicago: Moody, 1975.

Petts, David. "The Baptism in the Holy Spirit in Relation to Christian Initiation." MTh Thesis, University of Nottingham, 1987.

Pinnock, Clark. Review of Michael Green, *I Believe in the Holy Spirit. HIS* June (1976): 21.

Poirier, John C. *The Tongues of Angels.* Tübingen: Mohr Siebeck, 2010.

Powers, Janet Evert. "Missionary Tongues?" *Journal of Pentecostal Theology* 17 (2000): 39–55.

Price, Randall, with H. Wayne House. *Zondervan Handbook of Biblical Archaeology.* Grand Rapids: Zondervan, 2017.

Rea, John. *The Holy Spirit in the Bible*. Altamonte Springs, FL: Creation House, 1990.

Reymond, Robert L. *"What about Continuing Revelations and Miracles in the Presbyterian Church Today? A Study of the Doctrine of the Sufficiency of Scripture."* Nutley, NJ: Presbyterian and Reformed, 1977.

Robeck, Jr., Cecil M. "How Do You Judge Prophetic Utterance?" *Paraclete* 11.2 (Spring 1977): 12–16.

———. "The Gift of Prophecy and the All-Sufficiency of Scripture." Pages 453–58 in *Strangers to Fire: When Tradition Trumps Scripture*. Edited by Robert W. Graves. Tulsa: Empowered Life Academic-Harrison House, 2014.

Robertson, A. T. *A Short Grammar of the Greek New Testament*. N.p.: privately printed, 1908.

———. *Word Pictures in the New Testament*. 6 vols. Nashville, TN: Broadman, 1930–1933.

———. *A Grammar of the Greek New Testament in the Light of Historical Research*. 4th ed. Nashville: Broadman, 1934.

Robertson, A. T., and W. Hersey Davis. *A New Short Grammar of the Greek Testament*. Grand Rapids: Baker, 1930.

Robertson, A. T., and Alfred Plummer. *A Critical and Exegetical Commentary on the First Epistle of St. Paul to the Corinthians*. 1911. Repr., Edinburgh, Scotland: T. & T. Clark, 1994.

Robinson, John A. T. *Can We Trust the New Testament?* Grand Rapids: Eerdmans, 1977.

Roddy, A. Jackson. *Though I Spoke with Tongues*. Rev. ed. Atascadero, CA: Scripture Research, 1974.

Russell, E. A. "'They believed Philip preaching,' (Acts 8.12)." *Irish Biblical Studies* 1 (1979): 169–176.

Ruthven, Jon [Mark]. *On the Cessation of the Charismata: The Protestant Polemic on Postbiblical Miracles*. Sheffield, England: Sheffield Academic Press, 1993.

———. *On the Cessation of the Charismata: The Protestant Polemic on Post-Biblical Miracles*. Rev. and exp. ed. Tulsa, OK: Word & Spirit Press, 2011.

Ryrie, Charles C. *The Holy Spirit*. Chicago: Moody Press, 1965.

Samarin, William J. *Tongues of Men and Angels*. New York: Macmillan, 1972.

Schreiner, Thomas R. *1 Corinthians: An Introduction and Commentary.* Tyndale New Testament Commentaries (Downers Grove, IL: Inter-Varsity, 2018.

Schutz, Vernon A. *Tongues and the Sign Gifts.* Grand Rapids: Grace Publications, Inc., n.d.

Schweizer, Eduard. "Pneuma, pneumatikos." Pages 389–455 in vol. 6 of *Theological Dictionary of the New Testament.* Edited by G. Kittel and G. Friedrich. Translated by G. Bromiley. 10 vols. Grand Rapids: Eerdmans, 1964–1976.

Scofield, C. I. *The New Scofield Reference Bible.* New York: Oxford University Press, 1968.

Shank, H. Carl. *More of Christ: Preliminary Thoughts Concerning a Reformed Antidote to the Current Charismatic Movement.* Cherry Hill, NJ: Mack Publishing, 1973.

Shelton, James B. *Mighty in Word and Deed: The Role of the Holy Spirit in Luke-Acts.* Peabody, MA: Hendrickson, 1991.

Smeaton, George. *The Doctrine of the Holy Spirit.* Carlisle, PA: Banner of Truth, 1974.

Smith, Charles R. *Tongues in Biblical Perspective: A Summary of Biblical Conclusions Concerning Tongues.* Rev. ed. Winona Lake, IN: BMH Books, 1973.

Smyth, Herbert Weir. *Greek Grammar.* Rev. ed. Cambridge, MA: Harvard University Press, 1956.

Spittler, Russell P., ed. *Perspectives on the New Pentecostalism.* Grand Rapids: Baker, 1976.

Starner, Rob. "Luke and Paul: Co-Laborers . . . and Collaborators?" Pages 194–240 in *Trajectories in the Book of Acts: Essays in Honor of John Wesley Wyckoff.* Edited by Paul Alexander et al. Eugene, OR: Wipf and Stock, 2010.

Stibbs, A. M., and J. I. Packer. *The Spirit within You: The Church's Neglected Possession.* Grand Rapids: Baker, 1979.

Stoner, Peter W. *Science Speaks.* 3rd ed. Chicago: Moody, 1969.

Storms, Sam. *The Language of Heaven.* Lake Mary, FL: Charisma House, 2019.

Stott, John R. W. *Baptism and Fullness: The Work of the Holy Spirit Today.* 2nd ed. Downers Grove, IL: IVP, 1977.

Stronstad, Roger. *The Charismatic Theology of St. Luke: Trajectories from the Old Testament.* 2nd ed. Peabody, MA: Hendrickson, 2012.

————. *The Prophethood of All Believers: A Study in Luke's Charismatic Theology*. Sheffield, England: Sheffield Academic Press, 1999.

————. "On Being Baptized in the Holy Spirit: A Lukan Emphasis." Pages 160–93 in *Trajectories in the Book of Acts: Essays in Honor of John Wesley Wyckoff*. Edited by Paul Alexander et al. Eugene, OR: Wipf and Stock, 2010.

Swete, Henry Barclay. *The Holy Spirit in the New Testament*. London: Macmillan, 1910. Repr., Grand Rapids: Baker, 1976.

Swindoll, Charles R. *Tongues: An Answer to Charismatic Confusion*. Portland, OR: Multnomah, 1981.

Synan, Vinson, ed. *Aspects of Pentecostal-Charismatic Origins*. Plainfield, NJ: Logos International, 1975.

Thiselton, Anthony C. "The 'Interpretation' of Tongues: A New Suggestion in the Light of Greek Usage in Philo and Josephus." *JTS* 30 (1979): 15–36.

————. *The First Epistle to the Corinthians*. NIGTC. Grand Rapids: Eerdmans, 2000.

————. *The Holy Spirit—In Biblical Teaching, through the Centuries, and Today*. Grand Rapids: Eerdmans, 2013.

Thomas, Robert L. *Understanding Spiritual Gifts: The Christian's Special Gifts in Light of 1 Corinthians 12–14*. Chicago: Moody Press, 1978.

Turner, Max. *The Holy Spirit and Spiritual Gifts*. Rev. ed. Peabody, MA: 1996.

————. "Early Christian Experience and Theology of 'Tongues': A New Testament Perspective." Pages 1–33 in *Speaking in Tongues: Multi-Disciplinary Perspectives*. Edited by Mark J. Cartledge. Paternoster, 2006. Repr., Eugene, OR: Wipf and Stock, 2012.

Twelftree, Graham H. *People of the Spirit: Exploring Luke's View of the Church*. Grand Rapids: Baker Academic, 2009.

Unger, Merrill F. *New Testament Teaching on Tongues*. Grand Rapids: Kregel, 1971.

————. *The Baptizing Work of the Holy Spirit*. Wheaton, IL: Van Kampen Press, 1953.

————. *The Baptism and Gifts of the Holy Spirit*. Chicago: Moody Press, 1974.

Van Den Herik, A. L. *The Shortest Leap: The Rational Underpinnings of Faith in Jesus*. Bloomington, IN: West Bow Press-Thomas Nelson/Zondervan, 2020.

Van Gorder, Paul R. *Charismatic Confusion*. Grand Rapids: Radio Bible Class, 1972.

Vander Lugt, Herbert. *Are Tongues for Today? What the Bible Says about the Sign-Gifts*. Grand Rapids: Radio Bible Class, 1979.

Walston, Rick. *The Speaking in Tongues Controversy: The Initial, Physical Evidence of the Baptism in the Holy Spirit*. Fairfax, VA: Xulon Press, 2003.

Walvoord, John F. *The Holy Spirit: A Comprehensive Study of the Person and Work of the Holy Spirit*. 3rd ed. Grand Rapids: Zondervan, 1977.

Ward, Horace S., Jr. "The Anti-Pentecostal Argument." Pages 99–122 in *Aspects of Pentecostal-Charismatic Origins*. Edited by Vinson Synan. Plainfield, NJ: Logos International, 1975.

Warfield, B. B. *Counterfeit Miracles*. 1918. Repr., Carlisle, PA: Banner of Truth, 1976.

Weil, Simone. *Gateway to God*. Edited by David Raper. 1952. Glasgow: Fontana Books-William Collins Sons, 1974.

Weiss, B. *A Commentary on the New Testament*. New York: Funk and Wagnalls Co., 1906.

Wenham, J. W. *The Elements of New Testament Greek*. 1965. Repr., Cambridge: Cambridge University Press, 1987.

Williams, Cyril G. *Tongues of the Spirit: A Study of Pentecostal Glossolalia and Related Phenomena*. Cardiff: University of Wales Press, 1981.

Williams, J. Rodman. *Renewal Theology: Salvation, the Holy Spirit, and Christian Living*. Vol. 2. Academie Books-Zondervan, 1990.

Williams, John. *The Holy Spirit: Lord and Life-Giver*. Neptune, NJ: Loizeaux Brothers, 1980.

Williams, Peter J. *Can We Trust the Gospels?* Wheaton, IL: Crossway, 2018.

Witherington, Ben, III. *Conflict and Community in Corinth: A Socio-Rhetorical Commentary on 1 and 2 Corinthians*. Grand Rapids: Eerdmans, 1995.

Zeller, George W. *God's Gift of Tongues: The Nature, Purpose, and Duration of Tongues as Taught in the Bible*. Neptune, NJ: Loizeaux Brothers, 1978.

Zerwick, Maximilian. *Biblical Greek: Illustrated by Examples*. 5th ed. Translated by Joseph Smith. Rome: Pontifical Institute, 1963.

Index of Persons

Index of Biblical Sources

Other titles by Robert W. Graves

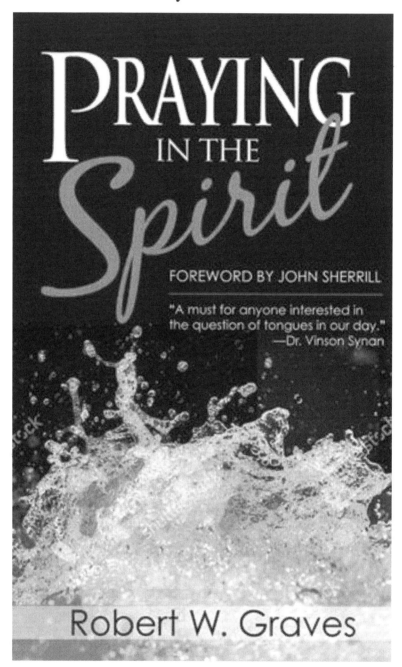

PRAYING
IN THE
Spirit

FOREWORD BY JOHN SHERRILL

"A must for anyone interested in
the question of tongues in our day."
—Dr. Vinson Synan

Robert W. Graves

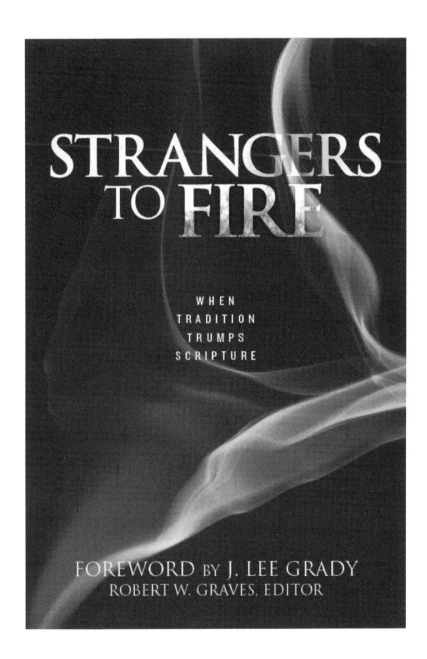

STRANGERS TO FIRE

WHEN
TRADITION
TRUMPS
SCRIPTURE

FOREWORD BY J. LEE GRADY
ROBERT W. GRAVES, EDITOR

Includes chapters by Craig Keener, Jack Deere, Wayne Grudem,
Robert Menzies, Doug Oss, Mel Robeck, and Gary Shogren

THE
KINGDOM CASE
AGAINST
CESSATIONISM

Embracing the Power of the Kingdom

Robert W. Graves
EDITOR

FOREWORD BY
CRAIG S. KEENER

Includes chapters by Michael Brown, Randy Clark, Gary Greig,
Derek Morphew, Jon Ruthven, Graham Twelftree, and Don Williams

Made in the USA
Columbia, SC
14 February 2024

31531501R00113